Beginning Breadboarding

Physical Computing and the Basic Building Blocks of Computers

Jennifer Fox

Apress®

Beginning Breadboarding: Physical Computing and the Basic Building Blocks of Computers

Jennifer Fox
Seattle, WA, USA

ISBN-13 (pbk): 978-1-4842-9217-4   ISBN-13 (electronic): 978-1-4842-9218-1
https://doi.org/10.1007/978-1-4842-9218-1

Copyright © 2023 by Jennifer Fox

Managing Director, Apress Media LLC: Welmoed Spahr
Acquisitions Editor: Aaron Black
Development Editor: James Markham
Coordinating Editor: Jessica Vakili

Distributed to the book trade worldwide by Springer Science+Business Media New York, 233 Spring Street, 6th Floor, New York, NY 10013. Phone 1-800-SPRINGER, fax (201) 348-4505, e-mail orders-ny@springer-sbm.com, or visit www.springeronline.com. Apress Media, LLC is a California LLC and the sole member (owner) is Springer Science + Business Media Finance Inc (SSBM Finance Inc). SSBM Finance Inc is a **Delaware** corporation.

For information on translations, please e-mail booktranslations@springernature.com; for reprint, paperback, or audio rights, please e-mail bookpermissions@springernature.com.

Apress titles may be purchased in bulk for academic, corporate, or promotional use. eBook versions and licenses are also available for most titles. For more information, reference our Print and eBook Bulk Sales web page at http://www.apress.com/bulk-sales.

Any source code or other supplementary material referenced by the author in this book is available to readers on the Github repository: https://github.com/Apress/Beginning-Breadboarding. For more detailed information, please visit http://www.apress.com/source-code.

Printed on acid-free paper

Table of Contents

About the Author

Jennifer Fox is an engineer, educator, and maker. After dabbling in dark matter (Occidental College, B.A. Physics), Fox studied engineering (UCLA, M.S. Mechanical Engineering) where she blended electronics, art, and education to tackle problems related to environmental and social justice. Fox founded her company, FoxBot Industries, in 2015 to provide an arts-based approach to STEM education and currently leads a team at Microsoft doing maker-related work.

About the Technical Reviewer

 **Massimo Nardone** has more than 22 years of experience in security, web/mobile development, cloud, and IT architecture. His true IT passions are security and Android.

He has been programming and teaching how to program with Android, Perl, PHP, Java, VB, Python, C/C++, and MySQL for more than 20 years.

He holds a Master of Science degree in Computing Science from the University of Salerno, Italy.

He has worked as a project manager, software engineer, research engineer, chief security architect, information security manager, PCI/SCADA auditor, and senior lead IT security/cloud/SCADA architect for many years.

Acknowledgments

This is my first book and I want to acknowledge that I am proud of myself for chugging away on it, slowly but surely. Next, A HUGE THANK YOU to my wonderful friend and part of my chosen family, Joshua Vasquez, for helping me "LEGO-tize" the transistor logic gates (and for the bomb cover photo!).

Another massive boat of thanks to my parents for instilling in me the importance of education and for their support and encouragement in the wild adventures of my life, many of which involve me "eating an elephant."

Thank you to the Adafruit folks, Phil and Limor, for the kit and for your long-term support. I appreciate and admire y'all.

And, of course, thank you to everyone who is part of my chosen family and my community. I deeply appreciate your questions about my book, your excitement, and your celebrations of my wins. I am truly grateful to be a part of a loving and supportive community. ☺

CHAPTER 1

Introduction, Supplies, and Circuit Diagrams

An average day for most of us involves walking around with a computer in our pocket, listening to music transmitted invisibly through the air, and flipping switches to generate artificial light when the sun sets (or if you're in a city like Seattle, sometimes during the day). Each of these technologies is truly miraculous, a feat of human ingenuity and persistence, scientific exploration collaborating with the meticulousness of engineering and creative design.

And yet, these technologies typically feel mundane. We (myself included) get annoyed when our maps app takes more than two seconds to load, frustrated when our music or videos glitch, and disgruntled when we run a vacuum cleaner and a hairdryer and inevitably have to reset a circuit breaker. When one of our precious (but replaceable) technologies breaks, it's easier and faster for most of us to toss the old and buy the new.

My goals with this book are threefold:

1. To give you a behind-the-scenes look at the wonderful world of electricity that we harness to build all sorts of useful gadgets so that you can better understand, and appreciate, how truly astonishing these everyday items are.

© Jennifer Fox 2023
J. Fox, *Beginning Breadboarding*, https://doi.org/10.1007/978-1-4842-9218-1_1

2. To provide you with some useful knowledge and skills so that if one of your electronics breaks, you have the option to try to repair it instead of replace it (it's satisfying and economically and environmentally friendly!).

3. To enable you to bring your own wild ideas to life! Want to build a smart watering system for your garden? You can do that! How about a potty-training device for your child? Doable! What about a robotic table? Not totally sure why, but possible! This book will give you a foundation in electricity and circuits that you can build on top of to make your ideas, or your ideal career, a reality.

This book is a beginner-friendly introduction to electronics and electricity, so **it's okay if you have no idea what "electronics" and "electricity" are or what those words mean**. We'll start from the basics, like "what is electricity?" and "what is a circuit?", and build up to an understanding of the fundamental building blocks of computers. This book is intended to give you both theoretical knowledge and practical skills. This means that as we learn new words and concepts, we'll learn how to **apply** our knowledge to build all sorts of electronic projects from a simple circuit for powering lights to a dark detecting circuit to logic gates!

To build these electronic circuits, we'll use a common tool used by engineers and hobbyists alike: the breadboard (Figure 1-1)!

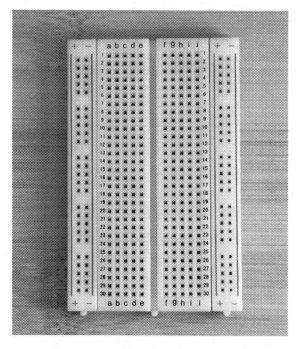

Figure 1-1. *A half-size breadboard for building electronic circuits!*

WHERE DOES THE TERM "BREADBOARD" COME FROM??

Engineers and hobbyists used to build circuits on wooden cutting boards by hammering nails into the board, wrapping wires around the nails, and connecting the wires between components like batteries and motors. In the 1970s, one might assume that whomever ruled the kitchen got fed up of having to replace their cutting boards, and, thus, the breadboard was born! (This is my interpretive take on the actual history.)

The breadboard is sometimes called a "plugboard" or "terminal array board." The version that is used today was designed by Robert J. Portugal in 1971. This model is made of white plastic with rows of small interconnected holes and often has two power rails on either side.

There are many benefits to building circuits on breadboards, including reusability and the ability to prototype or build temporary circuits without a soldering iron.[1]

The rest of this chapter introduces safety rules when working with electricity, gives you an overview of the kinds of parts we'll be working with, and ends with an overview on how to read circuit diagrams. Our exploration of circuits begins in Chapter 2, where we'll learn common words and concepts that show up throughout this book and beyond in electronics, and we'll build some simple circuits with the basic parts. We'll start building circuits on breadboards in Chapter 3, translating our learnings from Chapter 2 onto the breadboard and further exploring the wonderful world of circuits!

It is highly recommended to build the companion projects in each of the chapters because the best way to learn is to do! This is especially true with electronics, where theory is often abstract and may be confusing until you see it in action. Besides, electricity can be delightful, magical, and empowering as we wield the power of invisible particles to build useful, whimsical, and beautiful creations.

If you are new to circuits, it is recommended to go through the book in order. **If you have some prior experience with circuits**, you may skip around and work through the chapters that are of interest or that fill in any knowledge gaps.

This book also includes optional bonus projects that give you the opportunity to dig deeper into specific areas of electronics. These projects are designed for hands-on application – I'd highly recommend doing these projects if you are interested in learning electronics so that you can

---

[1] A soldering iron is a tool that melts metal to connect parts electrically. It can hold them together physically, too, but it is not a very strong physical, or mechanical, bond. It is recommended to avoid bending or otherwise stressing soldered parts because they are likely to break. This is why power cables for our computers and smartphones are coated in plastic and have bendy plugs!

go forth and build with electricity. If instead you are interested in learning *about* electronics, learning about circuit theory, or dipping your toes before deciding whether to go deeper, you may skip these bonus projects. Of course, you can always come back to them later!

Alright, with the house (book?) tour out of the way, let's dig into safety!

Safety Rules

Yay, safety! While the projects in this book don't involve dangerous parts (we are working with small, low-energy coin cell batteries for most projects), it's important to know electrical safety rules to avoid breaking or burning up components. And, hopefully, this book gets you excited about more advanced electronic projects! If/when you tackle advanced projects, it's helpful to have a solid understanding of safety.

As we go over the safety rules, it's okay if you don't understand some of the terms we are using just yet. You'll learn these new words as you go through the book. If applicable, projects will have notes on what to look out for. You can always return to this section if you're unsure about any projects in this book or beyond.

Safety Rule 1: Short Circuits

One of the most common mistakes when working with electricity is short circuits, or when electricity is given an easier path to flow than intended. Electricity is lazy and will always take the easiest path, even if it might not seem obvious to us.

We'll dig more into short circuits in Chapter 2, but for now let's look at the three main hazards that can happen with a short circuit:

1. Short-circuiting a battery or other source of electricity causes excess heat. With a high-energy battery like a car battery or the electricity that comes out of our walls, this can cause burns and/or fires.

2. Short-circuiting a battery or other source of
    electricity with our bodies, like with our hands, may
    cause electricity to flow through our bodies. This
    can cause burns and/or damage to the tissues and
    organs inside our bodies. More information on this
    is in the "Safety Rule 3" section.

    *Note: None of the batteries we will work with in
    this book have enough energy to travel through
    our bodies.*

3. Short-circuiting a component can result in excess
    electrical energy to a part which could cause the
    part to burn out and release smoke, or, in cases
    where there's a lot of electrical energy, the part may
    explode (having taught over 10,000 people, I've
    only seen this happen once). The battery we are
    using for the projects in this book does not have
    enough energy to make parts explode, but if you're
    ever concerned about exploding parts, wear safety
    goggles.

When building circuits, **check that the electricity does not have an
easier path to flow than where you want it to flow**. We'll explore this in
more detail in Chapter 2.

Safety Rule 2: Right-Hand Rule

The most important rule when working with high-energy electricity is the
right-hand rule: if you are unsure that the circuit or component you are
about to touch is live, place your left hand behind your back, ideally in a
pocket, and only use your right hand to touch the circuit or component.

However, the right-hand rule is a last resort. **Before touching any source of electricity, always double- and triple-check that it is powered off.**

Why one hand? If electricity travels across a human heart, it is often fatal. By only using one hand, the electricity will take the easiest path to the floor, or ground, and will not cross your heart. More details are covered in the "Safety Rule 3" section.

*Note: **The parts we will use in this book, including the batteries, are safe to touch with your hands because they don't have enough energy to be dangerous to us.** I'm including this rule in all its seriousness because it's good to practice safety protocols so they become automatic and for you to keep in mind when you build your own projects.*

Safety Rule 3: What's More Dangerous – Electrical Current or Voltage?

The answer is yes. Both electrical current and voltage are dangerous in different ways, although ultimately it is the flow of electricity, also called electrical current, through your body that causes damage and is potentially fatal.

How is voltage dangerous? The human skin has a high resistance to electricity, which means that if you touch the terminals of a battery with one hand or between both hands, a low-voltage battery won't shock you. **Above 50 Volts (50V)**, however, is enough energy to overcome our skin's resistance, which means that electrical current can flow into our bodies, damaging tissues and internal organs.

How is current dangerous? Even a small amount of current can damage our internal tissues and organs, like our heart which requires an electrical signal to function properly. A current as small as **0.007 Amps** (7mA) across a human heart for three seconds is enough to be fatal, and a current of **0.1 Amps** (100mA) passing through a human body is likely fatal because of internal burns.

For these reasons, it is important to take electrical safety seriously and always follow the rules. It is also recommended to work slowly and be overly cautious when handling potentially dangerous sources of electricity.

Safety Rule 4: Use the Right Tools and Components and Use Them Properly

All tools and components have limitations for both electrical current and voltage. When used within these limits, the tools and components are safe. Tools like multimeters can also offer added protection when working with potentially dangerous electrical sources.

However, tools and components will only function and work as expected when they are used within the manufacturer ratings. If you are unsure the part or tool you're working with is safe to use with the electrical source, check the datasheet and look for current and voltage limitations.

Why is this important? A tool that is not rated to work with a high-energy electricity source can fail and may result in electrical shocks or worse. (It may also melt… I've accidentally melted a few holes in more than one breadboard.) A component that is not rated to work with an electrical source may burn up or explode.

Wait… now I'm nervous… Is electricity super dangerous?!

Like driving a car, working with electricity is safe when we know and follow the rules. All of the parts used for projects in this book are safe to build **and** to make mistakes with. I purposefully designed all of the projects in this book to work with one or max two coin cell batteries, which are low voltage. We will use 9V batteries in a few projects for exploratory purposes – these have enough energy to burn out LEDs but are generally safe, and familiar, to work with. This book will give you a safe platform on which to experiment, test things out, and make mistakes.

So please, make mistakes!

The worst mistake you are likely to make as you work through these projects is to short-circuit the battery. If this happens, it's okay! The battery will burn up much more quickly than expected and will need replacing, but that happens sometimes.

Speaking of materials, onward to see what we will be playing with!

Tools and Materials

Table 1-1 provides the master supply list. You can purchase parts individually or grab all the materials from the Adafruit Kit #5696 (https://www.adafruit.com/product/5696).

Table 1-1. *Master Supply List*

Hardware – Nonconsumable Supplies		
3	Breadboards (half size)	**Adafruit Product ID: 64** *Self-Adhesive Solderless Half-Size Breadboard*
50	Breadboard jumper wires	**Adafruit Product ID: 1956** *M/M Jumper Wires, 26 AWG, Assorted Colors* *(3" and/or 6" recommended)*
6	Alligator clip wires	**Adafruit Product ID: 1008** *Small Alligator Clip Test Lead*
1	Balloon	**RUBFAC Party Balloon** *Any standard party balloon will suffice. Will be blown up with air. Can find on Amazon, Google, or your preferred party store!*
1	Safety glasses	**Grainger Part No: 4EY97** *CONDOR Safety Glasses: Uncoated, No Foam Lining, Wraparound Frame, Frameless, Clear, Clear, Unisex*

(*continued*)

Table 1-1. (*continued*)

Hardware – Consumable Supplies

2	9V alkaline battery	**Adafruit Product ID: 1321** *500mAh 9V Alkaline (MnO2 chemistry) battery*
4	Coin cell battery (CR2032)	**Adafruit Product ID: 654** *CR2032 Lithium metal 3V 250mAh*
2	Coin cell battery case, breadboard-friendly	**Aobao CR2032 Battery Holder with Switch** *Single CR2032 Battery Holder with On/Off* *Switch and colored Leads* *Note: Can purchase on Amazon or find via* *Google*
5–10	LED (5mm, red)	**Adafruit Product ID: 777** *5mm Basic Red LED, forward voltage = 2.0V,* *forward current = 20mA*
5–10	LED (5mm, green or blue)	**Adafruit Product ID: 779, 780** *5mm Basic Green LED, forward voltage = 2.0V,* *forward current = 20mA*
2	Buzzer	**Adafruit Product ID: 1536** *Breadboard-friendly 5V Buzzer*
2	Electric DC motor (5V or less)	**DigiKey Product No: 1528-1177-ND** *Vibration Motor 11000 RPM 5VDC*
1	Resistor variety pack (1/4Watt, variety between 1KΩ and 10KΩ; e.g., 10KΩ, 4.8KΩ, and 1KΩ)	**SparkFun Product No: 10969** *¼ Watt Through-Hole Resistor Variety Pack* *(pack of 500)*
2	Potentiometer (1KΩ or 10KΩ)	**Adafruit Product ID: 356** *TrimPot 10K with Knob*

(*continued*)

Table 1-1. (*continued*)

2	Electrolytic capacitor (100µF and 10µF)	**Adafruit Product ID: 2193 and No:2195** *Electrolytic Decoupling Capacitor, 100uF, 16V (pack of 10)* *Electrolytic Decoupling Capacitor, 10uF, 50V (pack of 10)*
2	Slide switch	**Adafruit Product ID: 805** *Breadboard-friendly SPDT Slide Switch*
20	Pushbutton (2-leg)	**DigiKey Product No: EG4378TB-ND** *Tactile Switch SPST-NO 0.05A, 12V, 2-leg pushbutton*
1	Photoresistor	**Adafruit Product ID: 161** *Photo cell (CdS photoresistor)*
1	Tilt sensor	**Adafruit Product ID: 173** *Tilt ball switch!*
1	Force-sensitive resistor (FSR)	**Adafruit Product ID: 1075** *Square Force-Sensitive Resistor (FSR) – Alpha MF02A-N-221-A01* *Note: Adafruit Product ID: 166 (round FSR) will also work*
1	IR break-beam sensor (3mm LEDs)	**Adafruit Product ID: 2167** *Infrared (IR) Break Beam Sensors with Premium Wire Header Ends – 3mm LEDs*
20	2N7000 transistor (N-Channel MOSFET)	**DigiKey Product No: 2721-2N7000-ND** *2N7000, TO-92, 60V, 0.2A MOSFET*
1	Optional: BS250 P-Channel transistor (MOSFET)	**DigiKey Part No: BS250P-ND** BS250, TO-92 P-Channel MOSFET, 45V, 230mA, E-LINE

(*continued*)

Table 1-1. (*continued*)

Tools: For bonus chapters and optional projects

1	Multimeter	**Adafruit Product ID: 2034** *Digital Multimeter Model 9205B+*
1	Conductive fabric tape	**Adafruit Product ID: 3961** *Conductive Nylon Fabric Tape – 5mm Wide x 10 meters long*
1	Wire strippers	**Adafruit Product ID: 4747** *Automatic Self-Adjusting Wire Strippers and Cutter*

Reading Circuit Diagrams

Circuit diagrams are pictures of circuits that show us how to build a specific circuit. In this book, we'll use **Fritzing diagrams**[2] which are cartoon-like images that show parts and wires that resemble reality. Grab your breadboard and let's look at some circuit pictures!

Circuit diagram   A picture that shows us how to wire, or build, a circuit.

Figure 1-2 shows what a Fritzing diagram looks like.

---

[2] Fritzing is a fantastic, open source program! You can download it here: https:// fritzing.org/

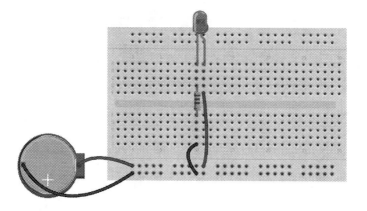

Figure 1-2. *Fritzing diagram for a simple circuit*

The gray block is the breadboard where we connect our battery, light (specifically an LED), and resistor (to limit the flow of electricity). The **red and black wires** show us how to connect the different sides of the circuit.[3] The colors of the wires we use to build our circuit do not have to match the colors in the picture, but it can be helpful to start by using two different colors as shown in the picture. We'll learn more about why we have two different colored wires in Chapter 2. Let's label the parts in our Fritzing diagram in Figure 1-3 below.

---

[3] Wait, wait, wait... isn't a circuit a circle? How can a circle have sides?! Great question, reader! Circuit circles have a positive (red) and a negative (black) side, which we'll dig into in more detail in Chapter 2.

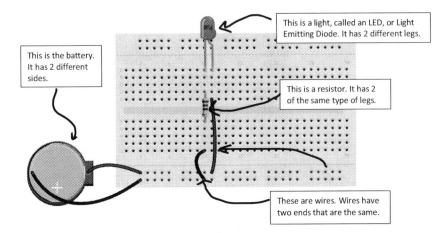

Figure 1-3. *A Fritzing Diagram with labeled parts*

What Other Information Is in This Diagram?

The breadboard has lots of small holes for plugging in wires and circuit parts. Like a spreadsheet, the holes are ordered into **rows** that are labeled with numbers and **columns** that are labeled with letters. The breadboard shown in Figure 1-4 below is called a **half-size breadboard**.

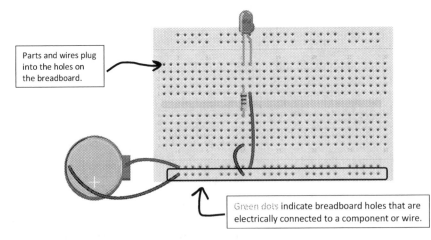

Figure 1-4. *A half-size breadboard showing how Fritzing Diagrams display parts that are electrically connected*

🔎 **Check it out:** Look on your breadboard and read the labels for the holes. How many rows are there? How many columns?

Half-size breadboards have two symmetric sides separated by a **trench** in the middle – the trench is handy if you have circuit parts that have multiple legs because you can place the part over the trench so that all of its legs are in different rows.

But wait... why does it matter if legs are in different rows?? Because **breadboard holes that are in the same row** (on one side of the trench) **are electrically connected**.

For example, look at Figure 1-5 where red boxes enclose the holes that are electrically connected on the left side of the breadboard, all of the holes in row 1, columns A–E, are connected; all of the holes in row 2, columns A–E, are connected; etc. Likewise, on the right side of the breadboard, the holes in row 1, columns F–J, are connected; the holes in row 2, columns F–J, are connected; etc. The groupings of holes for row 1 are shown in the picture to the right bounded by red rectangles.

On the outsides of the breadboard are **power rails**, additional holes for connecting power sources to our circuits. You might have noticed this is how we connected the battery in the Fritzing diagrams we saw earlier!

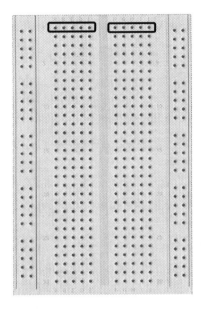

Figure 1-5. *Breadboard diagram with boxes showing how the breadboard holes are electrically connected*

Trench   The middle gap in a breadboard that electrically separates the two sides.

Power rails   Breadboard holes connected vertically for connecting power sources to a breadboard.

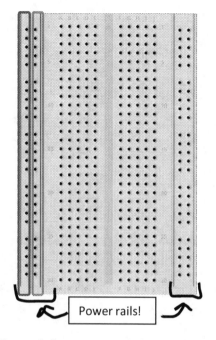

Power rails!

Figure 1-6. Breadboard diagram with boxes showing how the holes in the breadboard power rails are electrically connected

The holes that make up a single power rail are grouped differently than the holes in the middle of the breadboard: the holes in the outside column are connected, and the holes on the inside column are connected. **Each power rail is electrically separate.** This means we can connect two different power supplies to one breadboard. Yay!

17

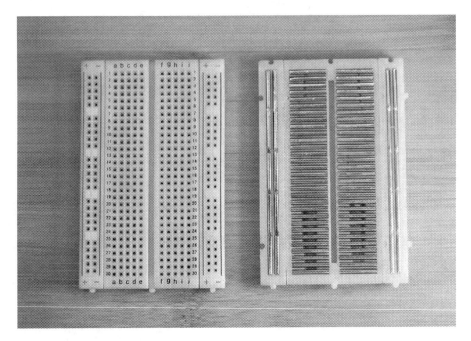

Figure 1-7. *Metal strips underneath a breadboard transfer electricity between the breadboard holes!*

🔎 **Check it out:** Peel off **part of** the adhesive backing of your breadboard and look at the metal underneath! If you have an extra breadboard, use pliers to remove one of the metal bars from the bottom to get a sneak peak at the metal pins on the inside!

HOW DOES THIS WORK??

If you peel off the sticky bottom of a breadboard, you'll see strips of metal on the bottom. The tops of the metal strips have metal pins, or clips, that are under the plastic holes on the breadboard. When we insert the leg of an electronic component, like an LED, the metal clips grab onto the component leg and provide an electrical connection to the rest of the pins in that row.

Each circuit we'll learn in this book will have a Fritzing diagram to show you how to connect the parts. As we get deeper into circuits and you get more practice, I'll challenge you to try on your own before you look at the Fritzing diagram. Remember: The best way to learn is to do, and I *want* you to make some mistakes along the way because you'll be more likely to remember what you learned.

Finally, **a quick mention on circuit schematics**. These are harder to read than Fritzing diagrams because schematics use symbols to represent parts. The Fritzing circuit we saw earlier would look like Figure 1-8 as a circuit schematic.

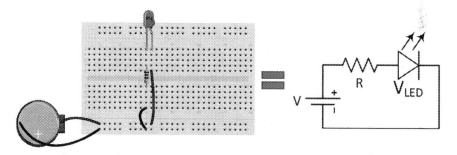

Figure 1-8. *How a Fritzing diagram (left) represents a circuit schematic (right)*

As we learn new electronic components, I'll also introduce the circuit schematic symbol for that part. You do not need to memorize these! My goal is to make it easier for you going forward, so when you see a schematic or a datasheet, you'll have a foundation to start from. Besides, you can always look up a part's schematic symbol using your favorite search engine. ☺

How to Read This Book

You're doing it already, yay!!

In all seriousness, you likely noticed that there are different types of content in this book.

First, we're working with lots of materials, so **material lists for a section** will be called out like this:

Grab These Materials

- Pencil

- Paper

- Stopwatch (a timer on your smartphone works great)

Make sure you have everything on the list unless it's labeled as optional. If you like interactive books (I do!), feel free to check off the parts as you gather them!

Next, helpful vocabulary are called out in text boxes for you to reference later more easily, like this:

Word   A way to share information with and convey meaning to other humans.

I've also included "the more you know" boxes, like this:

THE MORE YOU KNOW! (THERE WILL BE A TOPIC HEADLINE OR QUESTION HERE)

These are fun tidbits of history, deeper dives into specific topics, questions that commonly pop up in my workshops, and other interesting information that I thought you might enjoy. These are not "required" reading, and you may skip if you so choose.

… Although I hope you read this one. ☺

Finally, there are different ways for you to engage with the material in this book. Research studies on how people learn indicate that applying knowledge is the best way to get it to stick. Because I'm interested in your learning outcomes more so than your ability to follow instructions, I've included three ways to apply the knowledge you're learning. These are designed to help you better understand the information in this book and to get it to stick in your brain for longer (or at least be more easily recalled).

The first is what I call "**Questions for Thinking**," which are indicated as follows:

🫠 **Question 1:** What has stood out to you about this book so far?

🫠 **Question 2:** What are you most excited to learn? What are you dreading?

While I encourage you to truly consider the preceding Questions for Thinking, the ones that follow in subsequent chapters will focus on the learning content.

The second is "**Mini Observations**," like so:

> $\mathcal{P}$ **Check it out:** Bring awareness to your body in this moment. What do you hear? See? Taste? Smell? Feel? What is happening in your body? Are your shoulders tense, is your heart fluttering, your breathing slow and steady or rapid and shallow? Turn your attention inward for a few minutes (I recommend setting a five-minute timer) and take some deep breaths. If you are so inclined, write down your observations using the pencil and paper from earlier.

The third method of applying this book's knowledge is "**Experiment Callouts**," which are at-home explorations and/or deeper observations for you to conduct solo or with a friend or family member.

Like a cat engrossed and delighted in discovering the mysteries of a ball of string or a child testing the ratio of dirt and water that makes the best mud pie, experiments are a great way to let loose your curiosity, awaken your creativity, and probe the mysteries of the world around you.

In my honest opinion, these experiments are fun ways to discover the truly bizarre features of electricity, things we might have discovered as kids and thought, "Huh, this is weird and silly!" I hope the Experiment Callouts also inspire you to ask more questions and bring curiosity (and experimentation!) to your everyday life. Remember, **you do not need to *be* a scientist to *do* science**!

Finally, any time we build a circuit, I've included some "Troubleshooting Tips" at the end of the build section, like so:

TROUBLESHOOTING TIPS

1. Check the power source (e.g., the battery).

2. No, really, 90% of the time it's the power source. I have uttered, "Oh, wow, it's not turned on…" more times than I can count.

These are pulled from my own experience building circuits and from the most common questions I get from students, listed in descending order based on most likely/common problem. That said, these tips are not exhaustive and may not always cover a specific problem you encounter. If you run through the troubleshooting tips and your circuit still does not work, reach out to a friend, family member, colleague, or another human for a second set of eyes and brain to help you debug. If that still doesn't resolve the problem, you may search online or reach out to me directly (I can't promise a quick response, but I will do my best to get to your question).

I hope you find these tips help the book to be more engaging and fun! Now let's learn some science!

Summary

This chapter introduced the book that you're embarking on! We learned about the big-picture topics in this book as well as my educational approach, did a deep dive on safety (yay, safety!), looked at the tools and materials we'll need to build the projects in this book, and learned how to read the circuit diagrams that will help us along the way. Read on to learn more about the weird and wonderful world of electricity!

CHAPTER 2

Paper Circuits

In this chapter, we'll learn the basics of electricity starting from the building blocks of matter – protons, neutrons, and electrons. – We'll learn common terms and concepts that pop up when working with electricity and circuits. Let's get started!

What Is Electricity?

Grab These Materials

- Balloon
- 9V battery
- Coin cell battery
- 1 LED
- 2 alligator clips
- Safety goggles (glasses are fine)

When you think of electricity, what manifests in your mind?

Maybe you imagined a bright bolt of lightning illuminating the sky, or you were reminded that you need to charge your phone (always), or perhaps you chuckle at your childhood discovery that shuffling across carpet in socks gave you zapping powers. Electricity is all these things, and

© Jennifer Fox 2023
J. Fox, *Beginning Breadboarding*, https://doi.org/10.1007/978-1-4842-9218-1_2

so much more! Like gravity, electricity is one of those phenomena in this big, beautiful universe that pops up everywhere once you know where, and how, to look.

This also means that it can be tricky to define electricity because it often depends on context. I'll do my best, and there are tons of other great resources like Wikipedia to fill in any gaps or answer burning questions.

While gravity is due to matter, or mass, electricity is due to charges. There are two different types of electric charges: **positive** and **negative**. Like magnetic poles, **charges that are the same repel** each other, and **charges that are different attract** each other.

> 😵 **Question 1:** If you moved a positive charge close to another positive charge, what would happen?

> 😵 **Question 2:** If you moved a positive charge close to a negative charge, what would happen?

Electricity A form of energy due to charged particles. Similar charges repel; dissimilar charges attract.

Figure 2-1 can help us visualize how charges affect each other.

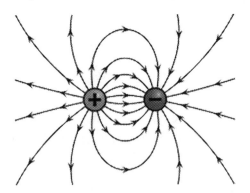

Figure 2-1. *Electric field lines between a positive and a negative charge. Source: Wikimedia Commons*

The positive charge is illustrated on the left and the negative charge on the right. The lines between the charges are called **field lines**. Field lines tell us the direction of a force between two objects. For example, in Figure 2-1, the field lines tell us that the two charges feel a pull toward each other because the arrows point from one charge to the other. If we have two of the same charges, like in Figure 2-2 below, we see field lines that show how the charges are pushing away from each other.

Electric field lines A representation of the force between two charges that points from positive charges to negative charges.

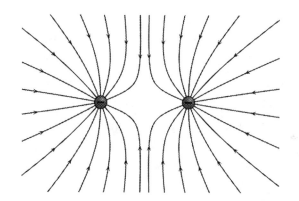

Figure 2-2. *Electric field lines between two negative charges. Source: Wikimedia Commons*

Electric field lines are defined to point from positive charges to negative charges – you do not need to remember this, but it's helpful to have a basic understanding of *why* the field line arrows are pointing the way that they do. This will also come up when we talk about electric current in the next section.

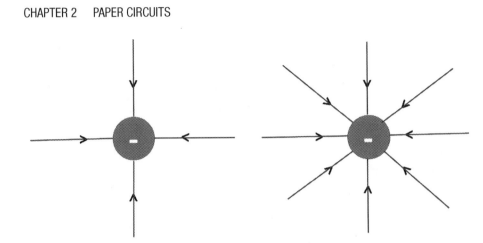

Figure 2-3. *Field lines showing the magnitude, or size, of two different negative charges*

Typically, field lines also tell us the size, or **magnitude**, of that force based on the proportion of the number of lines. For example, in Figure 2-3, the charge on the right is two times larger than the charge on the left. Even if the right-side charge wasn't labeled to tell us how big it is, we could figure out that it's got twice as much charge than the left-side charge because the right-side charge has eight field lines coming out of it, while the left-side charge only has four. Hooray for visual math!

The number of lines doesn't tell us exactly how strong the force is, it only gives us a relationship, or **proportion, between charges**. This means that all we can conclude about the preceding two charges is that the right-side charge is twice as strong. We don't know if it is a tiny charge or a huge charge, just that it's two times stronger than the left-side charge.

| WHAT DO THE TERMS "POSITIVE" AND "NEGATIVE" MEAN? |

Like most labels, "positive" and "negative" are arbitrary. The important thing is that there are two kinds of **different** charges. The difference between the charges determines how the charges behave under different conditions.

For example, even if we called "positive" charges "green" charges and "negative" charges "blue" charges, "green" charges would repel "green" charges and attract "blue" charges.

Wait, wait, wait... what exactly **are** charges?? Great question, my dear reader friend! This gives us a perfect excuse to learn about one of my favorite topics: atoms! If you are already familiar with atoms, you may skip the next section and move on to the first experiment.

Atoms: The Building Blocks of Nature

Everything that we can see, hear, feel, and touch is made up of the same types of building blocks called **atoms**. At the center of an atom is a teeny-tiny, super dense cluster of particles that we call the nucleus. The nucleus has two types of particles: protons, which are positively charged (hey, charges!!), and neutrons, which are neutrally charged. Surrounding the nucleus is a cloud of particles called electrons,[1] which are negatively charged (more charges!). An image of a helium atom is shown in Figure 2-4 below.

---

[1] Electrons are real bizarre particles (but then again, most of quantum mechanics is real weird and SUPER cool). They are both a particle and a wave at the same time 😵. Even when they are behaving as a particle, they are a "point particle" which means that they have mass but no volume. Yea... real weird. And super cool!! For the purposes of this book, we can treat electrons as mostly regular particles that absorb energy and bounce off things like billiard (pool) balls.

29

Atoms The basic building blocks of nature! Atoms have a heavy, dense nucleus at the center made of particles called protons and neutrons. The nucleus is surrounded by an electron cloud (it's real weird and cool; see the following footnote).

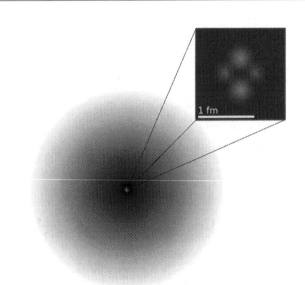

Figure 2-4. *A diagram of a helium atom (in ground state). Source: Wikipedia*

Atoms are hilariously small – like, 100 picometers across, which is 1 x 10^{-12}m (0.000000000001m). For context, our eyes can see things about as small as 0.0001m – atoms are nine times smaller than that!! That is so, so small.

Anyway! Back to how atoms affect electricity. With these three basic building blocks – protons, neutrons, and electrons – we get all the elements on the periodic table (hey, chemistry!). The simplest element is hydrogen, which has one proton, one neutron, and one electron, followed by helium which has two protons, two neutrons, and two electrons; the third is lithium which has three protons, three neutrons, and three electrons, and so on.[2] Yay for patterns in nature!

Protons and neutrons are really intensely attracted to each other (via a force called the strong nuclear force) and stay clustered close together at the center of the atom. Electrons are attracted to the nucleus because of the electromagnetic force (protons are positively charged so the nucleus has an overall positive charge), our first peek at atomic electricity! There are strict rules about how electrons can stack up around the nucleus because negative charges repel each other. I'm simplifying **a lot**, but these rules basically translate into specific distances, or orbitals, where only two electrons are allowed to be at a time (Figure 2-5). Once that orbital is full, a new electron must orbit the nucleus at a farther distance. A full orbital is more stable than a not full orbital, and atoms prefer stability (like most things in this universe, including us humans).

Figure 2-5. *The first two orbitals for atoms. Source: Wikipedia*

In the case of hydrogen, the first electron hangs out in the first orbital but doesn't fill it completely. Helium has two electrons, which fill its first orbital and makes it super, super stable – it doesn't want to add or give up its happy lil' electrons which is why helium doesn't interact with other substances. For lithium, the first orbital is full, and the third electron has to go farther away from the nucleus to the second orbital. Lithium

---

[2] … mostly. The pattern of increasing and equivalent numbers of protons, neutrons, and electrons holds for many elements on the periodic table, but not all. Since chemistry is not my wheelhouse, I'd recommend looking up the periodic table in your favorite search engine! Wikipedia is also a great resource.

(and hydrogen) is an example of why metals conduct electricity – there is a single electron in an orbital that it can "share" with other elements. This sharing causes atoms to bond with each other and to do things like allow electricity to flow.

Metals are good conductors[3] because there are what are called "**free electrons**": excess electrons that float freely through the metal. Without electricity, these electrons are moving randomly, and the net effect of all the electrons cancels out (like a bunch of fish swimming around in a lake). But, when an electric force is applied, the electrons move in the direction of the force (like how the fish will all swim away from a predator).

Free electrons Electrons within a conducting substance (e.g., metal) but not permanently attached to a specific atom.

Most atoms, or **elements**, are neutral because they have an equal number of protons (positively charged) and electrons (negatively charged). Some elements exist as **ions**, where there is an imbalance of either protons or electrons, giving the element a net charge (a net positive charge if there are fewer electrons than protons and a net negative charge if there are excess electrons).

Ion Atoms, or elements, that have an overall net charge (either positive or negative).

---

[3] Conductors are materials that easily conduct electricity. Most metals, e.g., copper, silver, and gold, are good conductors. Insulators are materials that resist the flow of electricity. Most materials besides metal are insulators, like plastic, wood, and glass.

Project 2-1: Static Electricity!

Okay, we've gotten into the weeds a bit. How does all this help us build circuits or do other cool projects?? Let's do a fun project!

Grab the balloon you gathered for this chapter and blow it up with air. Use the balloon to rub your hair (or kindly ask another person to do this) for a few seconds, and move the balloon away from your head. If your hair stands on end against the force of gravity, **you've just caused static electricity!**

Why does this happen? Rubbing the balloon on your hair makes it pull off negative charges, **electrons**, from the atoms in your hair. This leaves the balloon with lots of negative charges and your hair with lots of positive charges. Since negative and positive charges attract, the charge on the balloon attracts the charge on your hair. This allows your hair to defy gravity!

If you've ever accidentally on purpose shocked yourself or someone else after shuffling across a room in socks, you've experienced another form of static electricity. That said, we tend to be more familiar with moving charges. This is called **dynamic electricity**, and it's how we light our homes, heat our blow dryers, and send invisible signals to communicate across vast distances.

Current, Voltage, and AC vs. DC

When we talk about electricity, we are typically talking about electrical current. **Current is the amount of electricity (charge) that is flowing through a circuit,**[4] like when we have water flowing through a hose. Once the water is on, turning the hose spigot adjusts the amount of water flowing out of the hose nozzle. Similarly, with electricity, we can change the amount of current that flows through our circuit wires by adjusting our electrical power source (and the components in our circuit).

Electric current The amount of charge that flows past a point in a given amount of time. Current is measured in Amps (A).

But wait! There's more to electricity than just the amount of charge flowing! And it's slightly more confusing, so let's use a simple experiment to help us understand!

> 😊 **Question:** What happens when you plug a hose nozzle with your finger? (If you've never done this, try it! If you don't have access to a hose, use the faucet... but be warned, you *may* get wet!)

NO PEEKING.

Plugging the hose nozzle with your finger causes a small, fast jet of water to shoot out of the nozzle! In this experiment (or play), you didn't change the amount of water flowing, but you *did* change the space through which the water could fit. In other words, the same amount of water must fit through a smaller hole, so a smaller volume of water flowed faster. This is also known as water pressure.

---

[4] More specifically, current is defined as the amount of electric charge that flows past a specific point in our circuit over a given amount of time.

Water pressure is similar to (but not the same as) **electric potential**, or **voltage**. Voltage measures the amount of energy that we need to move a lil' charge from one place to another (and by lil' I mean, specifically, one unit of charge).

Voltage The amount of energy needed to move one unit of charge from one point in a circuit to another. Voltage is measured in Volts (V).

To recap: Current tells us how much charge is flowing, and voltage tells us how much electric pressure is pushing these charges. **Current has units of Amperes, or Amps (A) for short. Voltage** has units named after itself called **Volts (V).**

Cool! ... But how is this useful to building circuits? While there are many things you can explore and build with circuits without knowing what current or voltage is, a basic understanding is super helpful whenever you need to make your own decisions (or when you're curious about why electricity behaves the way it does).

For example, we need to understand current and voltage to choose the right power sources and appropriate components for our circuits, to problem solve and debug, to read datasheets, to build our own circuits, and so much more. Throughout the book, we'll learn how current and voltage affect our circuit, why the parts you're using were chosen, and how to apply this knowledge to explore new and bigger projects.

In case you're not convinced, let's do another project!

Project 2-2: Playing with Voltage

First, put on your safety goggles! Grab the rest of the materials you gathered for this chapter. (No need for the balloon unless you want to draw eyes and a smile on it and pretend that it's your scientific assistant... totally up to you.)

Insert the coin cell battery into the battery case. Take one of the alligator clip wires and connect one alligator clip to the **longer** LED leg and the other alligator clip to the red wire on the coin cell case. Connect a second alligator clip wire between the shorter LED leg and the black wire on the coin cell case. Observe what happens! (The built circuit is shown below in Figure 2-6.)

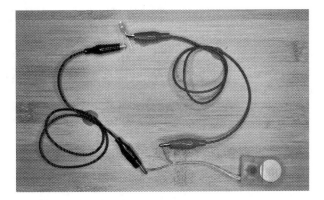

Figure 2-6. Our first circuit built with alligator clips, a battery, and an LED!

Hopefully, the light turns on! Huzzah! You just made your first circuit.

Now, unclip the second alligator clip from the black coin cell battery wire and clip that lead to the negative terminal on the 9V battery (the larger terminal, which should have a minus sign (-) label on the side of the battery). Unclip the other alligator clip wire from the red coin cell battery wire and clip to the other (positive) 9V battery terminal. Now your LED should be disconnected from the coin cell and connected to the 9V as its power source. What happens?? (The built circuit is shown below in Figure 2-7).

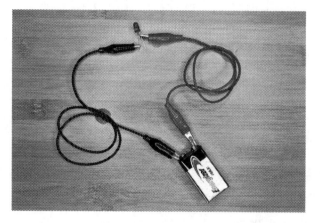

Figure 2-7. *A simple circuit made with alligator clips, a 9V battery, and an LED*

... womp, womp, womppppp. Our LED burned out!

Whyyyy ?? Although the coin cell battery can provide more current, or charge, over time, **the 9V battery has higher electric potential**, or pressure. This causes the LED to burn out because it can only handle maximum 3V of electric pressure.

And voila! A real-world demonstration as to why it's useful to know about current and voltage!

There's one more concept I like to cover before we get a'buildin: AC and DC! There have been far too many jokes about electricity and the rock band, so I'll let you crack your own and chuckle at your own ingenuity rather than groaning at mine.

.... You're welcome J (I make no such promises about bad jokes for the remainder of this book.)

Dynamic (moving) electricity comes in two main flavors:

1. **Direct current (DC)** electricity: This is either on or off, like a battery. It flows in one direction.

2. **Alternating current (AC)** electricity: This electricity changes direction very, very quickly and is basically a form of magic.

   Okay, okay, AC is not magic. It's a phenomenon that's fully understood by approximately 308 people.[5] For now, all that you need to know is that the flow of electricity changes in size and direction at consistent, or regular, intervals.

Here's a helpful image that shows how these two electrical signals look over time (Figure 2-8).

Direct current (DC) Electrical current that is constant in magnitude and flows in one direction.

Alternating current (AC) Electrical current that changes in magnitude and direction.

---

[5] I 100% made up this estimate.

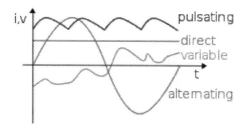

Figure 2-8. *Different types of dynamic electricity! DC is shown in red; AC is shown in green. Source: Wikipedia*

As we can see in Figure 2-8, the current and voltage of DC electricity don't change: the electrical output of a battery is (or should be) constant. (The real world is never that perfect, but it's generally accurate in practice.)

We can also see in Figure 2-8 that AC electricity, like what comes out of wall outlets, a motor, or a generator, **does** change over time.

WHY DO WE USE BOTH AC AND DC??

There are pros and cons to both AC and DC electricity. AC is what we use for our electrical grid largely because it's cheaper and easier to reduce power loss when transmitting electricity over (long) distances. AC electricity is made by turbines and generators.

DC is what we use for almost all our electronics because it's what the transistor (the building block of modern-day computers) needs to operate. It is easier to change the speed of a DC electric motor which is why it's preferred for electric and hybrid cars. DC electricity is generated by batteries and solar panels.

Alright, with that solid foundation in our brains (and as reference material whenever you need it), onward to building!

Let's Make Our First Circuit!

Grab These Materials

- 1 coin cell battery

- 1 coin cell battery case

- 2 alligator clips

- 1 LED (any color!)

Project 2-3: Let There Be Light!

First, let's wield our powers of observation!

> 🔎 **Check it out:** Get the coin cell and LED like shown in Figure 2-9. Remove the coin cell from its case. Observe these two circuit components – what do you notice about each of them?

Figure 2-9. *An LED and a coin cell battery*

Okay, now that you've had some time to observe these two components, your first challenge is to light up the LED with **only** the battery! I promise, **you do not need anything else**.

Try for at least three minutes before looking at a photo.

IT HASN'T BEEN THREE MINUTES YET, NO PEEKING.

Hint 1: How many legs does the LED have?

Hint 2: How many sides of the battery are there?

Okay, okay, either you've turned the light on (CONGRATULATIONS, you made your first circuit!!!), or you put in enough effort (HOORAY for effort!!) such that I'm willing to show you how (see Figure 2-10 below).

Figure 2-10. *An LED and a coin cell battery connected so that the LED turns on!*

☺ **Question:** Does it matter which way the LED connects to the coin cell? **Try a different orientation** if you haven't yet.

If you played around with different orientations of the LED and coin cell, I'm hoping you discovered that the LED does not turn on if you connect it like shown in Figure 2-11.

Figure 2-11. *An LED and a coin cell battery connected in a way where the LED is off*

These orientations look very similar, so what's the difference between the two??

This is why I wanted you to use your observation skills! While you were looking at the LED, you might have noticed that it has **two different legs**: one is longer than the other. (You might also have picked up on this from our earlier experiment.) **The longer LED is the positive leg.** This means that we connect the longer leg to the positive side of the battery.

But wait!! Which side of the battery is the positive side?!

Again, our powers of observation can give us critical knowledge. **You might have noticed a "+" and a "3V" written on one side of the battery.** (If you didn't, that's okay! Look at the coin cell until you can see those things or ask a friend for help if you can't find them.) These markings give us some information about the coin cell. The "+" tells us that this is the

42

positive side of the battery (more on that in a bit). The "3V" tells us... hey! You learned about voltage! You already know this one. ☺

> (But, in case you forgot or you're one of those people
> that skips around in books, the "3V" label means
> that the coin cell has a voltage of 3 Volts.)

To recap: We need to connect the longer LED leg to the positive side of the battery (the side with the "+").

The reason why we must connect the longer LED leg to the positive side of our battery is that electricity flows in a specific direction: **from positive to negative.**[6] This concept is called **polarity** – a term used to indicate the directionality of electricity. Some electronic components, like LEDs, need electricity to flow through them in one direction. Other components, like resistors (which we'll explore later), are not polarized and can have electricity flow through them in either direction.

Polarity Directional flow of electricity from positive to negative.

Polar components Electronic components that require current to flow through them in a specific direction.

We'll need to bring this knowledge of polarity to every circuit we build. Sometimes, this is a source of frustration because a polarized component may be why a circuit isn't behaving as expected. The good news is that there are consistent conventions to indicate whether a component

---

[6] For those of y'all who are like, "wait... isn't it the negative charges (electrons) that are moving??": YES. Well, in most situations, it's the electrons that are moving with some exceptions for things like batteries. But, the flow of DC electricity was defined to be from positive to negative before humans knew about electrons, and, well, it was easier to just go with the flow (see, bad jokes abound! Srynotsry). This is sort of similar to why the United States is still using inches and feet and miles instead of metric units. Maybe one day we'll update these things... Here's hoping.

is polarized. You just learned the most common method: **electronic components with one longer lead are polarized, and the positive lead is the longer one**.

Alright! Let's keep building and learning!

Project 2-4: Making It Bigger!

First, insert the coin cell back into its lil' case. **For all the projects going forward, I will assume that your coin cell is snugly in the coin cell case.** Next, get your two alligator clip wires which we will use to make our circuit bigger. A bigger circuit is helpful because we don't always want the battery to be right next to the component, especially if we have lots of components!

For this project, the circuit that we are building looks like Figure 2-12.

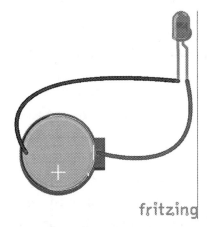

Figure 2-12. *Our first simple circuit with the basic parts: power source (battery), power sink (LED), and conductors (wires)*

Remember that this picture is a representation – you might have parts that look slightly different than the ones in the photo. It also does not show the alligator clips. That's okay! The goal of these circuit pictures is to show you how the different parts connect. It's important to learn how to apply a general picture like the one earlier to your specific set of circumstances because that will help you build circuits from sources outside this book.

Here are **step-by-step instructions** if you need them:

1. Grab your first alligator clip wire. Connect one of the alligator clips to the positive battery wire (red) and the other alligator clip lead to the positive (longer) LED leg.

2. Connect the second alligator clip between the negative battery wire (black) and the shorter LED leg.

Tada! A longer light circuit! (Just in case your light did not turn on, there are some troubleshooting tips at the end of this section. Every project in this book has its own set of troubleshooting tips in case things don't quite work out as expected, which, ironically, is to be expected in making and engineering.)

🔎 **Check it out:** Now that we've built two circuits (whoa, yea!), observe the different pieces that are common between both the small and larger circuits.

If we break down any circuit, there are three different necessary parts:

1. **Power source**: Every circuit needs a source of energy, which is where the electricity comes from. In this circuit, we are using a small battery. Other power sources include solar panels, generators, and turbines.

   What happens if we don't have a power source? Well.... Nothing! No source of electricity means our circuit is powerless.... Literally!

   The most common cause of failure in a circuit is that the power source is not connected or needs to be replaced. (For real, 60% of the time when I'm building something and it doesn't work, it's because I forgot to plug it in or turn on the power switch. It's good to be able to chuckle at ourselves when (not if, *when*) this happens. ☺)

2. **Power sink**: Every circuit also needs something to use the energy from the power source. In these first two circuits, our LED uses the electrical energy from our battery and converts it into light! Other components convert electrical energy into heat, motion, sound, or other functions.

   What happens if we don't have a power sink? If we have conductors between the power source, for example, a wire connecting the two sides of a battery, but there's no "official" power sink, the electrical energy still flows and loses some energy along the way. This causes the wires to heat up, and, if our power source is a battery, it means we will probably drain our battery super-duper fast.

Short circuit When conductive material connects the terminals of a power source without any load, or power sink, to use up the energy from the power source.

⚠ This is also known as a short circuit! If you touch the battery and it feels warm, immediately disconnect your circuit because you likely have a short circuit.

3. **Conductors**: Every circuit needs an easy path for the electricity to flow from the power source to the power sink (and back to the power source). The

most efficient way to do this is to use a conductive material, like copper wire. For safety purposes (for both ourselves and the components in our circuit), we typically want to use wires that are coated in an insulating material like plastic.

What happens if there are no conductors? In the circuits that we are building, the electrical energy of our power source is not large enough to overcome the resistance of air, and so current won't flow from the power source to the power sink. In other words, nothing will happen! Even a teeny-tiny air gap is often enough to stop the flow of electricity.

This is another common cause of failure in our circuits. If you build a circuit, check that the power source is on and connected properly, and then double-check that the metal parts of all the connectors are snugly touching the metal parts of all the other connectors as shown in Figure 2-13.

Figure 2-13. *How to properly connect an alligator clip lead to a circuit wire. The left image shows the alligator clip lead connected to the wire insulation - this is the incorrect connection. The right images shows the alligator clip lead connected to the metal of the circuit wire - this is the correct connection*

TROUBLESHOOTING TIPS

1. Check that the battery is securely in its connector and is oriented properly (positive to positive, negative to negative). Check that the battery case switch is on the "On" position.

2. Check that the alligator clip leads are fully and securely clipped onto the exposed metal ends of the battery connector.

3. Check that the alligator clip leads are fully and securely clipped onto the metal parts of the LED leg.

4. Check that the exposed metals of the alligator clip leads are **not touching.**

    a. Also, check that the LED legs are not touching.

5. Check that the longer (positive) LED leg is connected to the red (positive) battery case wire.

Schematic Symbols for an LED and a Battery

Since you've successfully built your first circuit (woo!), let's take a look at the circuit schematic symbols for the components we've used so far: LEDs and batteries!

The schematic symbol for an LED looks like Figure 2-14.

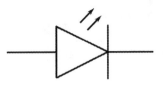

Figure 2-14. *A schematic symbol for an LED*

And a schematic symbol for a battery (any battery) looks like Figure 2-15.

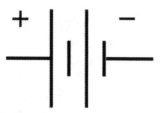

Figure 2-15. *A schematic symbol for a battery*

Project 2-5 (Optional): Paper Circuits!

If you're feeling ambitious or are curious about building paper circuits and/or wearables, here's another fun project to build!

Grab These Materials

For this project, we'll need

- **Conductive fabric tape**

- **Piece of cardstock** (a notecard size or larger, e.g., 3 x 5in or 7.6 x 12.7cm)

- 1 black permanent marker

- 1 ruler

- Regular tape (e.g., clear tape)

In this circuit, we'll use conductive tape as our wires instead of alligator clips.

Build Procedure

1. Using the permanent marker, mark the top of the **shorter** LED leg so that you can easily distinguish the two LED legs (Figure 2-16). When the ink dries, bend the LED legs so that the top of the LED sits flat on a surface.

Figure 2-16. *Marking the shorter (negative) LED leg*

2. Place the LED on top of the cardstock so that the
    light points toward the ceiling.

3. Cut two small pieces of conductive tape (about 0.5in/1cm).
    Remove the tape backing from one piece, then tape over
    the unmarked LED leg so that it is perpendicular to the
    leg. Tape the other piece of conductive tape over and
    perpendicular to the marked LED leg. Smooth out any air
    gaps with a fingertip. See Figure 2-17 below for an image of
    what this should resemble.

Figure 2-17. *Connecting an LED to a piece of paper to make a*
paper circuit

4. Use regular (nonconductive) tape to secure the coin cell battery case to the cardstock.

   a. I'd also recommend taping down the insulated part of the battery case wires so they don't move around.

5. Use the ruler to measure the distance from each of the LED legs to the coin cell battery case wires.

   a. **Remember to connect the black battery case wire to the marked LED leg.**

6. Using your measurements from step 5, cut two pieces of conductive tape that span the distance from the coin cell battery case wires to the LED legs.

   a. For example, if you measure the distance from the positive battery case wire to the positive LED leg to be 2in/5cm, cut a piece of conductive tape that is **at least** 2in/5cm.

   b. **I'd recommend giving yourself some wiggle room by adding ½ in/1cm to your measurement.**

7. One piece at a time, remove the backing from the conductive tape and use it to connect the LED to the coin cell battery. See Figure 2-18 below for an image showing what this might look like.

   a. Connect the black battery case wire to the marked (shorter) LED leg and the red battery case wire to the unmarked (longer) LED leg.

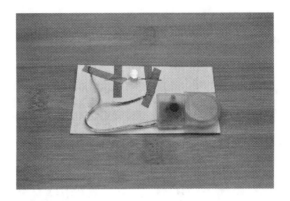

Figure 2-18. *The final paper circuit for an LED!*

Let there be light (again)!

Paper circuits are a great way to make unique birthday and holiday cards for friends and family. For these projects, **I'd recommend drawing out the circuit on the paper before building** it: mark where you want the light(s) to go and where you want to secure the battery. Then, draw lines between the battery wires and LED legs that show you where to put the conductive tape.

TROUBLESHOOTING TIPS

1. Check that the battery is securely in its connector and is oriented properly (positive to positive, negative to negative). Check that the battery case switch is on the "On" position.

2. Check that the conductive tape is fully and securely covering the metal ends of the battery connector. Use a fingertip to smooth out any wrinkles and air gaps.

3. Check that the conductive tape is fully and securely covering the metal parts of the LED leg. Use a fingertip to smooth out any wrinkles and air gaps.

4. Check that the conductive tapes on either side of the LED are **not touching**.

5. Check that the marked (shorter) LED leg is connected to the black (negative) battery case wire.

Add All the Lights! (a.k.a. Series and Parallel Circuits)

You now know how to build a circuit! And you deserve to celebrate your new knowledge and skills. Whenever we learn something new, it's important to celebrate our accomplishments as we go (even small progress is meaningful progress). I encourage you to share your first circuit(s) with a friend or family member and teach them what you learned!

Our next topic is learning how to add multiple lights to the same circuit in two different ways. Let's play around and see what we can discover!

Grab These Materials

- 2 coin cell batteries
- 2 coin cell battery cases
- 6 alligator clips
- 2 LEDs (same color)
- 1 LED of a different color

Project 2-6: Connecting Two LEDs to One Battery

First, make sure that your coin cell battery is snug in its case. Use two alligator clips, the coin cell battery, and one LED to build a circuit so that the LED light turns on (Project 2-5).

Once your light is shining bright, grab another LED of the same color (e.g., if you have a red LED, use another red LED).

Spend at least five to ten minutes exploring how you might connect the second LED to this circuit. This may not feel easy, but it's important to try for **at least five minutes** without looking up the solution because this helps you learn to think critically and creatively about building and debugging circuits. When we do this with simple circuits, we exercise our brain muscles so that they are ready to go for more complex circuits.

Things to consider for this exploration:

- Is it possible to connect the second LED without breaking the circuit? Try both ways (adding wires by breaking the circuit and adding wires without breaking the circuit).

- How is the first LED connected to the coin cell (i.e., what side of the battery does the longer LED leg connect to)? How can you repeat this same connection for the second LED (e.g., can you "stack" the second LED)?

If/when you figure out how to light up the second LED, what do you notice? Does the first LED change when the second LED turns on?

Then try a third, different colored LED! What do you notice about this circuit?

If you get stuck and/or frustrated, take a deep breath and maybe take a break. It may be helpful to go back to the first circuit we built with **only** the coin cell and LED (no case or alligator clips). Explore adding the second (and even third!) LED to that circuit. Once you've got those lights on, explore how you might make the circuit bigger by adding in alligator clips.

How did this experiment feel? Notice what sensations are in your body (sometimes, closing my eyes helps me tune in). Do you feel tension or tightness, warmth or butterflies, your brows furrowing and mouth frowning or relaxed and smiling? Are you holding your breath?

Learning and trying new things can be intense, a blend of euphoria and despair that is different for each of us depending on how familiar we are with the learning process, how we are feeling that day/week/month, and all sorts of other things both within and outside of our control.

As the projects in this book get more and more difficult, I challenge you to regularly check in with yourself and take breaks as you need them. For example, when I'm feeling frustrated by a failed project, I will give myself at least ten minutes before trying again. It can also be helpful to set reasonable deadlines. For example, **try to finish each chapter and its projects within a week** so the knowledge stays fresh, enabling you to build familiarity and expertise more easily. You got this! I've taught thousands of people, and I've found that every person is capable of learning these skills; it just takes practice, patience, and perseverance.

Alright, back to the electronics content! In the previous exploration, you may have discovered at least one way to add a second LED to your circuit (and if not, that's okay! I'm proud of you for trying, and now we can learn both ways together). Now that you've tried on your own, let's learn about the two different ways to add multiple components to our circuits!

Project 2-7: Our First Parallel Circuit

The previous exploration was intentionally difficult. This is my way of being kind to your future self: I want you to build resilience as you learn about and build circuits because at some point, things won't work and it will be really, really frustrating. The more you get used to this feeling, the more quickly and easily you can overcome it in the future.

The second reason why the prior experiment was particularly challenging was because of the coin cell battery. Even though there are two ways to connect multiple circuit components, the 3V coin cell battery only enables us to connect multiple LEDs in one way, like shown in Figure 2-19.

Figure 2-19. *A parallel circuit for two LEDs*

There are different ways to make this same connection, so your circuit might also look like Figure 2-20.

57

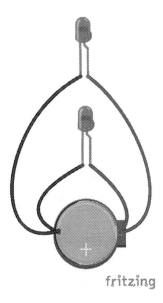

fritzing

Figure 2-20. *A second way to make a parallel circuit with two LEDs*

In both preceding diagrams, the two LEDs are connected **in parallel**. This means that the LEDs are connected in loops, or head-to-head and tail-to-tail – the longer LED legs are connected, either to each other or to the same battery wire, and the shorter LED legs are connected, again, either to each other or to the same battery wire.

If Project 2-7 did not work for you, go ahead and build one of the parallel circuits as shown in either Figure 2-19 or 2-20.

Parallel circuit Circuit components are connected in loops, or head-to-head and tail-to-tail.

Voltage is the same in parallel, while current is different.

WHICH PARALLEL CONNECTION (FIGURE 2-19 OR 2-20) IS BETTER?

Both circuits should behave the same. Personally, I think the Figure 2-19 circuit is easier to build, but if you prefer the Figure 2-20 circuit, go for it!

🔎 **Check it out:** How did the first LED change when you (successfully) connected the second LED? If you didn't notice anything, try removing one of the alligator clips and reconnecting.

If you pay close attention, you'll notice that the first LED got dimmer! Try adding more LEDs and observing what changes.

Project 2-8: More Parallel Circuits!

Whenever we discover something new, it is a great practice to ask what else you could change to test the limits of your discovery and to shed light on remaining mysteries. To do this, let's add a third LED of a **different color** (Figures 2-21 and 2-22)!

Figure 2-21. *Two red LEDs and one yellow LED in parallel*

fritzing

Figure 2-22. *Two red LEDs and one blue LED in parallel*

😵 **Question:** How do the first two LEDs change
when you add a third LED of a different color? Try
both a yellow LED and a blue LED as the third LED.

Wild, right?! The yellow turns on but is noticeably dim, and the blue
doesn't turn on at all! For a sanity check, remove the red LEDs and connect
the blue LED by itself to the battery.

61

⊚ **Question:** Does the order of the LEDs matter?
Try different combinations and observe what
happens.[7]

The LED brightness changes because **electric current** (the amount of
electricity flowing through our LEDs) **changes for circuit components in
parallel, although the voltage is the same.** This means that all the LEDs
in parallel have a voltage of 3V across the LED legs because the coin cell
has 3V across its terminals. But the current flowing through the LEDs is
different. This causes the LEDs to have different brightness.[8] We'll learn
more about why the yellow LED turns on and the blue does not later in this
chapter. (Hint: It has to do with the rainbow. Oh, fun! Cliffhanger!)

The current is different through each light because **parallel circuits
have multiple paths**, or loops, for the current to flow. In our LED parallel
circuit, the current can take two different paths: one through the lower
LED and one through the upper LED.

Tracing the path of the electricity is a helpful practice especially when
you are debugging or designing circuits. To do this, remember that current
flows out from the positive side of the battery, through the wire(s) and into
the connected component(s), then back to the negative side of the battery.
If we were to draw this current flow onto our parallel circuit diagram, it
would look like Figures 2-23 and 2-24.

---

[7] No, the order does not matter. But color does!

[8] Technically, the current through the parallel red LEDs is the same because they
are the same type of component, although the current through the first LEDs gets
smaller when you add the second LED.

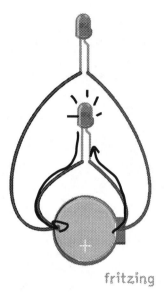

Figure 2-23. *Tracing the path of electricity through the first parallel circuit loop*

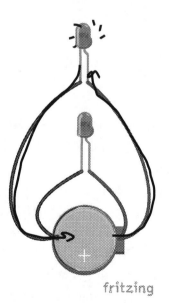

Figure 2-24. *Tracing the path of electricity through the second parallel circuit loop*

Tracing the path of the electricity helps us visualize that the current can take two different paths. This in turn reminds us that the current flowing through each LED may be different.

Project 2-9: Our First Series Circuit

We're not ready to tackle the second way to build circuits: **in series**! If you tried to build a series circuit in Project 2-6, it might have looked like Figure 2-25.

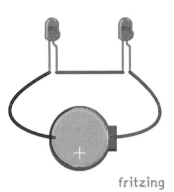

fritzing

Figure 2-25. *Two LEDs in series. Note: This will NOT work with one coin cell battery*

Series circuits are made by connecting parts in line with each other, or head-to-tail. In this figure, the negative leg of the first LED is connected to the positive leg of the second LED (a.k.a. head-to-tail! Er, tail-to-head?).

As you discovered if you tried this, it doesn't work! Sad panda.

The problem is that one coin cell battery does not have enough voltage to connect multiple LEDs in series. This is because **in a series circuit, the electric current is the same through each component, but the voltage across each component is different**. If we trace the path of the electricity, there is only one loop for the current to flow through. If there's only one path, the current must be the same through each component.

Series circuit Circuit components are connected in line, or head-to-tail.

Current is the same in series; voltage is different.

☺ **Question:** Trace the path of the electricity in Figure 2-26, starting from the positive side of the battery. (Remember, red wire = positive.)

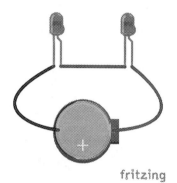

fritzing

Figure 2-26. *Two LEDs in series for tracing the path of the electricity*

Coming back to our series circuit dilemma: Because we have two (of the same) LEDs, the voltage across each LED is 3V / 2 = 1.5V. Sadly, this is not enough voltage to turn on the LEDs.[9]

How can we resolve this?? By getting a battery with higher voltage! Or by adding a second battery.

BUT FIRST! Let's apply what we've learned so far so that it sticks in our brain.

---

[9] How do we know how much voltage LEDs need? By looking at the datasheet for the LED or whatever circuit component we are working with! Datasheets are an excellent resource but can be tricky to read. If you're curious about datasheets, check out the Bonus Project 3 chapter! Red LEDs typically need about 1.7–2V.

🙂 **Question:** If our problem is that we don't have enough voltage, how should we add the second battery?

☐ In series!   ☐ In parallel!

Hint: Current is the same in series; voltage is the same in parallel.

In thinking this through, we know we need to **increase** the voltage of our circuit. Since voltage is the same in parallel, we need to add our second battery **in series** with the first battery, as shown in Figure 2-27.

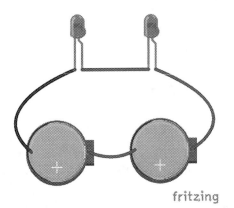

Figure 2-27. *Two LEDs in series with two coin cell batteries (also in series) to provide enough voltage for both LEDs*

As illustrated, we connect the batteries head-to-tail: the positive wire of the first battery connects to the negative wire of the second battery.

Go ahead and build the preceding circuit. Here's a procedure if you prefer written instructions:

1. Connect an alligator clip from the positive wire of the first battery to the **negative** wire of the second battery.

2. Connect a second alligator clip from the positive
    wire of the second battery to the positive (longer)
    LED leg.

3. Connect a third alligator clip from the negative
    (shorter) LED leg to the second LED's positive leg.

4. Connect a fourth alligator clip from the second
    LED's negative leg to the negative wire of the first
    battery.

Voila! Let there be (series) light! Swap out one of the red LEDs for the
blue LED – what do you notice??

**I'd highly recommend playing around with different series and
parallel connections, especially with different colors!** It's a great way
to get a feel for how to add multiple parts to one circuit and to better
understand how current and voltage behave ('cause they are real weird
and fun!).

BUILDING "GOOD" CIRCUITS

A quick note, it's sort of bad practice to build circuits without components
called **resistors** that limit the flow of electricity. Since we're learning the
basics and the worst thing that happens without a resistor is that our battery
dies a lil' faster, it's okay for now.

Summary of Parallel and Series Circuits

To summarize

- Parallel circuits are made in loops, or head-to-head and tail-to-tail. Voltage is the same in parallel; current is different.

  - Parallel circuits have multiple paths for the current to flow.

- Series circuits are made in line, or head-to-tail. Current is the same in series; voltage is different.

  - Series circuits have only one path for the current to flow.

We have one more topic to cover before we get into using breadboards to build circuits and adding some new types of circuit components. Trust me, it's spectacular and totally worth a few minutes. ☺

Electromagnetic Spectrum

"Electromagnetic spectrum" sounds like a superpower, and it might as well be! One of the reasons I **love** electronics is because it feels magical to wield the power of electricity and magnetism. If a witch were to visit us and saw how we could build tiny stars that fit our hands, she would be totally impressed with our powers.[10]

Science enables us to ask questions about the world and seek answers by observation, testing, analysis, and more testing (and more analysis and sometimes scrapping the whole thing and trying something entirely different). While building your first circuits, you discovered a wild mystery

---

[10] Remember: With great power comes great responsibility.

related to different colored lights, so now you may have (I hope!) a burning, scientific question: **WHY do different colored lights have different brightness in the same circuit with the same battery?!**[11]

If this were a book about physics, I would challenge you to develop a hypothesis, then design and build an experiment that enabled you to test that hypothesis.

But, although physics is awesome, this is an intro to an electronics book, so I'm going to spoil the mystery (but if you're motivated, please temporarily put this book down and create and run your own experiment!).

The reason why our lil' LEDs of different colors have different brightness is...

> *drumroll*
>
> *trying to maintain the suspense*
>
> *it tickles me so much how seemingly disparate phenomena are interconnected and I want to share my awe with you*

because of the electromagnetic spectrum! This is a fancy way of saying: light. Our LEDs have different brightness because they are emitting different colors of light! The Electromagnetic Spectrum is illustrated below in Figure 2-28.

---

[11] A quick note on formulating a scientific question: The more specific we can be about the mystery and the circumstances surrounding the mystery, the better our exploration, testing, and analysis will be.

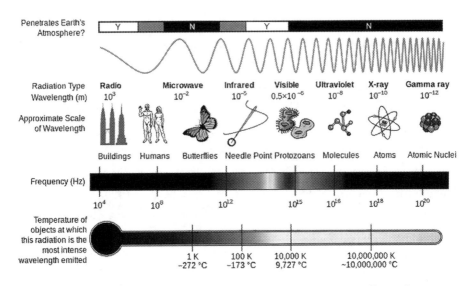

Figure 2-28. *The electromagnetic spectrum! Source: Wikipedia*

Light, which includes visible light, radio waves, microwaves, x-rays, and more, is a wave. Like other waves, for example, ocean waves, light waves have a **wavelength**, or how long they are in space from one wave peak to the next, and a **frequency**, how fast each wave peak passes a point. Higher frequency, and lower wavelength, light waves have higher energy.

We could spend the rest of this book on the electromagnetic spectrum (it's seriously fascinating), but I wanted to introduce you to this concept because it turns out that light, or the electromagnetic spectrum, pops up a LOT in electronics. It's handy to have a deeper understanding of what light **is** before getting further into electronics. I mean, hey, we're only in Chapter 2, and we already stumbled onto a mystery involving the electromagnetic spectrum! (Or EM spectrum for short because I like to be lazy.)

Getting back to the specifics of our mystery: **For visible light, red light waves are lower energy than blue and purple light waves.** This means that if we have a circuit with a red and a blue LED, the red LED will be brighter because the electricity can do less work (i.e., expend less energy). Turns out that electricity **also** likes to be lazy! What a silly and delightful universe we live in.

Going Further

Holy stars we've learned a ton already! We learned about atoms, the basic building blocks of matter, and how atoms have positive and negative (and neutral) charges. We learned that similar charges repel and dissimilar charges attract, which gives rise to the flow of electricity, and that some materials are better at enabling electrical flow (conductors) than others (insulators).

We learned that electricity is weird, and it's not only how much charge flows (current) that matters but also how much electric pressure (voltage) pushes charges from one location to another.

You learned all of that *and* you built your first circuit!! And then you learned about the direction of electrical flow (from positive to negative) and that some electronic components only allow current in one direction (polarity). We made our first circuit longer and learned about the three basic parts of a circuit: power source, power sink, and conductors. Then we learned about series and parallel circuits.

Oh and somehow we snuck in a lil' lesson about the EM spectrum. Phew!

You now know all sorts of handy skills to start building whimsical, fun, and practical projects. The following are a few of my ideas to get you started, but give yourself permission to explore all sorts of wacky and wonderful and WTF ideas.

Project Ideas!
Project 1: Light-Up Greeting Cards

Add lights to a store-bought card or design a card around your LEDs. For this, I'd recommend using conductive fabric tape and **drawing out the circuit** with the location of the battery and light(s) beforehand.

71

Project 2: Tiny Light-Up Furniture for Dolls, Action Figures, or Just Because Miniature Things Are Adorable!

You can build a doll-sized lamp with some paper for the lampshade, a paper tube (or a drinking straw), and a cardboard (or foam) base. What other tiny furniture could you make??

Project 3: Add Some Light-Up Flair to Your Halloween or Other Holiday Costumes!

Tuck coin cells with lights into a crown or behind horns, under a corsage, in a pocket, or wherever brings you joy! Use hot glue to hold the LEDs and/ or alligator clips in place. If you opt to forego alligator clips, use regular (nonconductive) tape to hold the LED to the battery.

Project 4: More Lights on Your Bike!! Or Model Train ☺

One can never have too many lights on a bike! Use hot glue to cover all metal parts and protect the circuit from the rain and other elements. Use hot glue if you want the lights to be temporary and duct tape if you'd like a more permanent solution.

Note: I recommend avoiding anything more permanent than duct tape as the circuits will likely need repair at some point.

Project 5: Tiny Lightsaber!

Ditch the alligator clips for this one. Grab a drinking straw, stick the LED into the bottom, and connect the coin cell directly to the LED. Use regular tape to hold it all together! This is a super fun project to do with kids of all ages.

HOW LONG WILL MY BATTERY LAST??

If left on, a single coin cell with one LED should last at least ten hours. You can calculate how long your battery will last with this formula:

1. A common battery capacity for a coin cell battery (specifically a CR2032) is 210mA hours (210mAh).

    a.   This means that a coin cell can provide about 210mA (0.21A) for one hour, or 21mA for ten hours.

2. Most LEDs consume about 20mA.

3. If we have one LED, our battery will last about ten hours (20mA × 10 hours = 200mA).

4. If we have two LEDs, our battery will last about five hours (20mA × 2 = 40mA, 210mAh / 40mA = 5.25 hours).

Have at it!

Summary

In this chapter, we learned the basics of electricity starting from the basic building blocks of matter: protons, neutrons, and electrons! We used this to build up a fundamental understanding of what electricity actually is (charges) and how it behaves – we did this because (1) it's interesting and cool and (2) it helps a ton when troubleshooting and coming up with new project ideas. We also learned about common terms and concepts that pop up when working with electricity and circuits as well as the difference between AC, the electricity that comes out of your wall, and DC, the electricity that comes out of batteries and solar panels. Finally, we applied our new knowledge to build simple circuits. I'm hoping that this was so fun that you gave some of the going further projects a try!

The next chapter is a special bonus chapter that teaches you how to use multimeters, an invaluable tool when working with electricity.

CHAPTER 3

Breadboards and Outputs

Breadboard Anatomy

Grab These Materials

- Half-size breadboard

Breadboards are made of conductors and insulators to make building circuits easier and quicker than with wires (like our alligator clips). Breadboards are also super convenient when we have lots of circuit components or when we are working with more complex parts that we'll see later in this book.

First, let's revisit the basic parts of the breadboard. Grab your breadboard and follow along! Personally, I like to speak new words and concepts out loud because it helps me remember. You are welcome to use whatever learning technique works best for you.

© Jennifer Fox 2023
J. Fox, *Beginning Breadboarding*, https://doi.org/10.1007/978-1-4842-9218-1_3

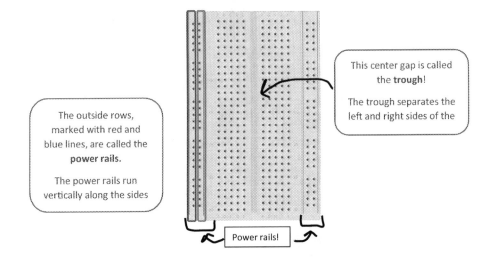

This center gap is called the **trough**!

The trough separates the left and right sides of the

The outside rows, marked with red and blue lines, are called the **power rails.**

The power rails run vertically along the sides

Power rails!

The **rows** of the breadboard are marked with numbers, like a spreadsheet! Each row has five holes for wires and other electronic components. The **columns** are marked with letters... also like a spreadsheet! There are lots of different sizes of breadboards, but most of them have the same number of holes in each row (i.e., the same number of columns), but have different amounts of rows.

Let's look at a breadboard in more detail to better understand how it works (Figure 3-1)!

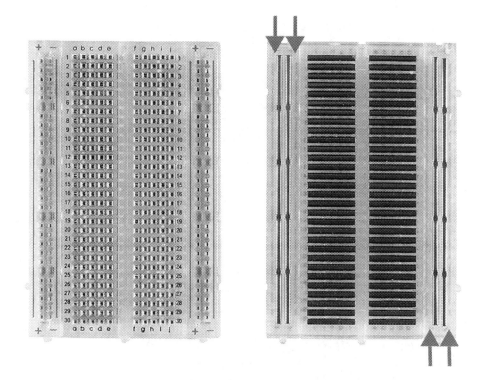

Figure 3-1. *Metal rows on the bottom of the breadboard*

If you flip a breadboard over, you'll typically find padded tape covered with a backing. Under the padded tape are metal strips, like shown in Figure 3-1.

*Note: I'd recommend keeping the tape and backing **on** to prevent your circuits from shorting, but if you didn't already do so in Chapter 1, it is worth peeking under one of the corners to see the metal strips for yourself!*

Figure 3-2. *Metal clip pulled out of a breadboard*

Figure 3-3. *Metal clip in a breadboard close up*

If we pull out one of the metal strips in our breadboard, like we see in Figures 3-2 and 3-3, we discover that they are connected to metal clips! These metal clips, like the one in Figure 3-3, sit directly underneath the breadboard holes. When you push a piece of wire or a component leg into one of the breadboard holes, the clip grabs onto it and holds it in place!

A wire or other conductive material pushed into a breadboard hole is electrically connected to the other holes in that row because each breadboard row is made up of a single piece of metal. But, each rows is electrically isolated from the other rows. The trough also separates the rows on either side of the breadboard, so each side of the breadboard is also electrically isolated.

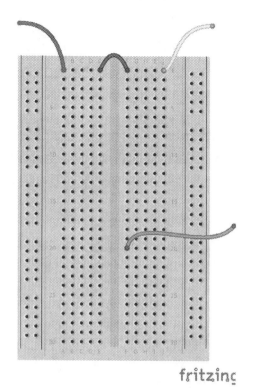

fritzinc

Figure 3-4. *Illustration showing how wires are electrically connected on a breadboard: Orange, blue, and yellow wires are all electrically connected. The green wire is not electrically connected to any of the other wires*

For example, in Figure 3-4, the orange wire is connected to the blue wire because they are both in row 1 on the left side of the breadboard. The yellow wire is **also** connected to the blue wire because they are both in row 1 on the right side of the breadboard. This means that **the orange wire is connected to the yellow wire** via the breadboard clips and the blue wire! If we were to remove the blue wire, the orange and yellow wires would not be connected.

The green wire on the bottom is **not** connected to the orange, blue, and yellow wires. It's doing its own thing down there!

Wait, what about those power rails?!

Aha, yes! Those are special and super helpful. Like we discovered in Chapter 1, the power rails make it easier to connect power sources to our circuits!

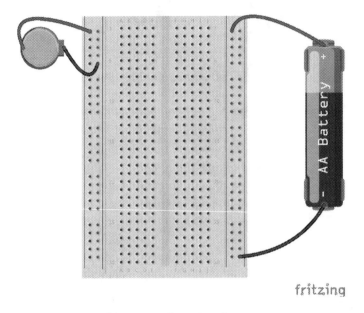

fritzing

Figure 3-5. A Fritzing diagram showing how to connect two separate batteries to the same breadboard using the two separate power rails. Note that the coin cell battery and the AA battery are electrically isolated

In the power rails, the connected holes are aligned vertically: all of the holes next to the red line are connected to each other, and all of the holes next to the blue line are connected to each other. The two vertical columns are **not** connected.

Finally, each set of power rails is isolated, which means we can have two separate power supplies for one breadboard circuit like in Figure 3-5. This is handy in situations where you have an energy-hungry component, like a motor, but you want to use a lower-power battery to switch the motor on and off.

WHY ARE SOME OF THE BREADBOARD HOLES GREEN??

The circuit diagram software we are using (Fritzing, yay!) uses green to highlight breadboard holes that are electrically connected to components we (virtually) plug in. This is handy as we can more easily trace the path of the electricity through our breadboard.

Breadboarding: Lights On!

Grab These Materials

- Half-size breadboard

- Coin cell battery with case

- 2+ LEDs

- 4 (or more) jumper wires (M-M)

Finally! We get to combine the skills and knowledge we've learned so far to build more circuits!

Building circuits on breadboards can be tricky because it's harder to trace the flow of electricity. And let's be real, the breadboard holes are tiny which makes it difficult to see if a component leg is in the correct row.

It's okay if you get frustrated. Remember to take breaks and to go slow, comparing your circuit with the diagram and double- or even triple-checking which row and column your component or wire is plugged into. And, of course, remember to check that the power supply is connected and turned on. ☺

STRUGGLING TO SEE WHICH HOLE YOU'VE PLUGGED THAT TINY COMPONENT INTO??

Get yourself a bright light and possibly a magnifying glass or use the zoom feature on your smartphone camera. This will make it easier to build circuits and reduce eye strain (and frustration) as we build more complex circuits with parts that have three or more legs.

Project 3-1: Light It Up on a Breadboard!

First, let's transfer our single LED and coin cell onto a breadboard. I'll walk you through one way to build this, but there are dozens of different ways you could build the same circuit using different rows, more or less wires, etc. Once you start to get a feel for the structure of the breadboard, explore some of the different ways you could turn the light on! You may start by observing the build diagram in Figure 3-6. The written procedure for this circuit follows the build diagram.

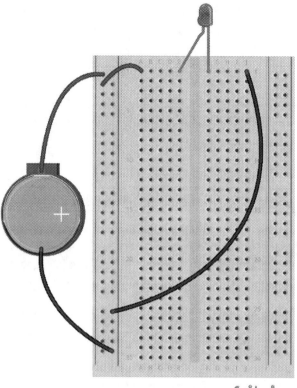

Figure 3-6. *A diagram showing how to connect an LED to a coin cell battery*

Procedure

1. Connect the positive battery wire to one of the holes in the positive power rail (red line).

2. Connect the negative battery wire to one of the holes in the negative power rail (black line).

3. Insert the positive (longer) LED leg into row 1 on the left side (column E).

4. Insert the negative (shorter) LED leg into row 1 on the right side (column F).

83

5. Connect your first jumper wire between the left row 1 (column A) and the **positive** power rail that the battery is connected to. (This is the red jumper wire in the diagram.)

6. Connect your second jumper wire between the right row 1 (column J) and the **negative** power rail with the battery. (This is the black jumper wire in the diagram.)

Congratulations!! You just made your first breadboard circuit. 👏👏

TROUBLESHOOTING TIPS

1. Check that the battery is securely in its connector and is oriented properly (positive to positive, negative to negative). Check that the battery case switch is on the "On" position.

2. Check that the metal tips of the battery wires are fully inserted into the breadboard holes.

3. Check that the battery case wires are in **different** power rails (negative to a hole next to the blue line, positive to a hole next to the red line).

4. Check that the jumper wires for the LED are in **different** power rails (negative to a hole next to the blue line, positive to a hole next to the red line).

5. Check that the LED legs are fully inserted into the breadboard holes and are in different rows, either different numbered rows or spanning the breadboard trough.

6. Check that the jumper wires are fully inserted into the breadboard holes.

7. Check that the positive (longer) LED leg is connected to the positive side of the battery.

8. Occasionally, a jumper wire is faulty. If you've checked everything else, try swapping out the jumper wires for different ones.

9. Finally, check that the battery has energy by connecting it directly to an LED.

Still not working? Compare it with the diagram, paying attention to the green holes on the diagram, the row and column labels. It may also be helpful to borrow another set of eyes and brain because sometimes the problem is so obvious we are overlooking it. Happens to me all the time. ☺

😵 **Try it:** Let's trace the path of the electricity because it will help us to better understand how breadboards and circuits work. In Figure 3-7 below, draw the path of the electrical current starting from the positive side of the battery through the light and back to the battery. Add arrows to show direction.

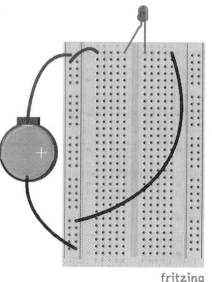

fritzing

Figure 3-7. *A circuit diagram for tracing the path of the electricity*

Now compare that to what I've got in Figure 3-8:

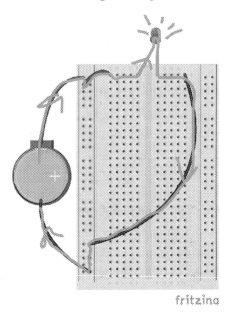

fritzing

Figure 3-8. *A diagram showing the path of the electricity from the positive side of the battery, through the LED, and back to the negative side of the battery*

If you're into descriptions more than pictorial representations, here's what's happening:

> The current flows out of the positive side of the battery
> through the battery case wire and into the positive
> breadboard power rail. Because we connected a wire
> into the positive power rail, the current flows into that
> wire and then into the first row on the left side of the
> breadboard. The current travels through that first row
> and reaches the positive leg of our light. Then, it flows
> into the light where it does work and loses some of its
> energy before flowing out of the light, through the first
> row on the right side of the breadboard, into and through
> the long black wire until it reaches the negative power

rail. The current can finally "go home" by traveling through the negative power rail into the negative battery case wire to the negative side of the battery.

Now that we better understand how the electrical current flows through a breadboard, let's add more stuff to our first circuit!

Project 3-2: All the Lights!!

Our next challenge is to build a circuit with two LEDs! I'd recommend starting with two of the same color or two colors close to each other in the rainbow (e.g., red and yellow or green and blue).

Since we're still getting comfortable building circuits on a breadboard, let's use a picture to get started (Figure 3-9).

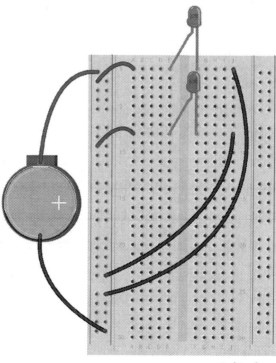

Figure 3-9. A diagram showing two LEDs connected in parallel

Procedure

1. Build the circuit for a single LED like you did in Project 3-1 earlier in this chapter.

2. Insert the second LED so that its positive (longer) leg is in row 8 on the left side of the breadboard, and its negative (shorter) leg is in row 8 on the right side of the breadboard.

3. Connect a jumper wire between the positive power rail and row 8 on the left side. (This is the second red jumper wire.)

4. Connect a jumper wire between the negative power rail and row 8 on the right side. (This is the second black jumper wire.)

Both lights should now turn on!

🔑 **Check it out:** Bonus circuits for all the knowledge points.

1. Change the color of one LED and observe what happens.

2. How many more LEDs can you add??

TROUBLESHOOTING TIPS

1. Check that the battery is securely in its connector and is oriented properly (positive to positive, negative to negative). Check that the battery case switch is on the "On" position.

2. Check that the metal tips of the battery wires are fully inserted into the breadboard holes.

3.   Check that the battery case wires are in **different** power rails (negative connects to a hole next to the blue line; positive connects to a hole next to the red line).

4.   Check that the jumper wires for the LED are in **different** power rails (negative to a hole next to the blue line, positive to a hole next to the red line).

5.   Check that both LED legs are fully inserted into the breadboard holes and are in different rows, either different numbered rows or spanning the breadboard trough.

6.   Check that the jumper wires are fully inserted into the breadboard holes.

7.   Check that the positive (longer) LED leg is connected to the positive side of the battery.

8.   Make sure that both LEDs are **in parallel**.

9.   Occasionally, a jumper wire is faulty. If you've checked everything else, try swapping out the jumper wires for different ones.

10.   Finally, check that the battery has energy by connecting an LED to it directly.

Still not working? Compare your circuit closely with the diagram or ask for help from friends, family, coworkers, etc.

There are many, many ways you can build a circuit with two, or more, LEDs! **Explore a few different approaches to building a circuit with two LEDs and one battery on your breadboard.** When you've made at least three different versions of the same circuit, explore adding more lights! Yay, light!

Some things to consider: How could you use fewer wires? How could you use more wires? How could you use the least amount of space on the breadboard? How might you use the most space?

Hint: With just one coin cell battery, multiple LEDs need to be in parallel. In other words, each LED should have its own circuit loop.

Making Sounds!
Grab These Materials

- Half-size breadboard
- 2 coin cell batteries in battery case
- 1 buzzer
- 4 jumper wires (M-M)
- 9V battery

Project 3-3: Circuit Sounds!

⚠ Auditory sensitivity note: If you have sensitivity
to high-pitched sounds, you may want to skip this
circuit.

Learning by doing is great fun, so let's start this section by building our
audible circuit. We'll use what we learn to better understand how we can
use electricity to make sounds, yay!

First, the diagram is shown in Figure 3-10.

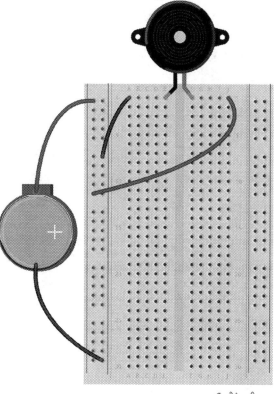

fritzing

Figure 3-10. *A diagram showing a buzzer connected to a battery*

Procedure

Try building the circuit as shown in Figure 3-10 **before** reading the procedure. If you get stuck, then use the procedure to help.

1. Plug the coin cell battery case into the breadboard power rails.

2. Insert the buzzer into the breadboard so that the two legs are in different rows. Note which row the longer leg is in.

3. Using a jumper wire, connect the positive power rail and the row with the positive (longer) lead of the buzzer. This leg is also typically marked with a "+" on the top of the buzzer.

4. Using a second jumper wire, connect the negative side of the battery case to the negative buzzer leg.

If the circuit is connected correctly (and your battery has energy), you will hear a constant, high-pitched tone from the buzzer!

Yes, this may be a terrible sound for your ears, and I completely understand if you immediately unplug the buzzer.

If it's so horrible sounding, why did we use it at all?! For better or worse, the buzzer is the easiest noise-making component to build circuits with. (That's pretty much the only reason I keep these around, although I have found that younger students get delight from them, so maybe it's just a "me" thing.)

TROUBLESHOOTING TIPS

1. Check that the battery is securely in its connector and is oriented properly (positive to positive, negative to negative). Check that the battery case switch is on the "On" position.

2. Check that the metal tips of the battery wires are fully inserted into the breadboard holes.

3. Check that the battery case wires are in **different** power rails (negative connects to a hole next to the blue line; positive connects to a hole next to the red line).

4. Check that the jumper wires for the buzzer are in **different** power rails (negative to a hole next to the blue line, positive to a hole next to the red line).

5. Check that both buzzer legs are fully inserted into the breadboard holes and are in different rows, either different numbered rows or spanning the breadboard trough.

6. Check that the jumper wires are fully inserted into the breadboard holes.

7. Check that the positive (longer) buzzer leg is connected to the positive side of the battery.

8. Occasionally, a jumper wire is faulty. If you've checked everything else, try swapping out the jumper wires for different ones.

9. Finally, check that the battery has energy by connecting the buzzer to it directly.

Still not working? Compare your circuit closely with the diagram or ask for help from friends, family, coworkers, etc.

Assuming you can put up with the sound of the buzzer, let's play around with this lil' noise maker to better understand how it works.

Our experimental question: Is it possible to adjust the tone of the buzzer?   Try adding or reducing wires, moving the buzzer around on the breadboard, and anything else you can think of.

What did you notice?

Let's try modifying our circuit by changing the amount of electrical power: What happens if we add a second battery **in parallel** (i.e., connected to the same breadboard power rails) with the first battery?

Why parallel? Remember that current adds in parallel and voltage adds in series. Like the LED, our buzzer can only handle 3V, so if we have just one buzzer, we need to add a second battery in parallel to avoid breaking the buzzer.

If you need some help with two batteries, a diagram is shown in Figure 3-11.

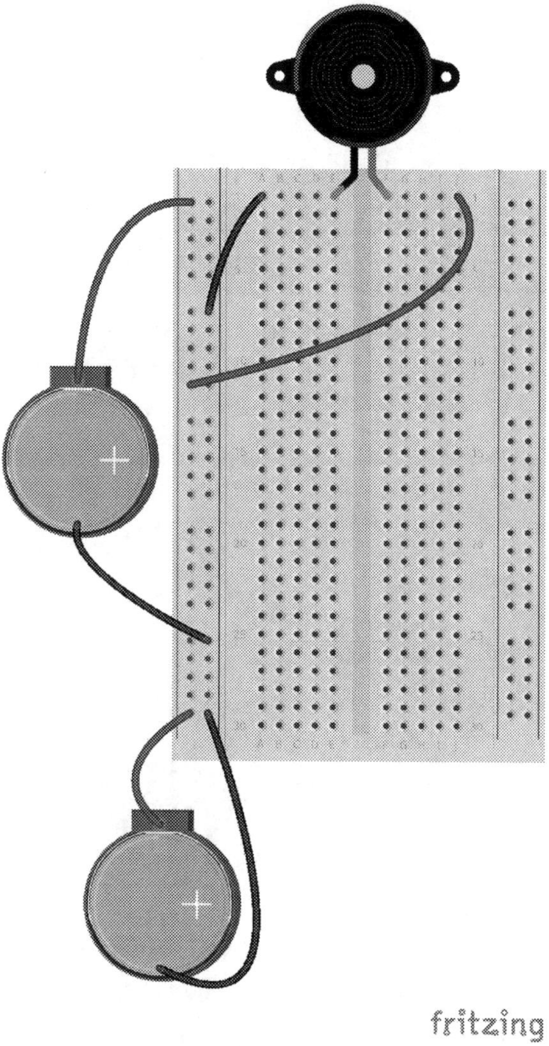

Figure 3-11. *A diagram showing how to connect a buzzer to two batteries (in parallel)*

Try unplugging the negative wire for the second battery. Listen to the buzzer tone, then plug the negative wire back in, and listen for any changes in the tone.

What else could you try?   If your ears are up for it, add another buzzer or try adding an LED!

Schematic Symbol for a Speaker

When looking at a circuit schematic, a speaker will have a symbol like this (Figure 3-12):

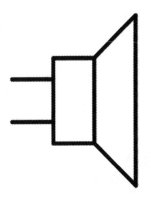

Figure 3-12. *Schematic symbol for a speaker*

(I love this one because it makes me feel like I'm practicing artistic drawings when I create my circuit schematics!)

How Does Electricity Make Sounds??

Now that we've heard firsthand (first-ear?) how we can make sounds with electricity (even though they might not be as pleasant as our favorite album), let's dig into how this works.

Like lights, there are a few different ways to use the energy in electricity to make sounds. The buzzer in our circuit uses what is called a "**piezo**" element, but most of us are probably more familiar with **speakers**, so let's start with those. (And yes, by speakers I mean the ones you crank to 11 when you're at band practice or really grooving out on a Saturday night... or Sunday morning!)

An Introduction to the Common Speaker

Let's look at the inside of a speaker to learn more about how it works (Figure 3-13).

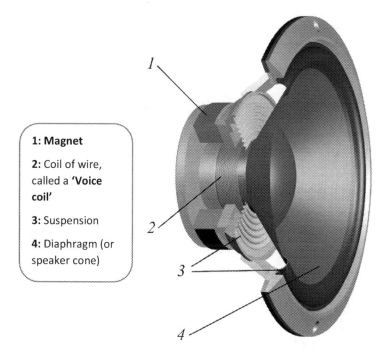

1: Magnet

2: Coil of wire, called a 'Voice coil'

3: Suspension

4: Diaphragm (or speaker cone)

Figure 3-13. *Diagram of a speaker (source: Wikipedia)*

As we discovered with our different colored LED experiment, electricity is delightfully more mysterious than it first appears. That experiment taught us more about the **electromagnetic spectrum** (a.k.a. light). You might have noticed the "magnetic" part in that word and wondered: What does electricity have to do with magnetism??

Everything!! Starting with Michael Faraday, physicists discovered that **electricity and magnetism are the same force** in the early 1800s. This means that **a moving electric field**, like a current, **generates a magnetic field**. Likewise, **a moving magnetic field generates an electric field**! This fantastic discovery is what enables the diaphragm of a speaker to rapidly move back and forth. Each time the diaphragm moves, it pushes air out of the way, or compresses it, to create a sound. This is just like the skin of a drum!

Faraday's Law   A moving electric field generates a magnetic field, and a moving magnetic field generates an electric field.

WAIT, WAIT, WAIT... HOW EXACTLY DOES THE DIAPHRAGM MOVE??

When electric current flows through the speaker's voice coil, it creates a magnetic field that is attracted (or repelled by) to the permanent magnet at the base of the speaker. As the voice coil moves, it pulls the diaphragm down (or pushes it away).

The voice coil is an electromagnet, which means that it becomes magnetized when electric current flows through it. There are TONS of different ways to use electromagnets, including in motors which we'll learn about in the next section!

If you are curious about learning more, I'd highly recommend the following experiment:

Get ahold of an old speaker that you can take apart – rummage through your electronics for one that's broken (or that you know you don't use or want) or go to a thrift store to find a cheap one that won't be missed.

Use a screwdriver to open the case and locate the black speaker, then remove it from its holding place. If you are okay destroying a working speaker in the name of education (or if it's already broken), use scissors to clip the speaker wires so you can pull it out and observe it more closely.

Identify the four main parts of the speaker   (1) permanent magnet, (2) voice coil, (3) suspension, and (4) diaphragm.

Next, grab a 9V battery and **connect the speaker wires to the 9V**. What do you notice visually and audibly? (If you don't hear anything, try removing some of the wire insulation to expose the metal bits inside.)

Swap the speaker wire connection to the 9V (e.g., if you connected red to positive and black to negative, switch that). What do you notice?

Try connecting and disconnecting the speaker wires as fast as you can! What do you notice?

What else can you explore??

An Introduction to How Piezo Elements Work

Now that we've explored how more common speakers work, let's get back to our buzzer (and why it sounds so... tinny).

Inside of our buzzer is a circular piezo element that is made of a ceramic disk ringed with metal, like Figure 3-14.

Figure 3-14. *A piezo element (source: Wikimedia Commons)*

When electric current is applied to the disk, the ceramic material contracts or expands. This causes the surrounding metal disk to vibrate, and the vibration compresses air to make a sound! In other words, our buzzer sounds tinny because it literally is using metal to make sounds. Not always the most pleasant of sounds, but, hey, it works!

We can change the pitch of our buzzer by changing how fast the piezo element vibrates or the **frequency** at which it vibrates. This is difficult (bordering impossible) to do by hand, but we can use "smart" circuits or computers to do this for us.

Making Movement!
Grab These Materials

- Half-size breadboard

- 2 coin cell batteries in battery case

- 1 motor

- 4 jumper wires (M-M)

Project 3-4: Motor Motion!

Our final project in this chapter explores using electricity to make things move with motors. Yay, motors! Motors use a lot of energy, so I'd recommend unplugging the battery when you're not actively observing or working with this circuit.

Just like with our sound circuit, **try building this circuit first using only the diagram (Figure 3-15)**. Read through the procedure only if your first (or second or third) attempt doesn't work as expected.

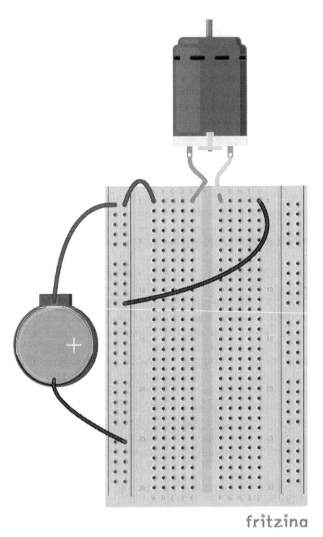

Figure 3-15. *A diagram showing how to connect a motor to a battery*

Procedure

1. Plug the coin cell battery case into the breadboard
    power rails.

2. Insert the motor leads into the breadboard into two different breadboard rows. Note which row each leg is in.

3. Using a jumper wire, connect the positive power rail and the row with one of the motor leads.

4. Using a second jumper wire, now connect the negative side of the battery case to the other motor lead.

    Is your motor spinning?? (I feel like this could be the start to a great nerdy joke.)

    If yes, awesome! Next step:

5. **Switch the orientation of the motor leads** (i.e., switch the positive and negative connections from the battery to the motor). What do you notice?

If not, great effort, onward to troubleshooting! (And then come back to step 5... it's worth it, I promise. ☺)

TROUBLESHOOTING TIPS

1. Check that the battery is securely in its connector and is oriented properly (positive to positive, negative to negative). Check that the battery case switch is on the "On" position.

2. Check that the metal tips of the battery wires are fully inserted into the breadboard holes.

3. Check that the battery case wires are in **different** power rails (negative connects to a hole next to the blue line; positive connects to a hole next to the red line).

4. Check that the motor jumper wires are in **different** power
    rails (negative connects to a hole next to the blue line; positive
    connects to a hole next to the red line).

5. Check that both motor leads are fully inserted into the
    breadboard holes and are in different rows, either different
    numbered rows or spanning the breadboard trough.

    a. **This can be a common issue** with the super small
        motor wires.

6. Check that the jumper wires are fully inserted into the
    breadboard holes.

7. Occasionally, a jumper wire is faulty. If you've checked
    everything else, try swapping out the jumper wires for
    different ones.

8. Finally, check that the battery has energy by directly connecting
    it to the motor.

Still not working? Compare your circuit closely with the diagram or ask for
help from friends, family, coworkers, etc.

Schematic Symbols for a Motor

The basic schematic symbol for a motor looks like Figure 3-16.

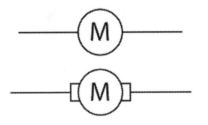

Figure 3-16. *Schematic symbol for a motor*

This basic symbol may have additional markings to indicate what type of motor it is, for example, whether it is DC, like Figure 3-17.

Figure 3-17. *An alternative schematic symbol for a motor*

Or whether the motor uses AC, which uses a wiggly line instead of a straight line (Figure 3-18).

Figure 3-18. *An alternative schematic symbol for a motor*

How Is Electricity Making the Motor Spin??

Motors convert electrical energy into mechanical energy, or motion. Just like speakers, motors use electromagnets (using electricity to generate a magnetic field). Here's a quick and "hand-wavy" explanation:

Inside many direct current or DC motors are small coils of wire that become magnetized when electric current runs through them. These electromagnets become attracted to, or repelled by, permanent magnets inside the motor. Motors have special connections that disconnect the first coil once it moves and connect to the next coil. This repeats and the continuous process makes the drive shaft spin!

In-Depth Overview of Motors for Those with Insatiable Curiosity

If we look inside a (brushed DC) motor, we'll find stationary permanent magnets, called the **stator**. These permanent magnets surround the **armature**, which rotates. In Figure 3-19, the permanent magnets are glued to the inside of the motor casing, and only the armature can be pulled out.

Figure 3-19. *The armature of a brushed DC motor. Source: Wikimedia Commons*

The armature has a few parts: small wire coils (our electromagnets!), a metal bar (or shaft), and a small metal cylinder with gaps (the commutator!) that sits over the shaft. The commutator is a cleverly designed part that connects to the motor terminals, via flexible brushes, so that **as the armature rotates, the current flow through the electromagnets is reversed** (see Figure 3-20 for another inside view of our brushed DC motor and Figure 3-21 for a labeled diagram)

But wait... why do we need to reverse the current flow??

Yes! Excellent question! Let's think about this for a moment, using our understanding of speakers to inspire our thought experiment.

> 😋 **Question:** What happens if we connect our battery directly to one of the electromagnets inside the motor (while it is in the stator and under the influence of permanent magnets)?
>
> *(It may help to explore what happens to a speaker when connected/disconnected to a battery in different ways.)*

With the speaker, when we connect the electromagnet to a battery, the wire coil moves the diaphragm in one direction. When we disconnect the battery, the diaphragm moves back. If we flip the polarity of the battery (i.e., swap the positive and negative leads), the diaphragm moves in the opposite direction when powered.

How does this help?! Aren't we looking at motors??

Well, yes! But the basic phenomenon is the same: to get motion in two directions or to achieve constant motion, we need to reverse the polarity of the battery and/or disconnect the battery. But we can't do that by hand very easily, especially if we're dealing with a spinning motor!

Figure 3-20. *Inside of a three-pole DC motor*

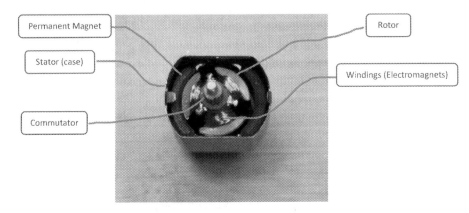

Figure 3-21. *Close-up of a three-pole motor*

This is why I love looking at the basic parts that make up everyday objects: the ingenuity of scientists and engineers shines bright in even mundane objects. The commutator, wiring of the electromagnets, and brushes in the DC motor all work together so that as the armature rotates, the direction of current flow changes in the electromagnets. This reverses their magnetic polarity so that instead of just moving something once, like our speaker diaphragm, the electromagnets in a motor keep moving:

> The electromagnet starts out by being attracted to one of the permanent magnets (e.g., North). When it has moved into place, the commutator reverses the magnetic polarity, and that same electromagnet is now repelled by the first permanent magnet and is attracted to the second permanent magnet (e.g., South), so it keeps rotating! This happens with each of the electromagnets. Reversing the battery connection to the motor leads changes the direction that the armature rotates.

Brushed DC motors can have two, three, or even more electromagnets (often called poles). When these motors have many poles (e.g., nine), the electromagnets are often connected in groups like how we might divide people into even teams – for example, electromagnets 1, 4, and 7 are connected, electromagnets 2, 5, and 8 are connected, and electromagnets 3, 6, and 9 are connected.

As you might have discovered, this is an area where static text may be limiting or difficult to comprehend completely. I'd highly recommend looking up a video showing how a three-pole brushed DC motor works.

Finally, there are tons of other types of electric motors. Here's a quick overview of some common ones:

- **Brushless DC motors**: These have the electromagnets on the stator (not moving) and the permanent magnets on the armature (moving). A computer controls the flow of current to the electromagnets, which is more precise and durable than brushed DC motors.

- **AC motors**: Electric motors driven by alternating current (AC). These typically have two parts: an outside stator with coils supplied by AC electricity to produce a rotating magnetic field and an inside rotor that produces a second rotating magnetic field via permanent magnets, AC or DC electromagnets, or a method called reluctance saliency that leverages some of the weird and wonderful properties of electric and magnetic fields.

- **Servo motors**: A motor with a feedback sensor to provide position information. These are common in robotics and other areas where you need precise motion.

- **Stepper motors**: This motor uses a pulsing electric current controlled by a computer to do precise, one-step movements via a gear. Stepper motors are also common in robotics and other precision applications.

Lights and Sounds and Motion, Oh My! But… Why?

In this chapter, we worked with three (3!) different kinds of electrical components: lights, speakers, and motors. These parts might seem wildly different, and they are in many ways, but there is one common thread linking them.

All the components we worked with in this chapter **do** something observable (by human senses) with electricity. In other words, we built our first breadboard circuits with **output devices**.

Output devices are incredibly helpful to learn about the behavior of electricity because we can see, hear, and/or feel if electricity is flowing in our circuit. Sometimes, we can also get information about **how** the electricity is flowing, especially when we add multiple components. Like when we used LEDs to visualize how electrical current and voltage split between parallel circuit loops!

Output device   A circuit component that does something observable by human senses.

There are lots of other types of "power sink" circuit components, and not all circuits need an output device. However, because my goal in this book is to help you better understand the flow of electricity, every circuit we build will have some kind of output device so we can see (or hear) how components affect current and voltage.

Going Further

Congratulations! You built circuits with output devices on a breadboard!

But, now what?? How can you apply this knowledge? Here are some ideas to get you started:

1. **Add lights to all the things!**

   Drawer too dark? Add some lights! Garage too spooky after dusk? Add some lights!

   While a breadboard might not be great for paper crafts like cards, lights on a breadboard can illuminate dollhouses (or other miniature installations), hats, jack-o'-lanterns, holiday decorations, and more. Coat circuits in hot glue for longer-lasting and semi-waterproof builds.

2. **Morse code communication system**

   Grab a friend and build two circuits (on two different breadboards) with the buzzer (or LED). Unplug and plug one of the breadboard wires to turn on/off the buzzer (or LED) and generate Morse code signals that you can send from afar.

   For extra security, work with your friend and make up your own alphabet code system!

3. **Avant-garde electronic music**

Explore using different materials and/or
components to change the sound of the buzzer. Can
you modify the sound of multiple buzzers so that
they create a "buzzer" band?

4. **Brush Bots!**

Brush Bots are super simple robots. Attach the
vibration motor to a small object with glue or tape,
then observe how the object moves. Turn this object
into a robot by giving it more features, changing the
legs/feet, adjusting the weight, etc.

Summary

We finally got to breadboards, yayy! This chapter taught you what a
breadboard is, some information about where they came from and why,
and what's inside of it that enables us to build circuits with it. We also
discovered more circuit components and learned about the inner workings
of buzzers, speakers, and (DC) motors. These parts are all around us! I
hope the knowledge in this chapter inspires you to take a closer look at
electronics and machines and observe the different parts that you've
learned about.

In the next chapter, we'll learn about more circuit components. These
will be in a category called "passive" components and include things like
resistors, potentiometers, and capacitors. If these funny sounding words
are confusing, that's okay! I was confused by these words at one time, also.
We'll walk through these components one at a time and look inside to
better understand what they are and how they work.

CHAPTER 4

Controlling Electricity (Passive Components)

Resistance: Limiting Electricity

You've used the power of electricity to turn on individual circuit components like LEDs and motors, hooray! But how do we control how much electricity goes into these parts?? One way to do this is with resistors! Resistors limit, or resist (oh, hey!), the flow of electricity.

The best (and most fun) way to learn is to do! That means we'll start learning about resistors by building a circuit. Well... technically three circuits, but most of the circuit stays the same.

A quick note on resistors before we begin: The size of a resistor is measured in Ohms, which use the Greek letter that looks like this: Ω. A larger resistor has a larger value in Ohms. For example, 100Ω is smaller than 1000Ω (or $1k\Omega$[1] because we like to be lazy).

---

[1] $k\Omega$ stands for "kilo Ω," where kilo is shorthand for 1×10^3. This means that a number, like 1, is multiplied by 1×10^3 to give us 1000!

© Jennifer Fox 2023
J. Fox, *Beginning Breadboarding*, https://doi.org/10.1007/978-1-4842-9218-1_4

Grab These Materials

- Half-size breadboard

- Coin cell in battery case

- 2 jumper wires

- 3 resistors of different resistances (e.g., 100Ω, 1kΩ, and 10kΩ)

- 1 LED

Project 4-1: Modifying Lights with Resistors!

First, build a circuit to turn on your LED like you did in Chapter 3. Then remove the negative jumper wire cable from the negative (shorter) LED leg and plug it into an empty row on the breadboard. Grab one of your resistors and connect it **between** the negative LED leg and the negative jumper wire.

Holy stars! If your LED turned on, what happened to it?? What do you notice? How is it similar and how is it different than your original circuit?

(If your LED didn't turn on, the build diagram and written instructions for a 100Ω resistor are shown in Figure 4-1.)

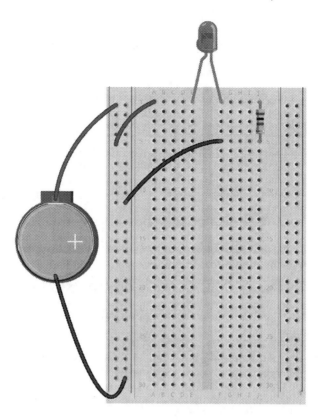

Figure 4-1. *A build diagram for an LED-resistor circuit*

Written Procedure

1. Insert the coin cell battery into its case and move the switch to the "On" position. Plug the red wire of the battery case into the positive breadboard power rail. Plug the black wire into the negative breadboard power rail.

2. Insert the LED into the top row. Its positive (longer) leg is plugged into the left-hand row 1. Its negative (shorter) leg is plugged into the right-hand row 1.

3.   Connect your first jumper wire between the positive breadboard power rail and longer LED leg (the red wire going into left-hand row 1).

4.   Grab a resistor (e.g., 100Ω) and connect it between the negative LED leg and row 5 on the right side.

5.   Connect your second jumper wire between the resistor (right-hand row 5) and the negative power rail (the black wire).

This is the end of the helpful parenthetical section! Let's take a closer look at how we just modified the flow of electricity.)

Adding a resistor to our circuit caused our LED to dim! Congratulations, you just wielded circuit skills to control the flow of electricity!

🔎 **Check it out:** Does orientation of the resistor legs matter? Does it matter which side of the circuit you add the resistor? What other things can you change and observe?

Now let's explore what happens when we try different types of resistors! Swap out the first LED (e.g., 100Ω) and replace it with a second LED. Do the same thing for the third LED.

I encourage you to jot down your observations:

- LED brightness with resistor 1 (_____ Ω): _____

- LED brightness with resistor 2 (_____ Ω): _____

- LED brightness with resistor 3 (_____ Ω): _____

In case you need some visual help, here are two more circuit diagrams (Figure 4-2) and 10kΩ (Figure 4-3) resistors:

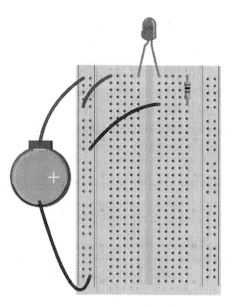

Figure 4-2. *Resistor circuit with a 1kΩ resistor*

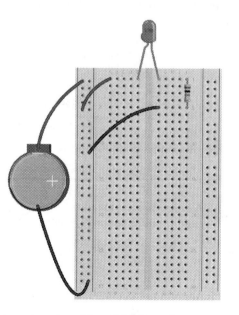

Figure 4-3. *Resistor circuit with a 10kΩ resistor*

What did you notice when you tried different resistors?

For me, the brightness of the LED changed! More specifically, as the resistance increased, for example, from 100Ω to $1k\Omega$ to $10k\Omega$, the LED gets dimmer.

Let's learn more about resistors to better understand how this new component works and how it regulates electricity.

> 🔍 **Check it out:** Look closely at the different resistors:
> What do you notice? How are they similar? How are
> they different? It may help to get a magnifying glass or
> use your phone to zoom in on the resistors.

TROUBLESHOOTING TIPS

---

1. Check that the battery is securely in its connector and is oriented properly (positive to positive, negative to negative). Check that the battery case switch is on the "On" position.

2. Check that the metal tips of the battery wires are fully inserted into the breadboard holes.

3. Check that the battery case wires are in **different** power rails (negative to a hole next to the blue line, positive to a hole next to the red line).

4. Check that the jumper wires for the LED are connected in **different** power rails (negative or black to a hole next to the blue line, positive or red to a hole next to the red line).

5. Check that the LED legs are fully inserted into the breadboard holes and are in different rows, either different numbered rows or spanning the breadboard trough.

6. Check that the resistor legs are fully inserted into the breadboard holes and are in different rows, either different numbered rows or spanning the breadboard trough.

7. Check that the jumper wires are fully inserted into the breadboard holes.

8. Check that the positive (longer) LED leg is connected to the positive side of the battery.

9. Occasionally, a jumper wire is faulty. If you've checked everything else, try swapping out the jumper wires for different ones.

10. Finally, check that the battery has energy by connecting it directly to an LED.

Still not working? Second-set-of-eyes time!

Resistor Schematic Symbol

The schematic symbol for a resistor is a zigzag line! Shown in Figure 4-4, it's super cute (at least, it reminds me of a cute monster mouth) and fun to draw:

Figure 4-4. *Resistor schematic symbol*

Most circuit diagrams will label each resistor with a capital "R" followed by a number, like R1, R2, R3, etc. To find the resistor value, look at the legend in the circuit diagram and find the resistor number (e.g., R1 = 100Ω). Resistors that have the same value will be labeled with the same number, for example, you might spot three R1 resistors, one R2 resistor, and four R3 resistors.

119

How Do Resistors Work?

As we discovered, using **a resistor limits the amount of electricity flowing** into our light. We can adjust how much electricity flows into our light by changing the resistor value. From an energy perspective, resistors reduce the amount of electrical energy flowing into our light.

Resistor   A circuit component that limits the amount of electricity flowing in a circuit. Units in Ohms (Ω).

How?!

In brief, resistors are made of a special material that somewhat conducts electricity – it's a material that is in between a conductor and an insulator – called a **semiconductor** (see! Somewhat conductive). For the resistors in our circuit, this material is usually either carbon, metal, or a metal-oxide film. But we can make resistors out of pretty much any material that is semiconductive, like graphite pencil lead (which means you can *literally* draw resistors!).

Resistors are special for two main reasons:

1.   They have a constant resistance.

2.   We can specify, and then measure, their resistance.

Unlike LEDs, resistors are nonpolar, so the orientation of their leads doesn't matter. Resistors are also **passive components**, meaning they only consume power and do not produce it. Resistors have lots of handy functions, like limiting electrical current and dividing, or changing, voltage in a circuit.

Passive component   A circuit component that only consumes power (does not produce power).

As we briefly touched on at the beginning of this chapter, the size of a resistor, how much a resistor restricts the flow of electricity, is measured in units of "Ohms." These units are represented with the Greek letter Omega: Ω. You will often see prefixes in front of resistance units, like kilo-Ohms ($k\Omega$), which means 1000Ω.

When we were exploring our three different resistors, you may have noticed colored markings on the resistor. These (intentional) markings are called **resistor color codes**, and I love them.

Resistor color codes are an ingenious way to communicate important information about a tiny component that can (generally speaking) be observed with our eyes. We read the four- or five-color bands as shown in Figure 4-5 below.

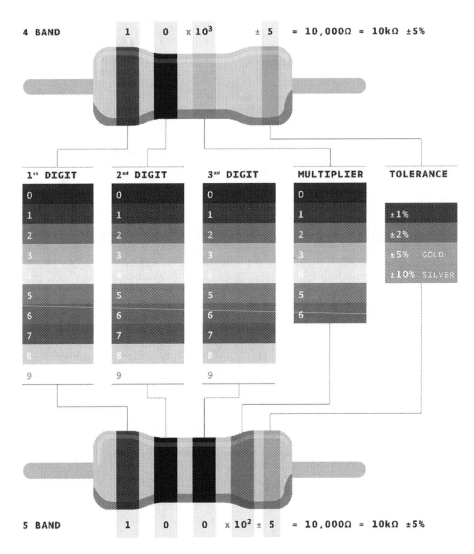

Figure 4-5. *Resistor color codes! Source: Wikimedia Commons*

In a resistor color code, the first two color bands (or the first three if there are five color bands) indicate the resistor value. The third color band indicates the multiplier (i.e., prefix, like kilo). The fourth color band indicates the tolerance, which tells us how accurate the resistance value is.

🔍 **Check it out:** Look at your three resistors from Project 4-1 and try to identify their values and tolerances using their resistor color codes! Are you surprised about the tolerance?

Resistor 1: _____ Ω ± _____ %

Resistor 2: _____ Ω ± _____ %

Resistor 3: _____ Ω ± _____ %

Project 4-2 (Optional): Draw a Resistor!
Grab These Materials

- Safety goggles
- 9V battery
- 3 alligator clips
- 1 LED
- Pencil with plenty of lead
- 1 square of paper about 1" x 1" (2cm x 2cm)

Remember when we used a 9V to power an LED and it burned out? Let's be adventurous again and try an experiment where we draw in a resistor for that circuit!

Procedure

1. Grab a piece of paper and use a pencil to draw a thick solid line. The line should be at least an inch long (2.5cm) and quarter of an inch thick (1/2cm) as shown in Figure 4-6. This is our resistor!

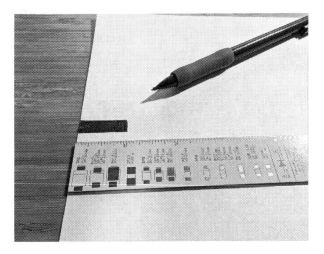

Figure 4-6. *Resistor drawn using standard pencil graphite*

2. Connect one alligator clip between the positive 9V battery lead and the positive LED leg.

3. Connect a second alligator clip between the negative LED leg and one side of the paper resistor. Make sure that the metal teeth of the alligator clip are clamped onto and covering the pencil graphite (Figure 4-7)

Figure 4-7. *Alligator clip connected to resistor drawn with graphite*

4. Connect a third alligator clip between the negative 9V battery clip and the other side of the paper resistor.

What do you observe??

If you have a multimeter handy, remove the alligator clips and measure the resistance of your homemade resistor!

Try drawing different resistors!

What happens when you draw a thicker line? Thinner line? What about different types of line designs? Get creative!

(Note: You may sacrifice an LED, but it's in the name of science! Science is all about asking questions and making (reasonable/safe) mistakes so experiment away!)

I WANT MORE DETAILS ABOUT RESISTORS!

The definition of 1Ω is the following: the resistance between two points in a circuit where 1 Volt (1V) of applied potential energy will push 1 Ampere (1A) of current. Resistors come in variety of power ratings. For hobbyist electronics, the most common power rating is ¼ Watt ("W").

The resistance of a resistor is calculated with the following equation (Eqn. 4-1):

$$R = \frac{\rho L}{A}$$

ρ = resistivity
L = length
A = cross sectional area

Eqn. 4-1

where R is the resistance, ρ is the resistivity, L is the length of the resistor, and A is the cross-sectional area. The resistivity depends on the material the resistor is made of (e.g., carbon). The length and cross-sectional area are physical characteristics of the resistor.

My preferred way to measure resistance is to use the ohmmeter function on a multimeter. However, this will only work if the resistor is disconnected from a circuit.

When there are multiple resistors in a circuit, the total circuit resistance is calculated differently for resistors in series (Eqn. 4-2) and in parallel (Eqn. 4-3):

Resistors in series:

$$R_{tot} = R_1 + R_2 + ... + R_{N-1} + R_N$$

Eqn. 4-2

Resistors in parallel:

$$\frac{1}{R_{tot}} = \frac{1}{R_1} + \frac{1}{R_2} + ... + \frac{1}{R_{N-1}} + \frac{1}{R_N}$$

Eqn. 4-3

A Mini Introduction to Ohm's Law!

When we add a resistor to our circuit, we reduce the amount of electrical energy flowing into our light (or motor, speaker, or other circuit components). There's a handy mathematical law that represents this phenomenon: Ohm's Law!

If you're nervous about math and equations, take a deep breath. You got this! It's okay to reread a sentence, paragraph, or section until it clicks. It's also okay to take a break and come back when your brain is feeling fresh.

Ohm's Law looks like this (Eqn. 4-4):

$$V = I * R \qquad\qquad Eqn.\ 4\text{-}4$$

In this equation, V represents voltage, like the voltage of our 3V coin cell or the 9V of our, well, 9V battery! It may also represent the voltage across a component in the circuit. I represents electric current, and R represents resistance. When we do calculations with this equation, we need to use consistent units to get accurate answers. The units in our equation should be Volts (V), Amps (A), and Ohms (Ω) without any prefixes.

For some of y'all, this may seem like a simple equation. So, of course, there's a catch: wielding Ohm's Law is much, much trickier than it appears on the surface (kind of like life?). We have to be very careful about **what** voltage, current, and resistance we are talking about (and using in Ohm's Law) because each part of our circuit may have different value for voltage, current, and resistance.

Let's try a simple application of Ohm's Law: let's calculate the amount of current flowing through our **whole** circuit in Project 4-1.

In this circuit, we are using a coin cell battery. The voltage of the whole circuit is 3V. In my example, I used a resistor of 100Ω (if you used a different value, then replace 100Ω with your resistor's value, in **Ohms, not kilo-Ohms**). The resistance of the whole circuit is 100Ω.[2]

Math process for applying Ohm's Law:

Step 1: Input known numbers into Ohm's Law:

$$3V = I * 100\Omega$$

Step 2: Divide both sides of the equation by the resistance:

$$\frac{3V}{100\Omega} = I$$

Step 3: Calculate the current!

$$I = 0.03A$$

This means that there is approximately[3] 0.03A (or 300mA [milliAmps]) of current flowing through our LED!

Bonus: Repeat this process for the other two resistors you used in Project 4-1! Note: The battery voltage stays the same; the resistance changes.

- Resistor 2 (_____Ω): _____A

- Resistor 3 (_____Ω): _____A

---

[2] Technically, there is some resistance from the wires and other components. But these are likely much less than the resistance of our resistor. This means it's okay to assume that the total circuit resistance equals the resistance of our resistor.

[3] Why approximately? Isn't math accurate? Yes! Math is accurate, but the real world is not. Theories, like Ohm's Law, help us approximate real-world phenomena and are usually good enough (i.e., accurate enough) for what we need. For example, we can use Ohm's Law to pick a resistor that will preserve our battery or to get a desired LED brightness. But, if we measure the current flowing through our LED with a multimeter (or ammeter), we may get a slightly different value. It's important to understand both the power and the limitations of theories like Ohm's Law so we can apply them appropriately.

HOW DO I APPLY OHM'S LAW WORK IF THERE'S NO RESISTOR?!

Aha! Sneaky, right? Great question, dear reader.

Every circuit has resistance even without an "official" resistor – wires are not perfect conductors and add some resistance to the circuit. Circuit components and batteries also add some resistance to the circuit, so there is always a small amount of resistance in every circuit.

It's considered "bad practice" to build a circuit without a resistor because resistors protect components, preserve batteries, and, assuming you choose a reasonable value, don't reduce the circuit's functionality. That said, if you are curious (or if you're just feeling lazy, which happens to me sometimes) and want to measure the current of a circuit with no resistor, for example, just a coin cell battery and an LED, I'd suggest either of the following:

1. Approximate the resistance as some low value like 1Ω.

2. Measure the resistance of the wires and sum them to get an estimate of wire resistance.

Happy math-ing!

Potentiometers: Adjustable Resistors!
Grab These Materials

- Half-size breadboard
- Coin cell in battery case
- 5 jumper wires
- 1 potentiometer
- 2 LEDs

Project 4-3: Dim the Light!

Now that we've discovered the power of resistance (or more accurately, how resistance consumes power), let's explore a special kind of resistor called a potentiometer! A potentiometer, or pot for short (yes, yes, jokes abound), has **three legs**, but we will only need two of them. Below in Figure 4-8 is a circuit diagram that shows you how to connect jumper wires to just two of the potentiometer legs:

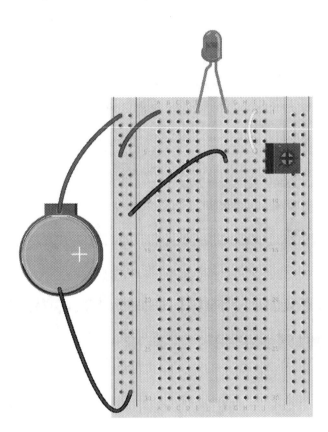

Figure 4-8. *Potentiometer circuit*

Written Procedure

1. Connect the battery case wires to the breadboard power rails.

2. Insert the LED so that its positive leg is in row 1 on one side of the breadboard trench, and its negative leg is in row 1 on the other side of the breadboard trench.

3. Insert the potentiometer so that its three legs are all in **different** rows (e.g., rows 5, 6, and 7 as shown in the diagram).

4. Connect your first jumper wire from the positive power rail to the positive LED leg.

5. Connect your second jumper wire from the negative LED leg to one of the outside potentiometer legs (e.g., breadboard row 5).

6. Connect your third jumper wire from the **middle** potentiometer leg to the negative power rail.

When you're done building the circuit, your light should turn on. Rotate the potentiometer! What do you notice? What do your observations reveal to you about the function of the potentiometer?

Keep your circuit intact as we learn how potentiometers work!

TROUBLESHOOTING TIPS

1. Check that the battery is securely in its connector and is oriented properly (positive to positive, negative to negative). Check that the battery case switch is on the "On" position.

2. Check that the metal tips of the battery wires are fully inserted into the breadboard holes. Wiggle them to check.

3. Check that the battery case wires are in **different** power rails (negative to a hole next to the blue line, positive to a hole next to the red line).

4. Check that the jumper wires for the LED are connected in **different** power rails (negative to a hole next to the blue line, positive to a hole next to the red line).

5. Check that the LED legs are fully inserted into the breadboard holes and are in different rows, either different numbered rows or spanning the breadboard trough.

6. Check that the potentiometer legs are fully inserted into the breadboard holes and are in **different rows**.

7. Check that the jumper wires are fully inserted into the breadboard holes.

8. Check that the positive (longer) LED leg is connected to the positive side of the battery.

9. Check that one of your jumper wires is connected to the **middle** potentiometer pin. This pin should be connected to the negative power rail, or ground.

10. Occasionally, a jumper wire is faulty. If you've checked everything else, try swapping out the jumper wires for different ones.

11. Finally, check that the battery has energy by connecting it directly to an LED.

Still not working? Second-set-of-eyes time!

Potentiometers: How Do They Work?

A potentiometer is an adjustable, or changing, resistor! This is super handy for making dimmer switches, volume controls, and speed controls. In fact, if you look under most (older) sound system volume knobs, guitar pedal knobs, and knobs that rotate on other music making or modifying devices, you'll find a potentiometer!

Potentiometer   A resistor that can vary when you move an adjustable terminal via a knob, slider, or other mechanisms. Units of Ohms (Ω).

The adjustable resistance in potentiometers is another cleverly designed mechanism as shown in Figure 4-9

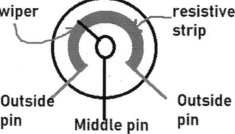

Figure 4-9. *The inside of a potentiometer! Source: Wikimedia Commons*

There are different shapes of potentiometers, but the mechanism is largely the same: a strip of resistive material is connected to leads on either side. These are the outside legs of our potentiometer. A metal wiper connects to the middle pin. When you rotate the knob on top of the potentiometer, it moves the wiper across the resistive material, like the windshield wipers move across your car windshield!

As the wiper moves closer to one of the outside pins, the resistance between the wiper (and thus the middle pin) and that outside pin decreases because there is less material between the two pins. At the same time, the distance between the wiper and the other outside pin increases. This means that the resistance increases between the middle potentiometer pin and that other outside pin.

> 🔍 **Check it out:** Move the jumper wire in your potentiometer circuit to the other outside pin. Rotate the potentiometer and observe what happens. How is this similar to the first circuit? How is it different?

IF THE RESISTANCE OF A POTENTIOMETER IS VARIABLE, WHY ARE THEY RATED WITH A SPECIFIC RESISTANCE?

You might have noticed that there are different ratings for potentiometers, like 1KΩ or 10KΩ. The **resistance rating is the maximum resistance** between the middle (wiper) pin and one of the outside pins. This happens when the wiper pin is at the far side of the resistive strip because that's when electricity must flow through the most material.

Some fun math with potentiometers:

- If the wiper is in the middle of the resistive strip, the resistance between the middle pin and the left outside pin is the **same** as the resistance between the middle pin and the right outside pin. This resistance is equal to ½ of the total resistance.

    - For example, if you have a 1KΩ potentiometer and the wiper pin is in the middle of the resistive strip, the resistance between the middle pin and either of the outside pins will be 500Ω (1KΩ / 2 = 500Ω).

- The resistance between the middle pin and the left outside pin plus the resistance between the middle pin and the right outside pin will always add up to the total resistance of the potentiometer.

  - For example, we have a 1KΩ potentiometer. If the resistance between the middle pin and the left outside pin is 200Ω, the resistance between the middle pin and the right outside pin must be 800Ω (because 1KΩ – 200Ω = 800Ω)!

Project 4-4: Dim More Lights!!

Let's put that second potentiometer pin to use! We'll add a second LED to our first potentiometer circuit and see what happens when we rotate the pot, yay!

😵 **Try to do this on your own first without looking at the circuit diagram (Figure 4-10)!**

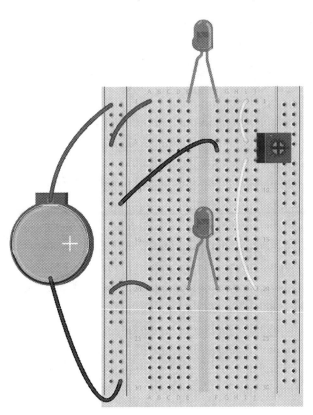

Figure 4-10. *Potentiometer Circuit with two LEDs!*

Written Procedure

1. Starting from the circuit in Project 4-3, insert a
    second LED into the breadboard so that its legs are
    in two different rows.

    a. For example, as shown in the preceding diagram, insert the
        positive LED leg into row 20 on the left side of the breadboard
        and the negative LED leg into row 20 on the right side of the
        breadboard.

2. Connect a jumper wire from the positive power rail
    to the positive (longer) LED leg.

3. Connect a jumper wire from the negative LED leg to the open outside potentiometer pin (e.g., row 7).

Rotate the potentiometer! What do you notice??

> 🔍 **Check it out:** What happens if you swap out one of the lights for a buzzer or motor? What other modifications can you make to this circuit?

Potentiometer Schematic Symbol

The schematic symbol for a potentiometer (Figure 4-11) is similar to the symbol for a resistor. In addition to the cute monster mouth (zigzag line), a potentiometer has a little line with an arrow showing that it can vary! So cute and clever:

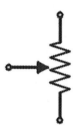

Figure 4-11. *Schematic symbol for a potentiometer*

Another helpful piece of information contained in the schematic symbol is that potentiometers have three legs, or poles. In the symbol, each circle at the ends of the lines indicates a pole, or connection point.

> 🔍 **Check it out:** We're starting to learn more about schematic symbols. Look up some circuit diagrams online and see what you recognize! For components that you do not recognize, what information can you gather?

TROUBLESHOOTING TIPS

1. Check that the battery is securely in its connector and is oriented properly (positive to positive, negative to negative). Check that the battery case switch is on the "On" position.

2. Check that the metal tips of the battery wires are fully inserted into the breadboard holes. Wiggle them to check.

3. Check that the battery case wires are in **different** power rails (negative to a hole next to the blue line, positive to a hole next to the red line).

4. Check that the jumper wires for the LED are connected in **different** power rails (negative to a hole next to the blue line, positive to a hole next to the red line).

5. Check that the LED legs are fully inserted into the breadboard holes and are in different rows, either different numbered rows or spanning the breadboard trough.

6. Check that the potentiometer legs are fully inserted into the breadboard holes and are in **different rows**.

7. Check that the jumper wires are fully inserted into the breadboard holes.

8. Check that the positive (longer) LED legs are both connected to the positive side of the battery via jumper wires.

9. Check that the negative LED legs are connected to different outside pins of the potentiometer.

10. Check that you have a jumper wire connecting the **middle** potentiometer pin to the negative power rail, which is also called ground.

11. Double-check that the legs of the potentiometer are where you think they are (it can be hard to see which holes the legs are connected to).

12. Occasionally, a jumper wire is faulty. If you've checked everything else, try swapping out the jumper wires for different ones.

13. Finally, check that the battery has energy by connecting it directly to an LED.

Still not working? Second-set-of-eyes time!

Capacitors: Flood Gate Components!

And now for something completely different! For this project, we'll first learn about capacitors by building a project. Then we'll dig into how capacitors work, yay!

Grab These Materials

- Half-size breadboard
- Coin cell in battery case
- 5 jumper wires
- 1 capacitor (100 µF ideal)
- 1 LED

Project 4-5: Light Flash!

In this project, we'll learn how capacitors work by building a "light flash" circuit. This circuit one is a bit tricky, so let's go through it together. First, build the following circuit shown in Figure 4-12 to charge up the capacitor:

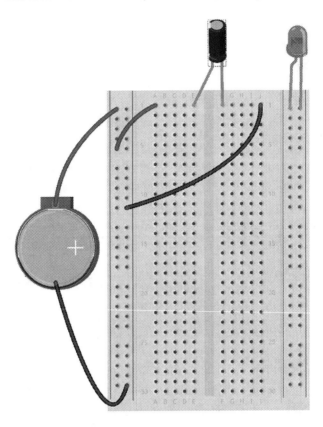

Figure 4-12. *Capacitor charging circuit*

Written Procedure (Charging Circuit)

1. Insert the battery case wires into the breadboard power rails.

2. Insert an LED into the unused power rails so that the positive lead is plugged into the positive power rail and the negative lead is plugged into the negative power rail.

3. Insert the capacitor into the breadboard. The positive (longer) lead plugs into the left-side row 1. The negative (shorter) lead plugs into the right-side row 1.

4. Connect a jumper wire between the positive battery power rail and the positive capacitor lead (left-side row 1).

5. Connect a second jumper wire between the negative battery power rail and the negative capacitor lead (right-side row 1).

Wait about one second, then build the next circuit shown in Figure 4-13 to flash the LED:

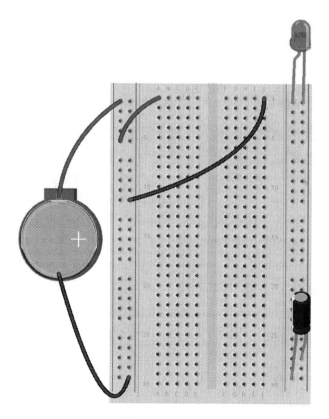

Figure 4-13. *Capacitor discharging circuit*

Written Procedure (Discharging Circuit)

1. Unplug the capacitor from the battery connections.

2. Plug the capacitor into the power rail with the LED. Insert the positive (longer) lead into the positive power rail and the negative (shorter) lead into the negative power rail.

AH! It happens so fast! Repeat the charging and discharging circuits a few times.

> 🔎 **Check it out:** Try a different capacitor! What is different between the two (or three... or four!)?

How Is a Capacitor like a Flood Gate?

As we discovered in our charging and discharging circuits, our **capacitor** stored energy for later use! This is similar to a battery, which also stores electrical energy. A capacitor stores energy in a different way than a battery, and it releases that energy much more quickly than a battery. A short description is that a capacitor stores electrical energy in an electric field. A longer explanation and in-depth look at capacitors can be found at the end of this section if you're super curious (yesss, be curious!).

Capacitor   A passive electronic component that stores a certain amount of charge and then releases it all at once. Units of Farads (F).

Capacitors help us to do things like make camera flashes, control the flow of electricity to sensitive components, smooth out the voltage and current of power sources, and build radio tuners and filters.

Capacitors are another type of passive component. They have two terminals, or leads. Some capacitors, like the one we used in our circuit, are polarized, which means that one of the leads is longer. Just like our LED, this longer leg indicates the positive leg. Heck yes for standards across circuit components!

BUT WAIT!! ISN'T THIS WHOLE CHAPTER ABOUT PASSIVE COMPONENTS WHICH CONSUME ENERGY AND DON'T PRODUCE IT?!

Well, yes! Great question. To flash the light with a capacitor, we had to first charge the capacitor using energy from the battery. Capacitors do not produce power on their own, they need a source of energy.

If you look closely at the capacitor (and maybe rotate it), you'll find a white band with a "-" in it. The leg with the minus sign above it is the negative lead. If you are working with a capacitor and it's not obvious which lead is longer, look for this minus sign!

Like we see in Figure 4-14, there are many ways to construct a capacitor. A common capacitor type is the parallel plate capacitor, which is made like a sandwich: two flat plates of metal with an insulating material called a dielectric in between. The conductive plates and the dielectric are the basic building blocks of different capacitor types.

Dielectric   An insulating material that can be polarized by an electric field.

Figure 4-14. *A variety of ceramic and electrolytic capacitors! Source: Wikimedia Commons*

Capacitors function like a flood gate (oh hey, we're getting to the chapter title!) in that they store a certain amount of charge and then release it all at once. The amount of charge a capacitor can store, also known as its threshold, is given by the capacitor rating. Capacitors are rated, or measured, in units of Farads. You'll most likely see capacitor ratings in smaller units, like microFarads (μF) or milliFarads (mF).

MORE INFO ON HOW CAPACITORS WORK, PLEASE!

Capacitors are a passive electronic component made of two or more conductive plates separated by a semi-insulative material called a dielectric. Nearly every electronic circuit uses one or more capacitors for a wide variety of functions, like local energy storage, voltage spike suppression, or complex signal filtering for electronic communication.

A common construction is a parallel plate capacitor. In this construction, two equally sized conductive plates are separated by a dielectric material in between. A **dielectric** is a material that can be polarized by an electric field.

When there is a potential difference across the capacitor plates, like when we connect the capacitor to a battery, an electric field occurs across the dielectric. This causes positive charge to gather on one plate and an equal amount of negative charge to gather on the other plate. The charges in the atoms of the dielectric are pushed by similar charges and pulled by different charges. In other words, the positive charges in the dielectric atoms move toward the negatively charged capacitor plate, and the negative charges in the electric atoms move toward the positively charged capacitor plate. We can visualize this phenomenon like this (Figure 4-15):

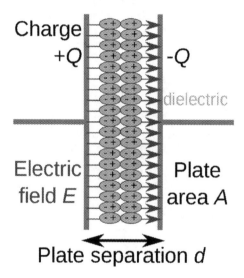

Figure 4-15. *Diagram of a charged capacitor with dielectric polarization. Source: Wikimedia Commons*

The capacitance of a capacitor depends mostly on the physical construction: the size (area) of the conductive plates (A), the separation distance (d), and a property of the dielectric called the permittivity (ε). You can use the following equation to calculate the capacitance of a capacitor:

$$C = \frac{\epsilon A}{d}$$

Another awesome thing you can use the preceding equation for is to explore how you can change capacitance by changing the dielectric or its other properties!

🔍 **Check it out:** Look up the permittivity of common materials like air, water, alcohol, wood, glass, etc. What patterns do you notice? What discoveries are surprising?

Schematic Symbol for a Capacitor

If you're looking for a capacitor on a schematic, look for this symbol shown in Figure 4-16:

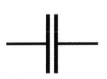

Figure 4-16. Capacitor schematic symbol

Wait a minute. This looks confusingly close to a battery schematic symbol!

Ah, yes, it does! That's because capacitors store electrical energy just like a battery. But, as we learned, the way that capacitors do this is different from a battery. This is why the lines of a capacitor schematic symbol are the same size.

Special Safety Note on Capacitors

The larger the capacitor, the more charge it can hold. Capacitors can hold so much energy that they are used to increase the power in a microwave! So cool.

But with all this power comes great responsibility (srynotsry). **Capacitors larger than your thumb are dangerous** (and potentially deadly) because of the amount of charge they can hold when charged. **Capacitors can store energy for a long time**, so even if your microwave is unplugged, the high-energy capacitor inside of it might still be charged.

While the capacitors we'll use in this book are safe to touch and fiddle with, even when charged, **here are some safety rules if you happen across a capacitor larger than your thumb:**[4]

1. **Don't touch the capacitor**!! Avoid touching anything metal on the board where the capacitor is.

2. Put the case back on and move the device to an out-of-the-way location. **Let the device sit unplugged for at least two weeks.**

3. After two weeks, the capacitor should have lost all its charge. Since we are safety-first oriented, we will double-check this! Grab a plastic-handled screwdriver. Put your left hand behind your back (one-hand rule), hold the plastic handle, and use the metal head of the screwdriver to touch both capacitor leads simultaneously.

4. If nothing happens, the capacitor is discharged.

    a. If you see a spark, well, the capacitor is now discharged.[5]

---

[4] Taking apart electronics is fun and educational, so rather than say "don't do it!", it's important to understand the consequences and how to take proper safety precaution. Always, always, always follow safety rules, even if you think it's fine, because your health and your life are worth waiting a few weeks and expending the energy to use the proper tools.

[5] Not ideal but technically safe.

And, you know, I'd advise you to avoid doing other silly, dangerous things like trying to open a capacitor because there are often hazardous materials inside. There's a reason they are tightly wrapped up, so let's keep them that way. ☺

Going Further

Woo-hoo!! You built at least four circuits with three different types of new circuit components!

But, now what?? How can you apply this knowledge? Here are some ideas to get you started:

1. **Project 1: Longer-lasting wearable lights!**

   With your knowledge of resistors, you can reduce the amount of electricity that flows in your circuits! This helps us make lights last longer, yay! Add a resistor to your wearable LEDs, and you can get light for days and even weeks!

2. **Project 2: Motor speed control!**

   Connect the potentiometer to the motor and rotate the potentiometer to control the motor speed. Use this to modify the Brush Bot you built in Chapter 3, make puppets that have adjustable movement (like a buzzing bee that buzzes more when it's close to a flower), or design another fun project that uses motor movement!

3. **Project 3: Electronic music with volume control!**

   Connect the potentiometer to the buzzer and adjust
   the volume! Try adding a resistor and listen to what
   changes. Explore how different resistors affect the
   sound output, and use the potentiometer to adjust
   the volume.

4. **Project 4: Explore different combinations of
   components!**

   Now that you can control the amount of electricity
   that flows in your circuit, explore using resistors and
   potentiometer(s) to power an LED and a motor with
   a single battery.

Summary

In this chapter, we learned how to control the flow of electricity! We did
this by using three different passive components, or components that don't
add power to circuits. Along the way, we learned about resistance and
capacitance and how engineers and chemists design these components.
We were also introduced to Ohm's Law!

The next chapter is another bonus chapter that does a deep dive into
Ohm's Law, yay!

CHAPTER 5

Interacting with Electricity via Buttons and Switches! (Electromechanical Components)

Pushbuttons: Hang onto Your Switch!

You made it to Chapter 5! If you haven't tried to build a circuit on your own yet, you've learned enough to give it a go (i.e., without a diagram). In this chapter, we'll learn about electromechanical components by building circuits with new kinds of components.

Grab These Materials

- Half-size breadboard
- Coin cell in battery case

© Jennifer Fox 2023
J. Fox, *Beginning Breadboarding*, https://doi.org/10.1007/978-1-4842-9218-1_5

- 3 jumper wires

- 1 pushbutton

- 1 LED

Project 5-1: Light at Our Fingertips

Let's build a circuit where we can turn off an LED! For this, I'll guide and give you some scaffolding, but I want you to try actually building the circuit without a diagram. If you get lost while trying on your own, you can skip forward in this section to look at the circuit diagram.

Alright, let's have at it!

First, pick up the pushbutton and look at it. What do you notice? How can you apply your observations to build a circuit with it? It may help you to write down your observations, thoughts, or to draw a picture of what a circuit could look like.

Next, start building the circuit with what you already know: the battery and LED. If you need them, written instructions are as follows.

Written Instructions (First Half)

1. Connect the battery case wires to the breadboard (power rails).

2. Insert the LED into the breadboard (so that its leads are in two different rows).

3. Connect a jumper wire between the positive battery wire and the LED.

    a. More specifically, connect a jumper wire between the positive power rail and the positive (longer) LED lead.

Next, we need to figure out how to connect the pushbutton into our circuit. **Like a resistor**, our pushbutton should be connected between the LED and the battery. This enables the button to interrupt the flow of electricity from our source of energy to the light that uses that energy.

Your challenge is to explore connecting the pushbutton into the circuit! Check out the following hints if you get stuck. (If you get super stuck and frustrated, skip ahead to the circuit diagram or take a break.)

> **Hint 1**: Look at the bolded text earlier.

> **Hint 2**: You may need two jumper wires, like we used for the resistor.

> **Hint 3**: The pushbutton is not polarized (it doesn't matter which orientation you connect the leads into the circuit).

Ready to test your circuit??

Press down on the top of the pushbutton and...

... what happened?!

If your circuit is wired correctly, pressing down on the pushbutton should cause the LED to turn on! When you stop pressing down on the pushbutton, the LED should turn off again.

If your circuit didn't work as expected, hooray for trying!! Now we can look at the diagram in Figure 5-1 to figure out where we made a mistake. Mistakes are a great way to learn and remember skills for next time.

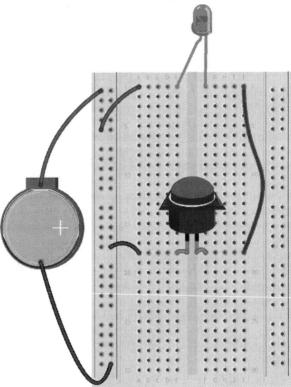

Figure 5-1. *Pushbutton circuit*

Written Instructions (Second Half)

1. Starting with the battery and LED in our breadboard, insert the pushbutton so that its two leads are in two different breadboard rows.

   a. In the diagram, the pushbutton leads are in two different rows that span the middle breadboard trench (row 18 on the left side and row 18 on the right side).

2. Grab a jumper wire and connect it from the negative LED leg to one of the pushbutton leads.

   a. In the diagram, this is the yellow jumper wire. It connects to the pushbutton via row 18 on the right side.

3. Grab a third jumper wire and connect it between
    the second pushbutton lead and the negative
    breadboard power rail.

    a. In the diagram, this is the black jumper wire. It connects the
        pushbutton via row 18 on the left side to the negative power
        rail (and thus to the negative side of the battery).

Test your circuit and wield your own energy to control electricity!!

(If your circuit still doesn't work as expected, compare your circuit with
the diagram again and/or check out the troubleshooting tips at the end of
this section.)

🔎 **Check it out:** Move the pushbutton to the other
side of the LED so that it's connected between the
positive battery lead and the positive LED lead. Test
your button! What do you notice? What does this
teach you about the pushbutton? About your
circuit?

TROUBLESHOOTING TIPS

1. Check that the battery is securely in its connector and is
    oriented properly (positive to positive, negative to negative).
    Check that the battery case switch is on the "On" position.

2. Check that the metal tips of the battery wires are fully inserted
    into the breadboard holes. Wiggle them to check.

3. Check that the battery case wires are in **different** power rails
    (negative to a hole next to the blue line, positive to a hole next
    to the red line).

4. Check that the LED leads are fully inserted into the breadboard
    holes and are in different rows, either different numbered rows
    or spanning the breadboard trough.

5. Check that the pushbutton leads are fully inserted into the
    breadboard holes and are in **different rows**.

6. Check that the jumper wires are fully inserted into the
    breadboard holes.

7. Check that the jumper wires are in the proper breadboard rows
    for each component.

8. Check that the positive (longer) LED lead is connected to the
    positive side of the battery.

9. Occasionally, a jumper wire is faulty. If you've checked
    everything else, try wiggling the wires or swapping out the
    jumper wires for different ones.

10. Finally, check that the battery has energy by connecting it
    directly to an LED.

Still not working? Second-set-of-eyes time!

Pushbuttons: A Lifetime of Bouncing Back

Ah yes, the **momentary pushbutton**, a symbol of resilience and remaining
unperturbed in the face of adversity. Or less dramatically, bouncing
back and returning to the same state before a disturbance. Perhaps still
dramatic for a circuit component, but accurate (and fun)!

Momentary switch   A switch that stays in place temporarily, for
example, until you remove your finger.

Pushbuttons are super fun to open and look inside. I'd recommend doing this if you have patience and a willingness to sacrifice a pushbutton and potentially search on your hands and knees for tiny metal parts (maybe with the help of a magnet). It also helps to have nimble fingers or tweezers.

Like most components, there are lots of ways to construct a pushbutton. Some pushbuttons look like Figure 5-2 on the inside:

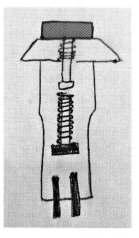

Figure 5-2. *Cross-section of a pushbutton momentary switch (open)*

🔎 **Check it out:** What do you notice about the pushbutton design? Do you think electricity will flow between the pushbutton leads? Why or why not? What mechanisms are inside the pushbutton that might cause it to move?

Despite how they are designed, all pushbuttons use **mechanical energy**, or energy of motion, to control electricity.

But wait! Where is this mechanical energy coming from?!

... From us!

Mechanical energy   Energy of motion, like a gear, pulley, or
baseball bat!

When we press down on the pushbutton, we convert our internal
chemical energy into mechanical energy. Our mechanical energy pushes
down the metal T inside the pushbutton so that it connects the two leads.
Inside, it looks like Figure 5-3:

Figure 5-3. *Cross-section of a pushbutton momentary switch (closed)*

Here's a more in-depth description: the top of the pushbutton is
connected to a metal **L** shape. Pushing down the top of the button pushes
down this **L** shape so that it makes electrical connection between the two
leads. When this happens, electricity can flow from one lead to the other. If
a switch is in this mode where it allows electricity to flow through it, we call
it a "**closed**" state.

At the same time the **L** shape is pushed down, a spring (or two) is
compressed. When you release the top of the pushbutton, the compressed
spring returns to its original (uncompressed) shape. This motion of the
spring pulls the **L** shape upward, and the button is open again! In this
mode where electricity cannot flow through the pushbutton, we call it an
"**open**" state.

158

A "**normally open**," or "NO," switch is like the one we just experimented with: in its rest state, it does **not** allow electricity to flow. In other words, NO electricity until we do some work! (Srynotsry for bad circuit puns.)

A "**normally closed**," or "NC," switch **does** allow electricity to flow in its rest state. It also requires work[1] to stop the flow of electricity.

Normally open (NO) switch   In its rest state, a switch that does not allow electricity to flow.

Normally closed (NC) switch   In its rest state, a switch that allows electricity to flow.

🫤 **Question:** When would you want to use a NO switch? When would you want to use a NC switch?

There are TONS of handy uses for both NO and NC switches. Normally open (NO) switches are often used to trigger actions, like pressing buttons on a TV remote, a garage door opener, or a video game controller. NC switches are often used for safety purposes, like only allowing electricity to flow when a microwave door is closed. Search around online for NO and NC switches or open up some (unused or broken) electronics around your house and see what kinds of switches you can find!

---

[1] I keep using this word "work"... is it intentional? Why yes, dear reader, it is! Work is both a term in English to describe, well, the expenditure of energy for some external purpose **and** a term in physics to describe a type of energy. In many ways, they are similar terms! The difference is that physics is ultra-precise. In case you're curious, work is defined as the transfer of energy by a force like mechanical energy (or gravity, electrical energy, chemical energy, etc.).

Pushbutton Schematic Symbol

In my humble opinion, the schematic symbol for a pushbutton begs me to interact with it. It closely resembles the actual pushbutton mechanism, and it's just sitting there, waiting to be pushed! Like shown in Figure 5-4:

Figure 5-4. Schematic symbol for a pushbutton

You may also see a small line perpendicular to the top line, like shown in Figure 5-5:

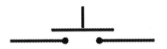

Figure 5-5. Another type of schematic symbol for a pushbutton

A helpful way to remember: If the schematic symbol looks like it should be pressed, it is probably a pushbutton. ☺

(Slide) Switches: Set It and Forget It

Continuing our exploration of electromechanical switches leads us to our next component and our next project!

Grab These Materials

- Half-size breadboard
- Coin cell in battery case
- 3 jumper wires
- 1 slide switch
- 1 LED

Project 5-2: Breadboard Flashlight

Using our own energy to trigger actions is pretty rad, but sometimes we just want the dang light to turn on and stay on! Like when we're going spelunking into a dark cave. A light that stays on is preferred.

Permanent switch   A switch that holds its state until acted on by an outside force, for example, your finger moves it.

Enter: **Permanent switches**! For our next project, we'll learn how to use a slide switch, a specific kind of permanent switch.

Grab the slide switch and observe it for a moment. What do you notice? What is different between the slide switch and the pushbutton? What is similar? What is similar with other components we've explored?

Starting with the circuit from Project 5-1, try to connect the slide switch into the circuit so that as you toggle the top of the slide switch, the LED turns on and off.

Spend at least three minutes trying. You can do this! ☺

(Schematic is on the next page in Figure 5-6 if/when you need it.)

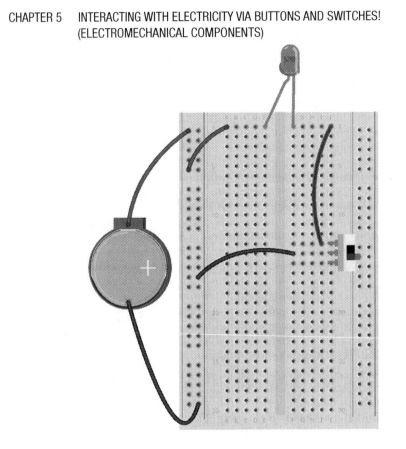

Figure 5-6. *Slide switch circuit*

Written Procedure

1. Connect the battery case wires to the breadboard (power rails).

2. Insert the LED into the breadboard (so that its leads are in two different rows).

3. Connect a jumper wire between the positive battery wire and the LED.

4. Insert the slide switch into the breadboard so
    that each of the three pins is in three different
    breadboard rows.

    a. In the diagram, the slide switch pins are in rows 13, 14, and 15
       on the right side of the breadboard.

5. Connect a jumper wire between the negative LED
    lead and the top slide switch pin (row 13 in the
    diagram).

6. Connect another jumper wire between the middle
    slide switch pin and the negative breadboard
    power rail.

Move the slider to turn the LED on and off! (Circuit not working? Check
the troubleshooting tips below.)

    🔍 **Check it out:** What happens if you move the
jumper wire on the outside switch pin to the other
side? What happens if you connect the LED to the
middle switch pin and the outside switch pin to the
negative power rail?

Now that you've built a circuit with adjustable light, you're ready to
take your breadboard on an adventure!

TROUBLESHOOTING TIPS

1. Check the battery on/off switch, its connections to the
    breadboard, and its orientation inside the case.

2. Check that the battery case wires are in **different** power rails.

3. Check that the LED leads are fully inserted into the breadboard
    holes and are in different rows.

4. Check that the slide switch leads are fully inserted into the breadboard holes and are in **three different rows** (rows are labeled with numbers, e.g., rows 13, 14, and 15 in the diagram).

5. Check that one jumper wire is connected between the middle switch pin and the negative breadboard power rail.

6. Check that a jumper wire connects the top switch pin to the negative LED pin.

7. Check that the jumper wires are fully inserted into the breadboard holes.

8. Check that the jumper wires are in the proper breadboard rows for each component.

9. Check that the positive (longer) LED lead is connected to the positive side of the battery.

10. Occasionally, a jumper wire is faulty. If you've checked everything else, try wiggling the wires or swapping out the jumper wires for different ones.

11. Finally, check that the battery has energy by connecting it directly to an LED.

Still not working? Second-set-of-eyes time!

Slide Switches: Stay in That State!

Now that we've explored using the slide switch, I wonder if you've guessed my next question: How does it work?!

Yes! I love understanding how things work because (1) it helps me better understand how it uses it, (2) it gives me ideas for other applications or projects, and (3) it makes me appreciate the ingenuity of the many humans who came before me. I hope some of this resonates with you and brings forth your curiosity (which resides in all of us!).

This means that we get to peek inside a slide switch! We'll also take a gander at some other common types of permanent switches.

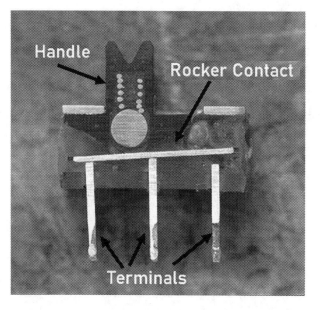

Figure 5-7. *Cutaway of a slide switch. Source: Wikimedia Commons*

Typically, a slide switch has either a metal contact that moves between the outside switch pins or a metal bar that rocks back and forth. As shown in Figure 5-7 above, when the handle is all the way to the left, it connects the left and middle pins together. In this state, the right pin is disconnected. When the handle is moved all the way to the right, the metal bar rocks over and connects the right and middle pins together (and the left pin is disconnected).

Straightforward and simple – a beautiful design!

Poles and Throws[2]

But... wait! Why do we need this extra unused pin? Couldn't we get an on/off switch with just two pins where the sliding contact doesn't connect to another third pin?

Why yes! Our three-pin slide switch would work with only two pins. We could also add **more** pins to control more components! This gets us into terminology in permanent switch land: poles and throws!

The number of **poles** on a switch tells us how many separate circuits the switch can control. For example, **a single pole ("SP")** switch can only control our own circuit. A two-pole or **double-pole ("DP")** switch could control our circuit **and** a friend's circuit!

Pole   The number of separate circuits a permanent switch can control.

With a two-pin permanent switch, we would only have two positions – on and off – compared to our three-pin switch which can also switch a second component on and off. This is known as the switch's **throw**, which refers to the position of the switch. A two-pin permanent switch is a **single throw ("ST")**, while our three-pin switch is a **double throw ("DT")**.

Throw   The number of positions a switch's poles can be connected to.

We can add lots of pins to our permanent switches to control all sorts of circuits and components! The four most common types of poles and throws are shown in Figures 5-8 to 5-11.

---

[2] Really, I didn't make these terms up! They are legitimate technical terms and they are too perfect.

Single Pole Single Throw (SPST): On-Off

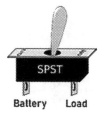

Figure 5-8. *SPST switch. Source: OpenClipArt*

Single Pole Double Throw (SPDT): On-On

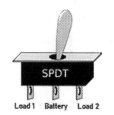

Figure 5-9. *SPDT switch. Source: OpenClipArt*

Double Pole Single Throw (DPST): On-Off

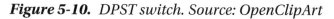

Figure 5-10. *DPST switch. Source: OpenClipArt*

167

Double Pole Double Throw (DPDT): On-On

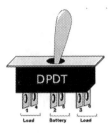

Figure 5-11. *DPDT switch. Source: OpenClipArt*

Okay! That's a lot of terminology. If it feels overwhelming, take a breath. **The two most common switches you'll encounter are SPST**, like household light switches**, and SPDT**, like the slide switch we played with. Also, you do not need to memorize these. You can always come back here for reference or use your favorite search engine.

Why do we need all these different pins?!

Great question! Sometimes, we want to use one battery to share energy with multiple components, like using one coin cell to power two LEDs that switch on in different ways. Other times, we might want to power two different components that use different amounts of energy, like turning on a light with a lower-energy battery when a motor that uses a higher-energy battery turns on.

There are all sorts of combinations for how we can power on (and turn off) different components. Different types of switches make our lives easier by enabling us to use a single component instead of smooshing a bunch of switches together to do what we want.

Other Types of Permanent Switches

Figure 5-12 below shows an assortment of permanent switches. Some of these, like the light switch on the bottom left, you use every day. Others, like a reed switch on the top right (switched on/off using magnets) are rarer but still super fun.

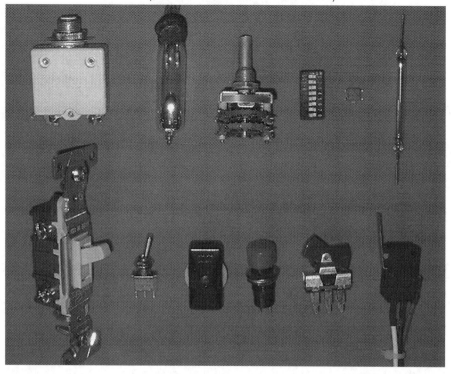

Figure 5-12. *Toggles and rockers and magnetic switches, oh my!*
An assortment of permanent (and momentary) switches. Source:
Wikimedia Commons

There is an abundant array of permanent switches! Too many to cover
here (for real, there are SO many switches!), but let's check out some of the
common ones:

- **Toggle switch**: This one uses a movable stick to switch
  between pins. These are often used for light switches.
  We saw toggle switches when learning about poles and
  throws earlier.

- **Rocker switch**: This switch has a handle mechanism
  that rocks from side to side when pressed. In other
  words, one side of the handle raises while the other
  side lowers, similar to the way a rocking horse moves!

- **Latching buttons**: Pushbuttons that latch, or click (so satisfying), into place until they are pressed again.

- **Rotary switches**: A switch with a handle that rotates between its pins. This is the kind of switch that our multimeter uses to switch between different throws.

Permanent Switch Schematic Symbol

A (NO) permanent switch has the following schematic symbol as shown in Figure 5-13:

Figure 5-13. *Schematic symbol for a permanent switch*

Technically speaking, this is a Single Pole Single Throw (SPST) switch. In case you're curious (or you make wild switch circuits), Figures 5-14 through 5-16 show the various pole and throw symbols:

SPDT:

(like our three-pin slide switch)

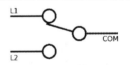

Figure 5-14.

DPST:

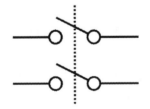

Figure 5-15.

DPDT:

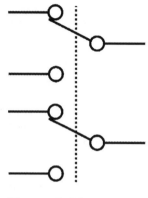

Figure 5-16.

🔍 **Check it out:** Use the schematic symbols to think about how the multipole and multithrow switches connect to different components, like lights, motors, and different circuits!

Project 5-3: Find and Record All the Switches!

Our houses are filled with all kinds of momentary and permanent switches. This experiment challenges you to use 15–30 minutes (or more if you're feeling ambitious and excited!) and explore your house for switches. Record where you find permanent and momentary switches. Bonus points for identifying the different switch subtypes (e.g., pushbutton, slide switch, toggle switch, etc.).

I've done the first row for you to give you an idea of how to fill in the table (and let's be honest, the light switch would have been way too easy for you).

Switch Function	Momentary or Permanent?	Type of Switch
Light switch	Permanent	Toggle

Project 5-4: Lights and Motors!

We've finally figured out how to connect an LED *and* a motor to the same coin cell battery: with an SPDT switch! In this project, we'll explore how to share electrical energy between the two components using our slide switch.

Grab These Materials

- Half-size breadboard

- Coin cell in battery case

- 3 jumper wires

- 1 slide switch

- 1 motor

- 1 LED

Start from the circuit in Project 5-2, as shown in Figure 5-17 below.

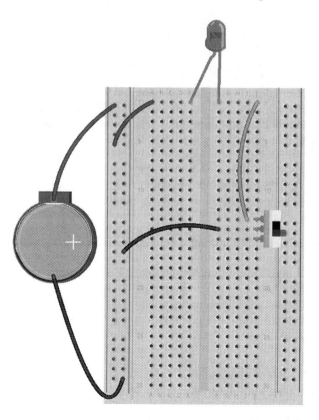

Figure 5-17. *Starting circuit for switching between an LED and motor*

Next, take the motor and use two jumper wires to connect it between the bottom switch pin and the positive battery terminal.

If you need it, the full written procedure and schematic are below in Figure 5-18.

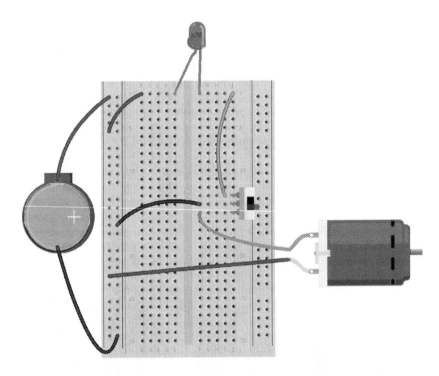

Figure 5-18. *Full circuit for switching between an LED and motor*

Written Procedure (Full Instructions)

1. Connect the battery case wires to the breadboard (power rails).

2. Insert the LED into the breadboard (so that its leads are in two different rows).

3. Connect a jumper wire between the positive battery wire and the LED.

4. Insert the slide switch into the breadboard so that each of the three pins is in three different breadboard rows.

5. Grab a jumper wire and connect it between the negative LED lead and the top slide switch pin.

6. Connect another jumper wire between the middle slide switch pin and the negative breadboard power rail.

7. Connect one motor lead to the positive power rail.

8. Connect the other motor lead to the bottom switch pin.

Move the switch handle and watch how we can help the battery share energy between the LED and the motor! (Not working? Troubleshooting tips at the end of the section should help!)

This is a great example of why an SPDT switch is useful: without our switch, our lil' coin cell doesn't have enough energy to control both components.

TROUBLESHOOTING TIPS

1. Check the battery on/off switch, its wire connections to the breadboard, and its orientation inside the case.

2. Check that the battery case wires are in **different** power rails.

3. Check that the LED leads are fully inserted into the breadboard holes and are in different rows.

4. Check that the slide switch leads are fully inserted into the breadboard holes and are in **three different rows**.

5. Check that one jumper wire is connected between the middle switch pin and the negative breadboard power rail.

6. Check that a jumper wire connects the top switch pin to the negative LED pin.

7. Check that one motor lead is connected to the positive breadboard power rail.

8. Check that the other motor lead is connected to the bottom switch pin.

9. Check that the jumper wires are fully inserted into the breadboard holes.

10. Check that the jumper wires are in the proper breadboard rows for each component.

11. Check that the positive (longer) LED lead is connected to the positive side of the battery.

12. Occasionally, a jumper wire is faulty. If you've checked everything else, try wiggling the wires or swapping out the jumper wires for different ones.

13. Finally, check that the battery has energy by connecting it directly to an LED.

Still not working? Ask another human to help!

Going Further

Hooray! You have a new way to control electricity and build more cool projects! Here are some ideas to get you going:

1. **Project 1: Physical status light**

   Connect a red LED and a green LED to the slide
   switch so that it can switch between the colors. Cut
   small holes in a piece of cardboard so that the LEDs
   poke through. Under the red LED, write something
   like "Please Leave Me Be," and under the green LED,
   write something like "Open to chatting!"

   Install at school, work, or wherever else you want
   to use it. Turn the light to red when you need focus
   time (or just don't feel like talking to folks) and
   green when you're open to being sociable!

2. **Project 2: Morse code version 2.0**

   Grab a friend and build two circuits (on two
   different breadboards) with a buzzer (or LED) and
   a pushbutton. Use Morse code signals or come up
   with your own binary code to send from afar!

3. **Project 3: Make your own switches!**

   Grab some cardboard, aluminum foil, and other
   common household items to make your own
   switches!

   One of my favorite switches to make is a NC
   momentary switch built with a clothespin. To do
   this, first glue the clothespin onto the cardboard.
   Cover the open clothespin ends with foil (the part
   that you pinch with your fingers to open and close
   the clothespin). Connect alligator clips to the foil, or
   snugly tape the metal ends of wires to the foil. Push
   down on the ends to close the switch!

What other switch ideas can you come up with? Some of my other favorite materials to make switches with are paperclips, brads, and rubber bands.

Summary

This chapter introduced electromechanical components that use our energy to control the flow of electricity. We focused on switches and learned about momentary and permanent switches, building projects and looking inside at the mechanisms that make them work. With both types of switches, we learned about the different kinds, like NO and NC momentary switches, and the pole and throw terminology of permanent switches.

In our next chapter, we will learn about and build more complex circuits. These circuits will teach us more about how computers and other fancy electronics work!

CHAPTER 6

Encoding Information into Electricity! (Logic Gates Part 1)

Why Records Sound Better Than CDs

Figure 6-1. *Vinyl records and CDs encode music with electricity in different ways. Source: Wikimedia Commons*

Wielding the power of electricity expands and amplifies our abilities in all sorts of ways: powering lights to read and write and make things at night, moving motors so we can quickly visit distant lands, and encoding

© Jennifer Fox 2023

J. Fox, *Beginning Breadboarding*, https://doi.org/10.1007/978-1-4842-9218-1_6

information like conversations and books and music. Like you see in Figure 6-1 above, it's this latter category, music, that we'll use to explore how to encode information with electricity!

The following statement may ruffle some feathers, but often the best way to get knowledge to stick is to use a potentially controversial statement like this: **records (or, if you prefer, albums) sound better than CDs.** (I will die on this tech hill.)

In the early days of CDs, this was true! This is because music encoded onto records and played back for our ears to enjoy is done using **analog signals, a quantity that can have any value** (sometimes in a limited range). This is also known as a **continuous signal**.

Analog signal   A continuous value over time. In other words, a signal that can have any value, like age, gender, or temperature.

Some examples of analog values include temperature, age, height, and air waves (i.e., sound). Alternating current (AC) electricity, like what comes out of (most) electrical outlets, is an example of an analog signal because it changes over time.

An analog signal may look like a wave, like we see in Figure 6-2.

Analog signal

Figure 6-2. *An example of an analog signal over time! Source: Wikimedia Commons*

😵 **Question 1:** What are some other real-world examples of analog signals?

CDs, on the other (1990s) hand, use **digital signals**, a quantity that can only have two values. This is also known as a **binary signal** or a **discrete signal**.

Digital signal   A binary value over time. In other words, a signal that can have only two values, like on/off, 1/0, or true/false.

Some examples of digital values are true/false, on/off, read/unread, and alive/dead. Direct current (DC) electricity, like what is generated by batteries, is a digital signal because it is either on or off.

A digital signal may look like what's shown in Figure 6-3.

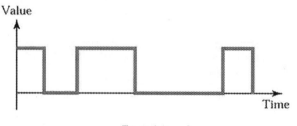

Digital signal

Figure 6-3. *An example of a digital signal over time! Source: Wikimedia Commons*

😵 **Question 2:** What are some other real-world examples of digital signals?

When we want to encode electricity, we can choose between analog and digital signals.

Records are imprinted with an analog signal that mirrors the actual sound waves generated by instruments – the same sound waves that we hear when we hear the vibration of a guitar string, vocal chords, or the skin and body of a drum. Recording music (onto a record) converts the mechanical energy of the musical sound waves into electrical energy (using a transducer made of a stylus, magnets, coils, a cantilever, and a body in a cartridge). When you play the record, the electrical energy is converted back into mechanical energy to generate sound waves! An example of sound waves for white noise is shown below in Figure 6-4.

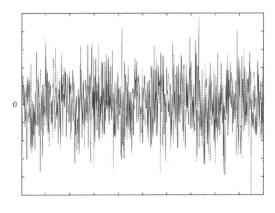

Figure 6-4. *A sound wave of white noise! The plot shows the amplitude (in this case, volume) of the wave over time. Source: Wikimedia Commons*

Newer systems that play records often have digital conversion in between the record and our ears, so there is, technically speaking, a digital signal in the mix. In older record systems, a phonograph passively amplifies the sound waves. These systems are exclusively analog signals. In my humble opinion, this is as close as you can get to live music.[1]

CDs (and our computers and smartphones) play music using digital signals.

---

[1] Okay, okay, I'm simplifying again. With recent technological advances, digital music is more *accurate* than analog recordings. But there's a warmth to analog recordings, or conversely there's too much "crispness" to digital recordings that cause many musicians (myself included) to prefer records. Despite all this, the analog vs. digital analogy is still relevant and useful. ☺

But... How do you make a continuous, analog sound wave with a digital signal??!

Right!

Wild.

Humans can be pretty clever.

We can approximate sound waves with digital signals by quickly turning the digital signal on and off, like we see in Figure 6-5.

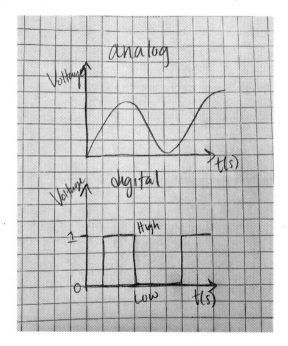

Figure 6-5. *Using a digital signal to imitate an analog signal!*

As shown in Figure 6-5, the digital signal can only have two values: high (1) and low (0). As mentioned earlier, this is also called a binary signal. Humans like to count in base ten because most of us have ten fingers. Binary numbers are a way of counting with only two numbers. If we met an alien species that only had one finger on each hand, they'd probably count in binary!

There are all sorts of fun things we can do with binary. We'll dig into this in more detail in Chapter 9, but for now let's start with counting! Counting in binary looks like this in Table 6-1:

Table 6-1. *Decimal and binary counting*

Decimal (Base 10)	Binary (Base 2)
0	0
1	1
2	10
3	11
4	100
5	101
6	110
7	111
8	1000
9	1001
10	1010
11	1011
12	1100
13	1101
14	1110
15	1111

🔑 **Check it out**: What patterns do you notice in binary number counting? What would the binary numbers for 16–20 be? How about 21–30? 100?

One of the cool things we can do when we combine binary numbers and electricity is to make **logic gates**! But enough theory, let's build some circuits to better understand what logic gates are and how they use binary numbers to encode information with electricity!

Logically Delicious! (Building Basic Logic Gates)

In this section, we'll replicate logic gates with pushbuttons to understand how logic gates function. We'll also learn to use logic gates to add, well, logic to our circuits!

Grab These Materials

- Half-size breadboard
- Coin cell in battery case
- 6 alligator clips
- 6 jumper wires
- 2 pushbuttons
- 1 LED

First, let's explore without the breadboard so we can more clearly see the path of the electricity!

Project 6-1: Combining Two Pushbuttons!

For this experiment, you will need the coin cell battery in its case, the alligator clips, the two pushbuttons, and the single LED. You will **not** need the breadboard (yet).

Your challenge for this experiment is to **combine two switches in one circuit**. There are two ways to do this. Each approach behaves a bit different, so press (all) the pushbuttons to check if the light turns on. (Finally! An excuse to push all the buttons!)

Hint 1: How can you combine two switches in series so that there is only one path for the electricity to flow? (Remember: In series means connecting components head-to-tail or in line with each other.)

Hint 2: How can you combine two switches in parallel so that there are two paths for the electricity to flow? (Remember: In parallel means connecting components head-to-head or in loops with each other.)

Once you've built both circuits , explore how they are similar and different.

Try for at least five minutes.   You're smart and capable and you can do this! It can also help to draw out the circuit on paper.

If you get stuck, check the section below to see the two methods.

Solutions to Experiment

Figures 6-6 and 6-7 below show the two ways to combine switches in one circuit.

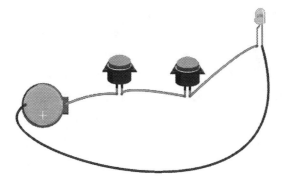

Figure 6-6. *Two switches **in series!***

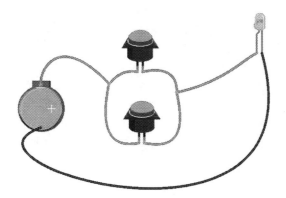

Figure 6-7. *Two switches **in parallel!***

Logic gate   A circuit component with one or two binary inputs and one binary output that changes based on the inputs.

If you didn't quite figure out the circuits during the experiment, build and explore them now. (Making these circuits with alligator clips before attempting on a breadboard can help a ton.)

🔎 **Check it out**: Trace the path of the electricity on both preceding circuits! (Yesss for drawing!)

Oh hey, look at you! You just built replicas of two **logic gates**!! (We'll build actual logic gates in Chapter 9.) Logic gates are special circuit components that have one or two (binary) inputs and one (binary) output. The electricity flowing (or not flowing) into the inputs changes the output.

Looking at your logic gate circuits from our preceding experiment, think about and write down your thoughts for these questions (even better: test out your hypotheses!):

> 😵 **Question 3:** When does the light turn on in the series circuit?
>
> _____

> 😵 **Question 4:** When does the light turn on in the parallel circuit?
>
> _____

> 😵 **Question 5:** Based on your exploration to questions 3 and 4, which circuit do you think is an AND gate? Why?
>
> _____
> _____
> _____

😜 **Question 6:** Based on your exploration to questions 3 and 4, which circuit do you think is an OR gate? Why?

_____

_____

_____

Using knowledge from our scientific exploration of logic gate circuits, let's transfer our learnings to the breadboard!

Project 6-2: Gotta Push 'Em All! (Pushbuttons in Series)

Let's build the **series pushbutton circuit** first.

Try to do this on your own first without peeking at the diagram (Figure 6-8). Start with the components you're familiar with (i.e., battery and LED). Then insert the pushbuttons into the breadboard and connect them between the battery and the LED.

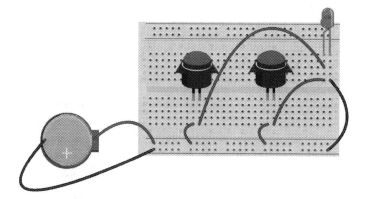

Figure 6-8. *Circuit diagram for two switches in series*

Written Instructions

1. Connect the battery case wires to the breadboard (power rails).

2. Insert the LED into the breadboard (so that its leads are in two different rows).

3. Connect a jumper wire between the negative power rail and the LED.

4. Insert the first pushbutton so that its two leads are in two different breadboard rows.

5. Connect a jumper wire between the positive power rail and the left-hand pushbutton pin.

6. Insert the second pushbutton so that its two leads are in two different breadboard rows.

7. Connect a jumper wire between the first pushbutton's right pin and the second pushbutton's left pin.

8. Connect a jumper wire between the second pushbutton's right pin and the (positive) LED lead.

Test your circuit!!

If your circuit is wired correctly, pressing down on **both** pushbuttons causes the LED to turn on! When you let go of either pushbutton, the LED turns off.

> *(If your circuit doesn't work as expected, compare your circuit with the diagram again and/or check out the troubleshooting tips at the end of this section.)*

This happens because our pushbuttons are in series, so there is only one path for the electricity to flow. Both pushbuttons must be pressed for the electricity to have a complete path of conductive material. In other words, we must press the first button **and** the second button.

AND gate A logic gate where both inputs must be true for the output to be true.

Oh hey! You just built a replica of an AND logic gate! If you've ever written computer code or taken discrete math, you've come across this concept. For those of us who haven't seen it (or as a refresher), **an AND gate output is on when both inputs are on**. (This can also be represented as "true" or 1 in binary.) For any other combination of inputs, the AND gate output is off.

TROUBLESHOOTING TIPS

1. Check the battery power switch and that the wires are in different power rails.

2. Check that the LED leads are fully inserted into the breadboard holes and are in different rows.

3. Check that both pushbutton leads are fully inserted into breadboard holes and are in different rows.

4. Check that the jumper wires are fully inserted into the breadboard holes.

5. Check that the jumper wires are in the proper breadboard rows for each component.

6. Check that the positive (longer) LED lead is connected to the positive side of the battery (via the pushbuttons).

7. Check for those rare faulty jumper wires by wiggling the wires or swapping out jumper wires.

8. Finally, check that the battery has energy by connecting it directly to an LED.

Still not working? Snag another human for assistance!

AND Logic Gate Schematic Symbol

Logic gate schematic symbols get away from "this sort of looks like the part" and into "we're dealing with pure symbolism" territory. The good news is that logic gates have similar shapes and there is a consistency to the symbolism. Once you recognize the general shape of a logic gate, when you see it on a circuit diagram you can look up the table of logic gate schematic symbols.

The schematic symbol for a logic gate looks like a sideways bell (or a sideways *Pac-Man* ghost) with two inputs and one output, like illustrated in Figure 6-9:

Figure 6-9. *Schematic symbol for an AND logic gate*

A and B are the two inputs into the logic gate. In our replica AND gate circuit, these are the two pushbuttons.

The output, Y, is the electricity that comes out of the logic gate. The value of the output (i.e., whether it is on or off) depends on the values of the two inputs (i.e., whether these are on or off). For an AND logic gate, both inputs A and B must be on for the output Y to be on.

In our AND gate, when electricity flows out of the gate it does work to turn on our LED. (This is handy because we can see what the logic gate output is and how it changes when the inputs change.)

Project 6-3: Push Any Button (Pushbuttons in Parallel)

Next, let's transfer our parallel pushbutton circuit onto the breadboard. Again, you've built lots of circuits now, so try to build this on your own before looking at the diagram or written instructions.

Start with what you know and think about how you can make two paths for the electricity to flow: one path through the first pushbutton (and to the LED) and a second path through the second pushbutton (and to the LED).

If you get stuck or frustrated, use the breadboard build diagram for our parallel pushbutton circuit (Figure 6-10).

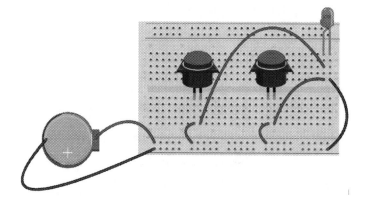

Figure 6-10. *Circuit diagram for two LEDs in parallel*

Written Instructions

1. Connect the battery case wires to the breadboard (power rails).

2. Insert the LED into the breadboard (so that its leads are in two different rows).

3. Connect a jumper wire between the negative power rail and the LED.

4. Insert the first pushbutton so that its two leads are in two different breadboard rows.

5. Connect a jumper wire between the positive power rail and the left-hand pushbutton pin.

6. Connect a second jumper wire between the pushbutton's right pin and the (positive) LED lead.

7. Insert the second pushbutton into the breadboard.

8. For this second pushbutton, connect a jumper wire between the positive power rail and the left pin.

9. Connect a jumper wire between the second pushbutton's right pin and the (positive) LED lead.

Again, test your circuit!

When our parallel pushbuttons are wired correctly, pushing **either** button turns on the light.

> *(If your circuit doesn't work as expected, compare your circuit with the diagram again and/or check out the troubleshooting tips at the end of this section.)*

This happens because our pushbuttons are in parallel, so there are **two paths** for the electricity to flow. Pushing the first button creates a complete path for the electricity to flow: through the pushbutton, to the LED, and back to the (negative side of the) battery. The second pushbutton creates a similar path when we press it.

In other words, we can press either the first button **or** the second button.

Look at that!! You just built a replica of an OR logic gate! **An OR gate output is on when any of the inputs are on.** This happens when one or both buttons are pressed.

OR gate   A logic gate where any input can be true for the output to be true.

TROUBLESHOOTING TIPS

1. Check the battery power switch and that the wires are in different power rails.

2. Check that the LED leads are fully inserted into the breadboard holes and are in different rows.

3. Check that both pushbutton leads are fully inserted into breadboard holes and are in different rows.

4. Check that the jumper wires are fully inserted into the breadboard holes.

5. Check that the right pins of **both** pushbuttons connect to the positive LED lead via the same breadboard row.

6. For both pushbuttons, check that the left-hand pin is connected to the positive power rail.

7. Check that the jumper wires are in the proper breadboard rows for each component.

8. Check that the positive (longer) LED lead is connected to the positive side of the battery (via the pushbuttons).

9. Check for those rare faulty jumper wires by wiggling the wires or swapping out jumper wires.

10. Finally, check that the battery has energy by connecting it directly to an LED.

Still not working? Hit up a friend, family member, or a random person for a second look.

OR Logic Gate Schematic Symbol

The OR logic gate symbol looks like a rad spaceship (Figure 6-11):

Figure 6-11. *Schematic symbol for an OR logic gate*

Like the AND gate, A and B represent the inputs to our logic gate. For the circuit we just built, our pushbuttons are the inputs A and B. The output, Y, changes based on the inputs A and B.

The electricity flowing out of our OR gate goes to the LED. This helps us see what the electricity is doing, yay!

196

How to Count with Just Two Fingers (a.k.a. Binary Numbers)

This is all fine and dandy, but **why should we care about making logic gates?**

Great question, my lovely reader, please continue asking "why"! **Logic gates are a way for us to make decisions with electricity (or code or math).** As we learned earlier, computers encode information using digital signals which are either on or off.[2]

One way to think about encoding information in digital signals is the game "20 Questions": one person thinks of a noun (a person, place, or thing!), and the other person gets 20 questions to guess what the first person is thinking of using only "yes" or "no" questions.

For example, if I was thinking of a salamander, my friend might ask, "Is it smaller than a toaster?", to which I would reply, "Yes!" They might then ask, "Is it alive?" I would again say, "Yes!" And so on until they guess the object (or run out of questions).

Despite only having yes/no (i.e., binary) answers in the "20 Questions" game, it is possible to navigate through complex information. "Talking" in binary also enables us humans to use electricity to store and transmit information over space and time.

Like all good programmers, early computer programmers leveraged prior knowledge to figure out how to "talk" in binary. This prior knowledge

---

[2] Why digital signals?? The main reason is that digital signals are easier and more reliable to measure than analog. This is because your signal is either on or off (or high/low). The real world is messy/complicated, and electrical signals can degrade or change even over small distances. It's not a big deal if a digital signal changes a lil' bit, you can still tell if the signal is on (or not). If an analog signal changes a tiny bit, it can make your measurements and circuits all sorts of confused and wrong!

was Boolean Logic![3] In addition to having a name that's super fun to say, Boolean Logic is a way to express logical statements with binary values.

Boolean Logic also gives us a framework for doing calculations with binary numbers. This is helpful because we can't add binary numbers in the same way we do with base ten numbers! Before we get into binary addition, let's look at some simple examples.

Let's say I want to turn a light on when it gets dark. I can rephrase this in a **conditional statement**: if it gets dark, turn on the light.

Conditional statement   A command for handling binary decisions.

This is a classic phrasing for computer programming: if <something happens >, then do <this other thing>. This is also called an "if-then" statement.

While it would be unnerving if we talked to other humans only using if-then statements, it's exactly what we need when converting human information into electrical information. The pushbutton logic gates we built do exactly this! The two inputs are the conditions: the "if" part of our "if-then" statement. The output is the "then" part.

Truth table   A summary of the possible inputs and outputs for a logic gate.

We can summarize logic gate behavior using **truth tables**, which are tables that list all possible inputs and subsequent outputs. **The truth table for our AND gate looks like this (Table 6-2):**

---

[3] Boolean Logic is named for George Boole who wrote books about it between the 1840s and 1850s.

Table 6-2. *AND Gate Truth Table*

A	B	Output
0	0	0
1	0	0
0	1	0
1	1	1

We read the truth table like this:

1. If A and B are false, then the output is false.

2. If A is true and B is false, then the output is false.

3. If A is false and B is true, then the output is false.

4. If A is true and B is true, then the output is true.

   Note: I swapped "true" for 1 and "false" for 0 because I believe it helps connect abstract math stuff to our everyday reality. ☺

   😄 **Question 7:** Your turn!! Finish the truth table **for an OR gate (Table 6-3)**.

Table 6-3. *OR Gate Truth Table*

A	B	Output
0	0	0
1	0	
0	1	
1	1	

Read your truth table!! It might not be quite as fun as reading your horoscope, but it is definitely informative.

(Just in case you need some help or you want to check your work (I'm a huge fan of checking work to figure out if I'm learning what I think I'm learning), the solution to the OR gate truth table is below in Table 6-4.)

Table 6-4. *OR Gate Truth Table (Filled In)*

A	B	Output
0	0	0
1	0	1
0	1	1
1	1	1

Boolean Logic and binary numbers are a massive topic. For now, this is enough to better understand and map out other logic gates.[4] Let's get back to building things!

Project 6-4: Flip It and Reverse It! (NOT Gate)

The final logic gate that we'll build with only pushbuttons is tricky and rad. That said, it's not exactly "best practice" in circuits. This is okay for now because we're building this circuit for educational purposes, but it's important to call out these things so that when you're building circuits in the wild, you can make appropriate (or at least informed) choices.

---

[4] If you are curious about binary numbers, Wikipedia is a great source! What you read here will give you a foundation from which to start. Remember: Take it slow; it's okay to reread things as many times as you need.

Grab These Materials

- Half-size breadboard

- Coin cell in battery case

- 4 jumper wires

- 1 pushbutton

- 1 LED

The logic gate that we're building for this project is called a NOT gate. This logic gate flips the electrical signal: if the input is on, the output is off. If the input is off, the output is on.

Our goal is to use the NOT gate to turn the light **off** when we press the button. In other words, the light is normally on, and when we press the button, the light turns off.

To do this, we'll use the pushbutton to **intentionally** make a short circuit. This is where the "not so best practice" part comes in... ☺

> 😵 **Question 8:** How can you do this on your own? Think about how you might use the pushbutton to create an easier path for electricity to flow when you press it.

If you get stuck, check out the following hints. And if you're super-duper stuck and **have attempted on your own for at least five minutes**, flip to the build diagram in Figure 6-12.

Hint 1: Connect the LED directly to the battery so that it is on when the battery is on/plugged in.

Hint 2: Connect the pushbutton in parallel with the LED.

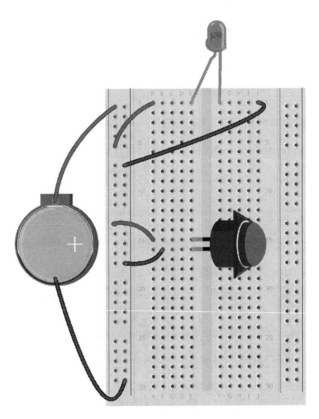

Figure 6-12. *Circuit diagram for a simple NOT gate*

Written Procedure

1. Connect the battery case wires to the breadboard (power rails) and insert the LED into the breadboard.

2. Connect a jumper wire between the positive power rail and the LED. Connect another jumper wire between the negative power rail and the LED.

3. Insert the pushbutton into the breadboard.

4. Connect a jumper wire between the positive power rail and one of the pushbutton leads.

5. Connect another jumper wire between the negative power rail and the other pushbutton lead.

For this circuit, the LED should be on by default. Test your NOT gate by pressing the button!

> *(Circuit not behaving as expected? Analyze the preceding diagram and/or check out the troubleshooting tips at the end of this section.)*

Woo-hoo! We flipped the electrical signal!

TROUBLESHOOTING TIPS

1. Check the battery power switch and that its wires are in different power rails.

2. Check that the LED leads are fully inserted into the breadboard holes and are in different rows.

3. Check that the pushbutton pins are fully inserted into breadboard holes and are in different rows.

4. Check that the jumper wires are fully inserted into the breadboard holes.

5. Check that one of the pushbutton pins is connected to the positive power rail. Check that the other pushbutton pin is connected to the negative power rail.

    a. Note: It doesn't matter which pin because the pushbutton is not polarized.

6. Check that the jumper wires are in the proper breadboard rows for each component.

7. Check that the positive (longer) LED lead is connected to the positive side of the battery. Check that the negative LED lead is connected to the negative side of the battery.

8. Check for those rare faulty jumper wires by wiggling the wires or swapping out jumper wires.

9. Finally, check that the battery has energy by connecting it directly to an LED.

Still not working? This is where we benefit from a second brain to get a fresh look!

NOT Logic Gate Schematic Symbol

A NOT gate schematic symbol, like shown in Figure 6-13, looks (to me) like a sideways stick figure wearing a large dress (so cute!):

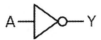

Figure 6-13. *Schematic symbol for a NOT logic gate*

As we discovered, a NOT gate has just one input, A, that reverses, or flips, the output, Y. The circle on the output side is how logic gate schematic symbols identify a "NOT" gate – we'll see more of these later in this chapter!

Project 6-5: Making Decisions with Logic Gates!

Grab These Materials

- Half-size breadboard

- Coin cell in battery case

- 12+ jumper wires

- 6+ pushbuttons

- 1 LED

Hooray! You've made it to your first independent project! For this project, we'll use logic gates to build a circuit to help you make decisions.

To get you started on this project, I'll walk you through a simple example and give you some tips. Take my example and adapt it to make it your own circuit! For your project, you'll likely need more jumper wires and pushbuttons (maybe even all the pushbuttons, yesss!!). The key is to **start simple and add one part/wire at a time**.

We are also getting into circuits where drawing diagrams is super helpful. You can use schematic symbols or make rough sketches of components. Doing this before you tackle the project helps you think about and work through the circuit. Even a simple drawing can save a ton of time (and mental confusion and frustration). Figure 6-14 shows an example of a circuit drawing for my sample decision tree.

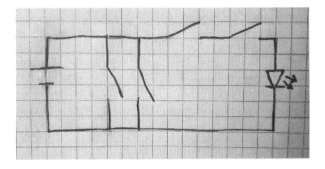

Figure 6-14. *An example circuit drawing for a pushbutton logic decision tree*

For my project, I am making a "Pet Adoption" decision maker. I'll use two logic gates to help me decide if a pet is a good choice for me to take home.

I have two criteria:

1.   If the pet is a cat, it is large and fluffy.

2.   If the pet is a dog, it is large or likes going on walks.

I can represent the preceding scenario with an AND gate to represent the cat criteria and an OR gate to represent the dog criteria. Both logic gates connect to the same light. This is because there is an implicit "OR" between my two criteria: either #1 is true or #2 is true for me to adopt the pet.

Tip   Connect your LED to the unused power rail. This will give you lots of space for wires!

Based on the criteria above, I can build a Pet Adoption decision maker like Figure 6-15.

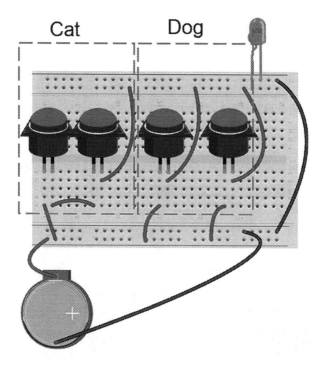

Figure 6-15. *Example of a Pet Adoption decision maker using two logic gates*

In this example, the left AND gate represents the cat criteria – it is large AND fluffy. Both of these conditions must be true for the light to turn on.

The right OR gate represents the dog criteria – it is large OR likes going on walks. Either of these conditions must be true for the light to turn on.

Bonus Points: Logic Gate As Input

The downside to my existing logic gate circuit is that I have to keep track of which logic gate corresponds to which pet type (the AND logic gate is used for the cat and the OR for the dog).

A better solution might be to **use the logic gate inputs to represent the pet type**. For this circuit, the output of each pushbutton goes to one or more logic gates that track the pet characteristics (e.g., large, likes going on walks, etc.).

For simplicity (and space), I'll remove one of my criteria. My new criteria are as follows:

1. If the pet is a cat, it is large.

2. If the pet is a dog, it is large or likes going on walks.

Figure 6-16 shows how I might update my Pet Adoption decision maker using a logic gate as input to another logic gate.

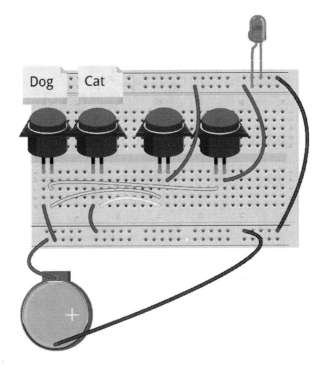

Figure 6-16. *Example of a Pet Adoption decision maker with the logic gate as input to the second logic gate*

In this example, the left OR logic gate represents the type of animal I'm considering for adoption: a dog or a cat. The output of this OR logic gate goes to another set of OR conditions: the left (unlabeled) pushbutton represents the characteristic "large," and the right (unlabeled) pushbutton represents the characteristic "likes going on walks."

If you trace the path of the electricity, the "dog" pushbutton connects to both the "large" and "likes going on walks" pushbuttons (cyan wires). The "cat" pushbutton connects only to the "large" pushbutton (yellow wire).

If this starts to get overwhelming, take a deep breath. Trace the path of the electricity on your breadboard. **Build the preceding circuit one pushbutton at a time.** Then convert your own project. Trust yourself; you can do this!

If you get stuck, it's totally okay to remove some wires, completely start over, go back to your drawing, or come back later. Do whatever you need to do to feel okay, but do give this a try!

Going Further: More Logic Gates and Project Ideas!

Quick Intro to Other Logic Gates: NAND and NOR!

In this chapter, we built replicas of AND, OR, and NOT logic gates. But there are all sorts of other logic gates to explore! NAND and NOR gates are fairly common, so let's do a quick intro on these.

A NAND gate, which stands for "NOT AND," is the reverse of an AND gate: the output is exactly opposite of the AND gate (i.e., the output is true when any of the inputs are false). The truth table for the NAND gate is seen in Table 6-5:

Table 6-5. *NAND Logic Gate Truth Table*

A	B	Out
0	0	1
1	0	1
0	1	1
1	1	0

The NAND gate schematic symbol looks like the AND gate, but it has a circle at the output that tells us it's a NOT version of this gate (Figure 6-17):

Figure 6-17. *Schematic symbol for a NAND logic gate*

A NOR gate, or a "NOT OR" gate, is the opposite of an OR gate. Oh hey, yay for naming patterns! For this logic gate, the output is the opposite of an OR gate (i.e., the output is true only when all of the inputs are false). The NOR truth table looks like this (Table 6-6):

Table 6-6. *NOR Logic Gate Truth Table*

A	B	Out
0	0	1
1	0	0
0	1	0
1	1	0

And, in keeping with communication patterns, the NOR gate schematic symbol looks like an OR gate with a circle at the output as illustrated in Figure 6-18:

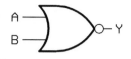

Figure 6-18. *Schematic symbol for a NOR logic gate*

Build All the Projects!

We can use logic gates to represent some of the information we deal with in our daily lives. Here are some ideas for expanding on this further:

1. **Project 1: Build more logic gates by adding another pushbutton.**

   Add a third pushbutton to the AND and/or the OR gates.[5] Explore different ways to use this third input to change the (single) output. Name your logic gates by looking up other types of logic gates or making up your own naming system (we'll learn more about them in Chapter 9).

2. **Project 2: More decision makers!**

   What other ways can you combine AND, OR, and NOT gates to help make decisions? Try building one with a friend to see what you create together!

3. **Project 3: Use logic gates to explore the flow of electricity.**

   Build different combinations of pushbuttons and trace the path of the electricity. What do you discover about electricity? What mysteries do you encounter?

---

[5] Srynotsry for the bad logic gate pun there. ☺

4. **Project 4: Teach a friend about logic gates.**

   Demonstrate one of the logic gate circuits you
   built (or your decision maker project!) to a friend
   or family member and explain how electricity is
   traveling in the circuit. Let them test out the buttons
   and ask questions.

What other ideas can you come up with for using logic gates to
represent electricity?? I always love sharing my learnings, ideas, and
questions with friends and family because they often give me novel ideas
or insights. I encourage you to do the same!

Summary

This chapter was all about translating human-readable information into
electricity with logic gates! We learned about the two main ways to encode
information with electricity: analog, or continuous signals, and digital,
or binary signals. We put on our empathy caps and thought about what it
would be like to count if we were an alien with only two fingers – that is, we
learned how to count using binary numbers!

We built replicas of logic gates using pushbuttons so that we could
observe how we actually represent and control binary information
with electricity. This introduced us to conditional statements (if-then
statements) which may be familiar from programming or mathematics.
We also learned how to use truth tables to keep track of the behavior of
logic gates!

Phew! We learned a TON! In the next chapter, we'll take a break from
logic gates to learn about sensors so that we can gather information from
the world around us and add it to our circuits.

CHAPTER 7

Sensors!

Using Our Senses to Detect Sensors

The human body is an incredible interface for the world around us. Our modes of sensing phenomena like light, wind, waves, and heat give us information that helps us to perceive, interact with, and understand other living creatures and nonliving objects.

In a similar way, most electronics need "senses," or sensors, to interact with the world. So far, we've mostly worked with output devices like lights, motors, and buzzers. The input devices that we've worked with include pushbuttons and switches.

Input device A component that takes in information from the world and converts it to an electrical signal.

Input devices take in physical information and convert that information into an electrical signal. Some inputs like buttons and touchscreens are designed for human interaction. Other inputs take in information from the world around us, for example, light and sound, similar to our human senses. These types of inputs are called sensors (makes sense, right!). There is an impressive array of sensors that detect all sorts of phenomena from gases to invisible light (e.g., infrared and

© Jennifer Fox 2023
J. Fox, *Beginning Breadboarding*, https://doi.org/10.1007/978-1-4842-9218-1_7

radio waves) to temperature. The best way to get a feel for the plethora and diversity of sensors is to observe them! And with the stage set, onward our next experiment!

Project 7-1: The Wonderful World of Sensors

Electronic inputs are all around us! Your challenge for this experiment is to **observe and record as many different types of electronic input devices as possible**.

If you're feeling lazy or are pressed for time (I can personally relate to both of those), take at least ten minutes to walk around your home, maybe even go outside, and record each different input you notice.

If you're feeling motivated or curious, explore different spaces like grocery stores, libraries, coffee shops, parks, your school or office, and any other public (or private) spaces that you frequent!

*Wait, wait… **HELP**! What qualifies as an input device? How will you know when you see one??*

An input device is anything electronic that takes in information from the physical world. When you see that it uses electricity, take a moment to stop and observe. How is the device interfacing or interacting with the physical world? If you only notice outputs, like lights or sounds or motors, think about how real-world information might be influencing the behavior of those outputs.

Log your observations in the following table! I did one example for you so you can get a sense of how you might fill it out. Feel free to log information in a different way or make your own table!

Input Device	Location/Object	Description (How It Works and/or What It Does)
Touchscreen	*Smartphone*	*Human interface device for fingers to type, search, etc.*

A Brief Inventory of Sensors

A few minutes spent observing electronic inputs reveals that there are dozens of ways that electronics gather information! A single smartphone has all sorts of inputs: a touchscreen, microphone, camera, accelerometer (which measures acceleration), GPS, light sensor, proximity (or distance) sensor, fingerprint sensor, thermometer, and more! (If you're curious, you can look up a list of the sensors in your smartphone using your favorite search engine. Be curious, it's an impressive list!)

One of the delightful benefits of electronics is that we can augment our human senses and detect things that are normally invisible to us, like magnetic fields, infrared radiation (i.e., heat), and air pressure. The number of different kinds of sensors is impressively extensive. We'll focus on the most common categories and types of sensors.

Analog vs. Digital

Hello again our new friends: analog and digital! All sorts of stuff in electronics can be bucketed into these two categories, including sensors!

As we learned last chapter, analog sensors have a continuous signal. Examples of analog sensors include light sensors, microphones, and strain gauges (a type of weight sensor). Most analog sensors like these convert physical information into a voltage or a resistance that varies. A lot of analog sensors have built-in **analog-to-digital converter (ADC)** circuits to make it easier to measure the sensor value with a computer. Yay for engineers making it easier for us to measure things!

Analog-to-digital converter (ADC)   A circuit used to convert analog signals into digital signals.

With digital signals fresh in your mind, hopefully you inferred that digital sensors output a signal that is either on or off. A fun example of a digital sensor is an infrared (IR) break-beam sensor – these are the sensors that prevent your garage door from crushing you when you walk under it (another big YAY for safety!). IR break-beam sensors are fun sensors in spy and action thriller movies where they are used as invisible security sensors that the heroine (or villain) has to dance around to get to a prized object.

What Kinds of Things Can We Sense with Electricity?

All the things!!

Well okay, maybe not *all* the things. We're still learning a ton about the brain, so using electronics to detect feelings like love or joy is probably difficult. But, for the most part, if it's a physical phenomenon, there probably exists a sensor to detect it.

Some examples of things we can sense with electronic sensors include

- Temperature

- Pressure (air, water, etc.)

- Gravity (via accelerometers and inertial measurement units (IMUs))

- Weight and mass

- Distance/proximity

- Speed

- Acceleration

- Sound and vibration

- Humidity

- Magnetic fields

- Radiation

- Fluid properties (like density, viscosity, etc.)

Most of the physical phenomena listed earlier have more than one type of sensor. This makes for a wide array of sensors to choose from and play with! An assortment of sensors that you're likely to find in an electronics kit is shown below in Figure 7-1.

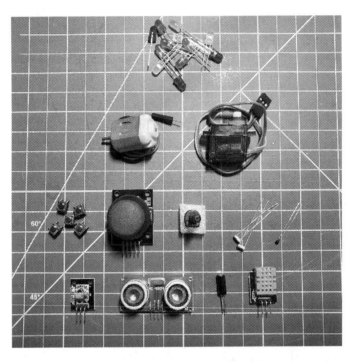

Figure 7-1. *Some of the sensors we can use in electronic circuits!*

Many sensors require a "smart" circuit called an **integrated circuit**, or IC[1] for short, to read and analyze the information coming out of it. More complex ICs also require instructions via computer programming (and a computer or a microcontroller[2]). Because learning to program is not the purpose of this book, **the sensors we'll explore in this chapter can change an output device like an LED without an IC or code instructions**. This means that we'll only explore resistive sensors and sensors that act like switches. That said, I will mention other sensors along

---

[1] As we'll learn later, ICs are made of semiconductor material with a LOT of tiny logic gates connected together. ICs make building complex circuits easier and are the foundation of modern computers!

[2] What is a microcontroller?? A microcontroller is a simple computer that runs one main program, like an Internet router or a garage door opener!

the way so you can learn more about what sensors are available for you to use. The end of this chapter will have a bit more info on other useful and common sensors.

Integrated circuit (IC)   An electronic circuit built on a small piece of semiconducting material. This circuit performs the same function as a larger circuit made of discrete parts.

Hold up... Why are we bothering with sensors at all??

One reason is that there are lots of sensors we can use without code! Sensors make our circuits way more interactive and fun (and useful).

Also, while learning to code will expand your electronic powers, I believe it is useful to explore sensors with basic circuitry because it deepens our understanding of how these sensors work. This exploration also gives us more insight into the weird and wild phenomenon of electricity! And this knowledge makes it easier to debug a nonfunctioning circuit later on if (when!) we end up in the world of hardware programming.

Alright, enough reading, let's play!

Electronic Eyes: Photoresistors!

In this section, we'll learn how to use photoresistors to detect light in our circuits!

Grab These Materials

- Flashlight (the one on a smartphone will work)
- Half-size breadboard
- Coin cell in battery case

- 3 jumper wires

- 1 photoresistor

- 1 LED

  😵 **Question 1:** What information can you glean about a photoresistor simply by its name? What else do you notice about the sensor?

Project 7-2: Light-Sensitive Light

If we break apart the word "photoresistor," there are two familiar words: "photo" and "resistor." We've already encountered resistors in our circuit explorations, so that tells you a bit about how this component behaves.

The word "photo" comes from the Greek word for light (phos). This tells us that our sensor is something that interacts with light. Observing and exploring the sensor can help us figure out where it takes in light (since a photoresistor looks way different than eyes or a camera aperture!).

Your first sensor challenge is to **build a circuit that uses a photoresistor to change the LED**. Try to build this circuit using your knowledge of resistors. If you get stuck, look at the following hint or read on to see the build diagram (Figure 7-2) and written instructions.

Hint: Flip back to your LED and resistor circuit. How might you replace the resistor with your photoresistor?

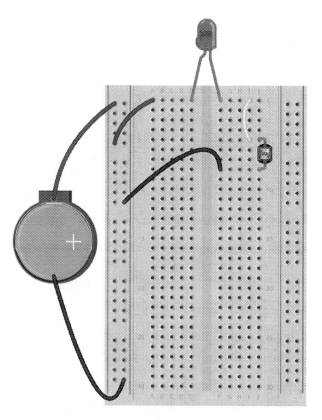

Figure 7-2. *Circuit diagram for a photoresistor*

Written Instructions

1. Connect the battery case wires to the breadboard (power rails).

2. Insert the LED into the breadboard (so that its leads are in two different rows).

3. Connect a jumper wire between the positive power rail and the LED.

4. Insert the photoresistor so that its leads are in two different breadboard rows.

221

5. Connect a jumper wire between the negative LED
    lead and one of the photoresistor leads. (This is the
    yellow wire in the preceding diagram.)

    a. Note: The photoresistor is not polarized, so the orientation of
       its leads does not matter.

6. Connect a third jumper wire between the remaining
    photoresistor lead and the negative power rail.

What do you notice??

If your circuit is wired correctly, your battery has sufficient power, and
there is some ambient light in the room, the LED should be lit up ever so
slightly. It might help to shine a flashlight on the photoresistor.

If your LED is totally off, even after shining a flashlight on the sensor,
run through the troubleshooting tips at the end of the section.

> 🔍 **Check it out**: What happens when you cover the
> top of the photoresistor with your finger?

> 🔍 **Check it out**: What happens when you shine a
> flashlight onto the photoresistor (or if it's daytime,
> take the circuit outside)?

> 😃 **Question 2:** Once you've run the two "Check it
> out" explorations, what hypotheses can you make
> about the photoresistor?

> *Hint: Grab your multimeter and use it to measure
> the resistance of the photoresistor as the light
> levels change!*

TROUBLESHOOTING TIPS

1. Check the battery power switch and that the wires are in different power rails. Wiggle the wires to ensure they are making good electrical connection with the breadboard holes.

2. Check that the LED leads are fully inserted into the breadboard holes and are in different rows.

3. Check that both photoresistor leads are fully inserted into breadboard holes and are in different rows.

4. Check that there is enough light to turn on the LED by shining a flashlight on the photoresistor, turning on the room lights, or taking your circuit outside in the daytime.

5. Check that the jumper wires are fully inserted into the breadboard holes.

6. Check that the jumper wires are in the proper breadboard rows for each component.

7. Check that the positive (longer) LED lead is connected to the positive side of the battery.

8. Check for those rare faulty jumper wires by wiggling the wires or swapping out jumper wires.

9. Finally, check that the battery has energy by connecting it directly to an LED.

Still not working? Grab a friend, family member, or other humans to talk it out!

But Wait, Electronic Eyes?! How Does That Work??

As you may have discovered, our photoresistor changes resistance based on how much light shines on it! **More light means less resistance** and thus a brighter light. Less light means more resistance, which causes a dimmer light.

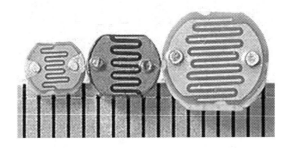

Figure 7-3. *Different sizes of photoresistors (in mm). Source: Wikimedia Commons*

The design of a photoresistor (Figure 7-3 above) is similar to that of a solar panel: light shining on the photoresistor transfers its energy to the sensor material. The energy from the light releases electrons in the sensor material. This makes it easier for electrical current to flow through the sensor material and reduces its resistance. With a lower resistance to the flow of current in our circuit, our LED shines brighter!

You can also use a photoresistor and other light sensors to turn on a light when it gets dark. This is how solar path lights and most street lights work! If you take apart a solar path light, you will likely discover a photoresistor at the top of the lid near the solar panel. There will also be an IC (maybe under a black blob) that reads in the sensor data and turns on the path light when the sensor reading is below a certain threshold.

While photoresistors are beautifully simple, it also means they are less accurate than other light sensors. **If you need a light sensor that is more accurate and/or responsive, check out photodiodes and phototransistors.**

Photoresistor Schematic Symbol

Photoresistors are just a variable resistor! This means that their schematic symbol is a variation of the resistor sawtooth, like illustrated in Figure 7-4:

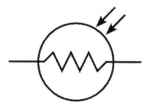

Figure 7-4. *Photoresistor schematic symbol*

The incoming arrows indicate light shining on the photoresistor! I must admit, I'm not 100% certain why there is a circle in the symbol (some photoresistor schematic symbols don't have the circle), but I like to believe it's because the photoresistor is circular. ☺

Electronic Touch: Force-Sensing Resistors

Onward to our next resistive sensor type! This project encourages poking and prodding.

Grab These Materials

- Half-size breadboard
- Coin cell in battery case
- 3 jumper wires

- 1 force-sensing resistor (FSR)

- 1 LED

Project 7-3: Touch-Sensitive Light

Time to wield your circuit knowledge of resistors to a new sensor: a force-sensing resistor, or FSR! You are 1000% capable of building this on your own, so try it before looking at the circuit diagram in Figure 7-5!

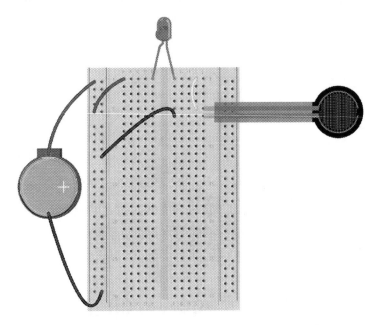

Figure 7-5. *Circuit diagram for a force-sensing resistor*

Written Instructions

1. Connect the battery case wires to the breadboard (power rails).

2. Insert the LED into the breadboard (so that its leads are in two different rows).

3. Connect a jumper wire between the positive power rail and the LED.

4. Insert the FSR so that its leads are in two different breadboard rows.

5. Connect a jumper wire between the negative LED lead and one of the FSR leads. (This is the yellow wire in the diagram.)

    a. Note: The FSR is not polarized, so the orientation of its leads does not matter.

6. Connect a third jumper wire between the remaining FSR lead and the negative power rail.

If you haven't done so yet, squeeze the FSR between your thumb and forefinger! (THIS IS SO FUN but be a bit careful to avoid crumpling the sensor.)

!!!

Right!!

I love these sensors SO much. They are delightful and silly and fun and simple! (You've probably realized I'm a huge fan of keeping it simple.) Show another human what you just made and encourage them to explore how to interact with the sensor!

(If your circuit is not working as expected, get some help via the troubleshooting tips at the end of this section.)

> 🔎 **Check it out**: What happens if you squeeze the FSR with more fingers? Fewer fingers? Does it matter where you squeeze the sensor? What happens if you gently hold the sensor? How else can you explore how the sensor works (and doesn't work)? What hypotheses can you make about how the sensor works? Test out all your hypotheses!

TROUBLESHOOTING TIPS

1. Check that the battery power switch is on and that the wires are in different power rails. Wiggle the wires to ensure they are making good electrical connection with the breadboard holes.

2. Check that the LED leads are fully inserted into the breadboard holes and are in different rows.

3. Check that both FSR leads are fully inserted into breadboard holes and are in different rows.

4. Check that the jumper wires are fully inserted into the breadboard holes.

5. Check that the jumper wires are in the proper breadboard rows for each component.

6. Check that the positive (longer) LED lead is connected to the positive side of the battery.

7. Check for those rare faulty jumper wires by wiggling the wires or swapping out jumper wires.

8. Finally, check that the battery has energy by connecting it directly to an LED.

Still not working? Get some help from a friend, family member, or anyone else in the vicinity!

FSR: Converting Touch into Electricity

A force-sensing resistor, or FSR, is also sometimes called a flex sensor. FSRs allow us to detect physical pressure, like squeezes and weight. These sensors are made of two layers. One layer is a semiconductor[3] (e.g., carbon-based ink), and the other layer is a conductive electrode. The two layers are separated by a nonconductive spacer, like shown below in Figure 7-6.

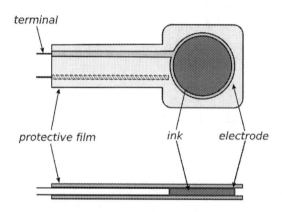

Figure 7-6. *Diagram of a force-sensing resistor! Source: Wikimedia Commons*

As you may have guessed by its name, an FSR changes resistance depending on how much pressure is applied. They are low cost and easy to use, but are not super precise. This is because FSRs can vary widely in how much the resistance changes in response to applied pressure. FSRs are great for fun, for prototyping, or to act as a pressure-sensitive switch (i.e., was it pressed or not). **I would not recommend FSRs for a project that requires known, consistent measurements**, like a weight scale.

---

[3] Semiconductive material is, well, semiconductive! It's a special kind of material that conducts electricity only under specific circumstances, like when squeezed, deformed, or under lights. Semiconductors are used for all sorts of handy applications, including solar panels!

That said, if you are willing to take the time to calibrate the sensor by taking measurements of its resistance against a known pressure or weight, you can use it to make rough estimates of applied pressure or unknown weights.

There are **tons of other sensors that measure pressure and weight**, including

- **Strain gauges**: These use a spring that deforms when a force, like weight, is applied. These are often used in bathroom scales and are handy for heavy loads and long-term usage.

- **Piezoelectric sensors**: Turns out air pressure is a form of pressure! In addition to measuring sound, piezoelectric sensors can also measure other types of physical pressure.

- **Capacitive sensors**: Parallel plate capacitors are made of two parallel conductive plates. When a pressure is applied, the plates move closer. This change in distance changes the capacitance of the sensor which allows us to get information about the applied pressure.

- **Manometers**: These sensors use glass tubes filled with liquid, typically in a U-shape. Applied pressure causes the liquid to move. This change in movement gives us information about the amount of applied pressure. These are the earliest type of pressure sensor!

This is by no means an exhaustive list, so if you are curious or have a specific pressure-sensitive need, you have lots of options to choose from.

FSR Schematic Symbol

Since our FSR is really just a fancy (and rad) resistor, the FSR symbol is sometimes just a resistor symbol with an "FSR" label, like we see in Figure 7-7:

Figure 7-7. *FSR schematic symbol*

You might also see a resistor symbol with an output arrow and a fancy "f," like below in Figure 7-8:

Figure 7-8. *A second type of FSR schematic symbol*

Electronic Proprioception: Tilt Sensors!

Proprioception is the super cool sensation that enables us to detect the location of our bodies in space (sometimes, this feels like a superpower, like when we catch a dropped object without consciously thinking about it). This project enables us to detect physical motion in our circuits.

Grab These Materials

- Half-size breadboard
- Coin cell in battery case
- 3 jumper wires
- 1 tilt sensor
- 1 LED

231

Project 7-4: Gravity-Sensing Light

For our next circuit, we'll use a simple sensor to detect orientation! Human bodies do this via proprioception, or kinesthesia, which allows us to sense our own body's movement, action, and location in the physical world.

For our circuit, we will use a **much** simpler mechanism: a tilt sensor! Grab your tilt sensor, observe it, **and try to build the circuit without looking at the schematic (Figure 7-9)**.

 🔎 **Check it out**: Shake the tilt sensor. What do you observe?

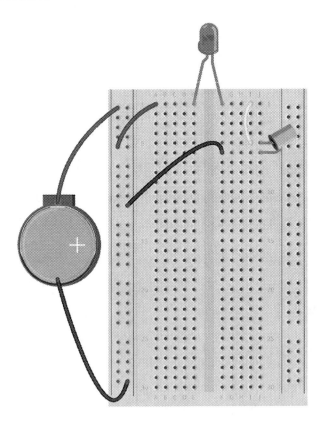

Figure 7-9. *Circuit diagram for a tilt sensor*

Written Instructions

1. Connect the battery case wires to the breadboard (power rails).

2. Insert the LED into the breadboard (so that its leads are in two different rows).

3. Connect a jumper wire between the positive power rail and the LED.

4. Insert the tilt sensor so that its leads are in two different breadboard rows.

5. Connect a jumper wire between the negative LED lead and one of the tilt sensor leads. (This is the yellow wire in the diagram.)

   a. Note: The tilt sensor is not polarized, so the orientation of its leads does not matter.

6. Connect a third jumper wire between the remaining tilt sensor lead and the negative power rail.

Once you've wired your tilt sensor circuit, rotate the breadboard toward you (or just flip it upside down). What do you notice??

Our tilt sensor turns off the LED when it tilts sideways and upside down!

(If your circuit doesn't' work as expected, double-check the build diagram and/or work through the troubleshooting tips at the end of this section.)

> 🔎 **Check it out**: Explore the tilt sensor more carefully. Slowly rotate the breadboard. At what angle (e.g., 45°) does the tilt sensor turn off the LED? How does it behave at this threshold?

⊕ **Question 3:** Once you've run the "Check it out" exploration, what hypotheses can you make about the tilt sensor? What do you think is inside that causes it to function as a tilt sensor?

TROUBLESHOOTING TIPS

1. Check that the battery power switch is on and that the wires are in different power rails. Wiggle the wires to ensure they are making good electrical connection with the breadboard holes.

2. Check that the LED leads are fully inserted into the breadboard holes and are in different rows.

3. Check that both tilt sensor leads are fully inserted into breadboard holes and are in different rows.

4. Check that the jumper wires are fully inserted into the breadboard holes.

5. Check that the jumper wires are in the proper breadboard rows for each component.

6. Check that the positive (longer) LED lead is connected to the positive side of the battery.

7. Check for those rare faulty jumper wires by wiggling the wires or swapping out jumper wires.

8. Finally, check that the battery has energy by connecting it directly to an LED.

Still not working? Talk it out with a friend, family member, or other human!

The Beautifully Simple Tilt Sensor

Our tilt sensor is another beautiful example of a simple and functional design. When you shook the sensor and/or explored its mechanism more closely, you may have hypothesized about its design. Figure 7-10 gives us a peek inside a tilt sensor.

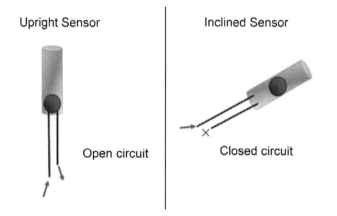

Upright Sensor   Inclined Sensor

Open circuit   Closed circuit

Figure 7-10. *The beautifully simple mechanism inside of a tilt sensor. Source: Wikimedia Commons*

Inside our tilt sensor case is a conductive ball. When the sensor is upright, the ball makes electrical connection between the sensor leads inside the case. This allows electricity to flow through the sensor leads.

When the sensor is tilted, the ball rolls off the sensor leads and breaks electrical contact. This prevents electricity from flowing through the sensor leads.

That's it!!

So elegant.

Tilt Sensor Schematic Symbol

A tilt sensor is a special kind of switch. Depending on context and where you are seeing the circuit diagram, a tilt sensor might be represented with a schematic-like drawing and a label, like shown in Figure 7-11:

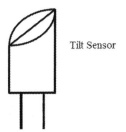

Figure 7-11. *Schematic symbol for a tilt sensor*

If you are searching for tilt sensor circuits and it's not obvious what component the tilt sensor is on the circuit schematic, it may be represented by a switch symbol with a box around it, like we see in Figure 7-12:

Figure 7-12. *Another type of schematic symbol for a tilt sensor*

If you happen upon a circuit diagram and it has a component that you believe is a tilt switch, check out the title, read the circuit description, or look for some other context on the circuit diagram.

Electronic Motion Sensing: IR Sensors!

For our final sensor exploration, we'll play with infrared sensors. Infrared (IR) light is just below visible light on the electromagnetic spectrum. Although humans can't see infrared, we can occasionally feel it on our skin as heat! Some animals, like snakes and mosquitoes (GROSS), **can** see infrared light waves, and it allows them to detect the heat given off by warm-blooded creatures (like mice and humans, eep!).

Grab These Materials

- Half-size breadboard

- Coin cell in battery case

- 3 jumper wires

- 1 IR receiver

- 1 IR transmitter

- 1 100Ω resistor

- 1 LED

Our IR sensor(s) has two parts:

1. **IR transmitter**: This emits an infrared light. It's really just an LED designed for IR wavelengths! The transmitter has two wires: positive and negative.

2. **IR receiver**: This receives infrared light and sends a signal when IR light is received (or not received). The receiver has three wires: positive, negative, and signal.

Project 7-5: Sensing "invisible" light

🔎 **Check it out**: Grab your smartphone and open the camera. Power on the IR transmitter and look at it through the camera. What do you notice??

Try to build this circuit using the color-coded wires on the transmitter and receiver. You only need one battery to power the transmitter, receiver, and LED that acts as our output device.

As before, start with the circuit components that you're familiar with: connect the battery to the power rails and insert the LED into the breadboard. Then connect the LED (positive leg) to the positive power rail.

If you test your circuit and it's not working as expected, **try turning off the room lights or moving to a darker location**. This is because the IR receiver may be saturated. To get a good signal, it needs a low level of ambient light.

And if it's still not working, check out the circuit diagram in Figure 7-13 and subsequent build instructions.

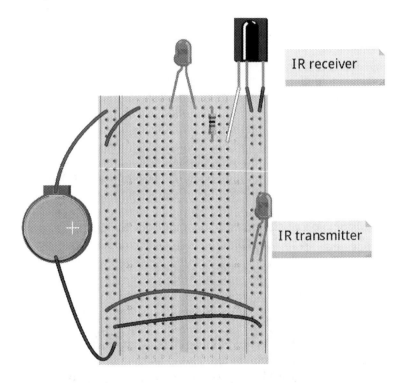

IR receiver

IR transmitter

Figure 7-13. *Circuit diagram for an IR breakbeam sensor (IR transmitter and receiver)*

Note: The IR transmitter and receiver in the diagram look different than yours. This is okay! There are lots of different types. The important part is to identify the positive wire (red), negative or ground wire (black), and data signal wire (white or yellow).

Written Instructions

1. Connect the battery case wires to the breadboard (power rails).

2. Insert the LED into the breadboard (so that its leads are in two different rows).

3. Connect a jumper wire between the positive power rail and the LED.

4. Connect your resistor between the negative LED leg and an open breadboard row.

5. Connect a jumper wire from the battery positive power rail to the open positive power rail.

6. Connect another jumper wire from the battery negative power rail to the open negative power rail.

7. Insert the IR transmitter so that its positive (red) wire connects to the open positive power rail and its negative (black) wire connects to the negative power rail.

8. Insert the IR receiver so that its positive (red) wire connects to the positive power rail and its negative (black) wire connects to the negative power rail.

    a. Note: Either power rail will work for this. Organize your circuit how you like it!

9. Connect the IR receiver data signal wire (white or yellow wire) to the open resistor lead.

You now have an IR break-beam circuit! If it's working as expected, the LED should turn on.

Move the IR receiver so that it faces the IR transmitter – the LED should turn off! Now place a finger, your hand, or another solid object between the IR transmitter and receiver.

Huzzah! Our LED turned off!! The IR break-beam sensor acts like a magical wireless switch!

TROUBLESHOOTING TIPS

1. Check that the battery power switch is on and that the wires are in different power rails. Wiggle the wires to ensure they are making good electrical connection with the breadboard holes.

2. Check that the LED leads are fully inserted into the breadboard holes and are in different rows.

3. Check that both IR transmitter leads are fully inserted into the breadboard holes. Check that the black wire connects to the negative battery power rail and that the red wire connects to the positive battery power rail.

4. Check that the IR receiver leads are fully inserted into the breadboard holes. Check that the red wire connects to the positive battery power rail, the black wire connects to the negative battery power rail, and the white (or yellow) wire connects to the negative LED leg via a resistor.

5. Check that the resistor is between the negative LED leg and the white (or yellow) wire of the IR receiver.

6. Check that the positive (longer) LED lead is connected to the positive side of the battery.

7. Check for those rare faulty jumper wires by wiggling the wires or swapping out jumper wires.

8. Finally, check that the battery has energy by connecting it
    directly to an LED.

Still not working? Throw it across the room! … Just kidding. You can totally
figure this out. Ask for help from a favorite human! (Or maybe someone who
happens to be sitting nearby.)

Sensing Invisible Light

This is the first time we've used a sensor to detect something that our eyes
cannot! There are all sorts of sensors that enable us to build circuits and
electronics that enhance our abilities. This is one of my favorite aspects of
science and engineering: we can use our knowledge to explore and better
understand the magnificent world around us.

Our IR break-beam sensors use invisible light to detect motion.
This happens by using the invisible infrared beam emitted from the IR
transmitter. The receiver is sensitive to the same wavelength of light. When
an object (that blocks IR light) moves between the transmitter and receiver,
the IR beam between the two is broken, and the receiver signal changes.

IR break-beam sensors have very quick reaction times and can be a
great way to sense motion that happens fast. The downside of break-beam
sensors is that you need both the transmitter and receiver, and there must
be an unbroken line of sight between the two.

Figure 7-14. *PIR sensor! Source: Wikimedia Commons*

Another type of IR motion sensing is done with passive IR sensors, or PIR sensors like the one shown in Figure 7-14 above. These use a receiver (no transmitter) to detect infrared heat from living creatures. PIR sensors are commonly used for simple motion detecting security systems or to trigger wildlife cameras.

IR Break-Beam Schematic Symbol

As you noticed in the circuit diagram, an IR transmitter is really just an LED. When you see one of these in a circuit, it will likely have the same schematic symbol as a regular ol' LED, like illustrated in Figure 7-15:

Figure 7-15. *Schematic symbol for IR transmitter*

Often, IR transmitters will be labeled with "IR" or "infrared" or a wavelength in nanometers (nm) that indicates it's not a visible LED.

IR receivers are typically represented by a rectangle with three inputs, a half circle that indicates the receiver (or its "eye"), and two incoming arrows indicating that it is receiving light – like our photoresistor! You may see labels on the schematic symbol, like what is shown in Figure 7-16:

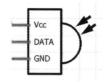

Figure 7-16. *Schematic symbol for an IR receiver*

If there are no labels on the schematic symbol, it is often labeled as "IR receiver" or some abbreviation like "IR rcvr."

Going Further: All the Sensors and Fun Project Ideas!

Sensor Stuff!

As we've discovered, there are sensors to detect an incredible variety of phenomena in this universe. Here's a high-level overview of some of the sensor categories:[4]

- **Motion**: Sensors that detect various forms of motion, like our tilt sensor, accelerometers, gyroscopes, and rotary encoders.

- **Location**: Sensors that provide data about location, like GPS, inertial measurement units (IMUs), and real-time location systems.

---

[4] There are *many* ways to divide up sensors. It's more of an art than an exact science, so some folks might prefer other ways of grouping. I chose these groups to help you better understand the wide variety of sensor capabilities and to get ya started exploring them! As you learn more about sensors, you may mentally (or even physically) group sensors in different ways based on what works best for your brain.

- **Force**: Sensors that measure physical inputs and pressure, like buttons and switches, strain gauges, capacitive touch sensors, and force-sensing resistors!

- **Acoustic**: Sensors that measure pressure waves (i.e., sound waves)! These include microphones, ultrasonic, piezoelectric (a.k.a. contact mics), and vibration sensors.

- **Environmental**: A catch-all for sensors that measure information about the world around us, like temperature, pressure, humidity, and gas concentrations (e.g., CO_2, carbon monoxide, propane, methane, etc.).

- **Optical**: Sensors that measure light, like IR and PIR sensors, photoresistors, cameras, and color sensors.

- **Electronic and magnetic**: Sensors that detect electric and magnetic fields, like reed switches, Hall effect sensors, and our handy-dandy multimeter (i.e., voltmeters, ammeters, and ohmmeters).

As mentioned earlier in this chapter, most of these sensors require more advanced circuits. Sometimes, this means a "smart" circuit with a computer chip to accurately read sensor measurements. The best way to learn how to use these sensors is to build projects! Find a project that you're passionate about, figure out what sensor(s) you need, and use your favorite search engine to find someone who shared instructions for the same or a similar project.

Websites that are particularly helpful for learning more about building with sensors include Instructables, Hackster IO, Adafruit Learn, SparkFun, and Make: Projects.

Build All the Projects!

We can use logic gates to represent some of the information we deal with in our daily lives. Here are some ideas for expanding on this further:

1. **Project 1: "The cat knocked it over again" monitor** (i.e., a "tipped over" monitor)

   Combine a NOT gate with a tilt sensor so that the tilt sensor turns on a light when it gets knocked over! This is handy if you have a cat that likes knocking things off shelves or if you want an alert if an object slips, tips, or otherwise falls over.

   a. **Project 1a: Bonus tilt sensor project: Build your own tilt sensor!**

   Use the beautifully simple design to design your own tilt sensor! Design it based on your needs or curiosities – it can be bigger, smaller, more or less sensitive, etc.!

   Some suggestions for materials: Paperclips (tilt sensor leads), ping pong balls or plastic cups (for the sensor body), and aluminum foil (to make a conductive ball).

2. **Project 2: Interactive robot**

   Combine the force sensor or the photoresistor with the motor and build a robot body using cardboard and other household materials!

   Note: You may need to use two batteries or a 9V (with a resistor) to power the motor.

3. **Project 3: Comparison scale for tiny objects, plants, or animals**

   Use the force-sensing resistor to compare weights of tiny things! Compare the LED and buzzer output – is one easier to "measure" with? Is there a way you can calibrate your scale?

4. **Project 4: DIY touch-sensitive doorbell**

   Use the force-sensing resistor to create a nonintrusive doorbell with the LED (or buzzer if you truly want to be disturbed) for when you're playing video games or otherwise engrossed in an activity. Add a label to let folks know to press the sensor when they want to get your attention.

5. **Project 5: Interactive sounds**

   Combine the force sensor or the photoresistor with the buzzer and build an instrument!

   Note: You may need two batteries for this project.

6. **Project 6: Build your own "traverse the invisible security beams" game!**

   Put a treasured object in the center of a room. Install IR break-beam sensors between the door and the object. Challenge your friends (or play solo!) to try to get the object without triggering a light!

What sensors surprised you? What sensors would you use to give yourself (or your favorite pet) superpowers? What sensors or projects do you want to explore further? Share your discoveries and creations with your friends and see what project ideas they come up with!

What other mysteries have you encountered? Look up questions using your favorite search engine, use Wikipedia to learn more about particular sensors, and explore projects made by other folks!

Summary

This chapter introduced the concept of electronic inputs or devices that enable us to take in information from the world around us and use it to modify our circuits. This gives us information to better understand this universe, to cause actions, and to make decisions.

In our exploration of sensors, we covered simple sensors – photoresistors, force-sensing resistors, tilt sensors, and IR sensors – to show you how sensors work and how they can be used to control and change the flow of electricity. We learned about the mechanisms behind these simple sensors and were introduced to the vast array of sensors that await exploration when you start working with more complex circuits and/ or programming electronics.

CHAPTER 8

Transistors: The Building Blocks of Computers!

Transistors As an Electronic Switch

With pushbuttons and switches, we explored how to use electricity to make simple decisions. But what if we wanted to make these decisions without using our fingers as much? This is where transistors come in! Similar to how DNA makes up the foundation of all life on earth, transistors are the fundamental building blocks of all computers and microcontrollers![1]

Transistor   An electronic component that uses semiconductive material to switch and amplify electronic signals.

---

[1] A microcontroller is a simple computer that performs one task forever (or until powered off), like a WiFi router.

In this chapter, we'll learn how to use transistors to switch and amplify electrical signals. We'll also learn the basics of how transistors work, and we'll dig into how transistors transformed electronics to enable modern computers, hooray!

Grab These Materials

- Half-size breadboard

- Coin cell in battery case

- 5–6 jumper wires

- 1 N-Channel transistor (2N7000 N-Channel MOSFET)

- 2 100Ω resistors

- 1 pushbutton

- 1 LED

Since a transistor is a **much** different component than anything we've worked with so far, let's learn about how they are structured before we use them in circuits.

Field-effect transistor (FET)   A specific type of transistor with three terminals that allow for the control of electric current flow. The control signal for a FET is voltage.

Also, since there are TONS of different kinds of transistors, let's be more specific about what kind of transistor we're using. For the purposes of this book, we are focusing on FET transistors, also known as "field-effect transistors."

With that background knowledge, grab your transistor and turn it so that the **flat side is facing you**. This transistor is a "2N7000." Our FET transistor has three pins that perform different functions, like we see in Figure 8-1.

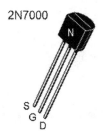

Figure 8-1. *FET N-Channel pinout diagram. Source: Wikimedia Commons*

Put on your "learning the alphabet hat" and let's learn what these letters mean for an N-Channel MOSFET:[2]

- **S is the Source pin**: Current flows out of the source pin. (Note: This is the lower voltage side of the transistor.)

- **D is the Drain pin**: This is where current flows into the transistor. (Note: This is the higher voltage side of the transistor.)

- **G is the Gate pin**: This is the control pin. An applied voltage turns the transistor "on" so that current flows from the drain to the source.

With the flat side facing you, the Source is the left pin, the Gate pin is in the middle, and the Drain is the right pin.

---

[2] All FETs use the same pin terminology (Source, Drain, and Gate), but they behave different for N-Channel and P-Channel MOSFETs. We'll explore this a bit later in the chapter!

The Gate pin acts as the switch for the transistor: when there is no voltage applied to the Gate pin, then no current flows from the Source to the Drain. In other words, the transistor is "off." When there is a voltage applied to the Gate pin, then a current flows from the Source to the Drain, and the transistor is "on."

🔎 **Check it out**: Look up "2N7000 transistor" in your favorite search engine. What do you discover?

Project 8-1: Make an Electronic Switch

Since this is a tricky circuit with a component unlike anything we've ever played with before, we will start with a diagram (Figure 8-2).

Let's gooo!

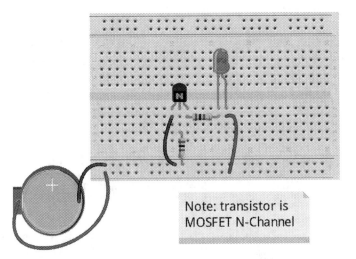

Figure 8-2. Circuit diagram for a MOSFET transistor used as a switch

Written Instructions

1. Connect the battery case wires to the breadboard (power rails).

2. Insert the LED into the breadboard.

3. Connect a jumper wire between the positive power rail and the positive LED leg.

4. With the flat side facing you, insert the transistor so that its pins are in three different breadboard rows.

5. Connect a jumper wire from the transistor Source pin (left pin) to the negative power rail.

6. Connect a resistor between the transistor Drain pin (right pin) and the negative LED leg.

7. Connect a resistor between the transistor Gate pin (middle pin) and the negative power rail.

But wait! What happened?

Nothing!

> 😕 **Question 1:** Why isn't our LED turning on??
> Hint: Go back and read the description of the Gate pin earlier in this section.

The transistor Gate pin acts as the switch for the transistor. Right now, the voltage between the Gate pin and negative power rail is 0V, which means no current is able to flow from the Source to the Drain! If you had the "Aha!" moment, go ahead and fix the circuit now.

If you're still a little stuck, that's okay! These are weird (and delightful once you get the hang of them) components. Check out the following build diagram in Figure 8-3 for some help.

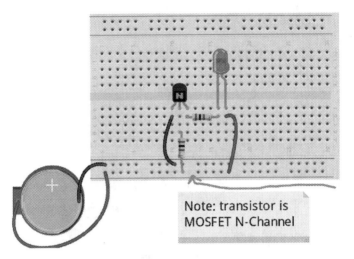

Note: transistor is
MOSFET N-Channel

Figure 8-3. Circuit diagram for a MOSFET as a switch (powered on)

Written Instructions

1. Move the resistor so that it connects the transistor Gate pin to the **positive** power rail.

    There we go! Our LED should now turn on, yay! (And if not, check the troubleshooting tips at the end of this section.) Move the resistor back to the negative power rail and the LED turns off again! Repeat to your heart's content.

    This is pretty wild; what exactly is happening in our circuit?! To start, let's look at how the electrical current is flowing in our circuit by answering the following questions.

    🤔 **Question 2A:** Trace the path of the electricity on Figure 8-4 below when the transistor is **OFF** (focus on the path through the Source and Drain pins; ignore the Gate pin):

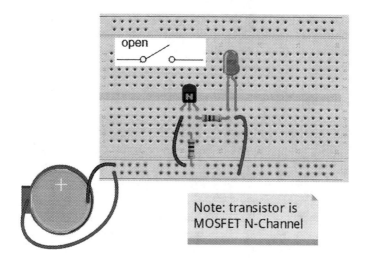

Figure 8-4. *Transistor circuit diagram for tracing the path of electrical flow (powered off)*

Question 2B: Trace the path of the electricity in Figure 8-5 below when the transistor is **ON**:

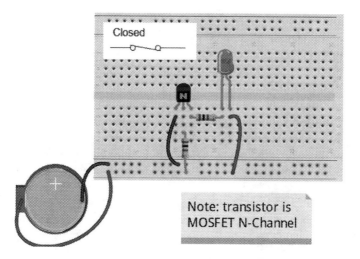

Figure 8-5. *Transistor circuit diagram for tracing the path of electrical flow (powered on)*

255

In case you want to compare, my answers are given in Figures 8-6 and 8-7:

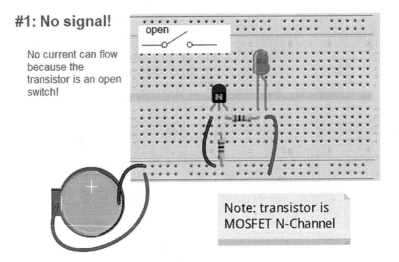

Figure 8-6. *Path of electrical current flow when the transistor is powered off*

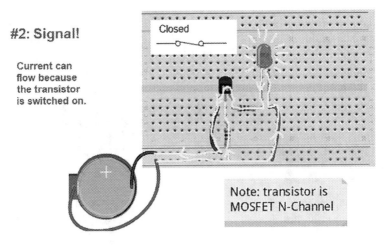

Figure 8-7. *Path of electrical current flow when the transistor is powered on*

In words, here's what's happening in our circuit:

1. When the Gate pin has no voltage across it, no current can flow[3] from the Drain pin to the Source – just like an open switch.

2. When the Gate pin does have voltage on it, current flows into the Drain pin and out of the Source pin, completing the circuit. This turns on the light because the current has a complete path!

Project 8-2: How Much Voltage on the Gate Pin?

How much voltage does the transistor Gate pin need to switch on?

We'll quantify this later, but it's much more fun to explore first! Grab an assortment of resistors, including the smallest and the largest values. Replace the resistor connecting the transistor Gate pin with different resistor values and record your findings in the following table.

---

[3] Note that I'm simplifying here; electrical current flow is much more complicated than this! For example, charges "know" if a circuit isn't complete and will not flow, even through a partial connection (this is because they flow under the force of an electric field which is not present if the circuit isn't complete). Another frustrating issue is that current flow is often backward because electrons are typically the charges moving in a circuit, and they move from negative to positive. Current flow was defined before humanity discovered electrons, so... here we are. Kind of like how the United States is stuck with the imperial measurement system instead of metric, we're stuck with current flow defined as positive to negative!

Bonus   Break out your multimeter and measure the voltage between the transistor Gate pin and the negative power rail!

Resistor Value   Observations

```
┌──────────────────────────────────────────────────┐
│              TROUBLESHOOTING TIPS                  │
└──────────────────────────────────────────────────┘
```

1. Check the battery power switch and that the wires are in different power rails. Wiggle the wires to ensure they are making good electrical connection with the breadboard pins.

2. Check that the LED leads are fully inserted into the breadboard holes and are in different rows.

3. Check that all transistor leads are fully inserted into breadboard holes and are in different rows.

4. Check that the transistor **Gate pin** is connected to the **positive power rail**.

5. Check that the negative LED pin is connected to the transistor Drain pin.

6. Check that the transistor Source pin is connected to the negative power rail.

7. Check that the jumper wires are fully inserted into the breadboard holes.

8. Check that the jumper wires are in the proper breadboard rows for each component.

9. Check that the positive (longer) LED lead is connected to the positive side of the battery.

10. Check for those rare faulty jumper wires by wiggling the wires or swapping out jumper wires.

11. Finally, check that the battery has energy by connecting it directly to an LED.

Still not working? Grab a friend, family member, or other humans to talk it out!

(FET) Transistor Schematic Symbol

The transistor schematic is infinitely helpful because it tells us **what** the transistor pins do. If you ever forgot which pin does what, look up the schematic symbol! Figure 8-8 shows the symbol for the 2N7000 N-Channel FET transistor:

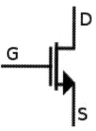

Figure 8-8. *Schematic symbol for an N-channel FET transistor*

I absolutely LOVE that there is an arrow pointing out to the Source pin – this tells us that current flows out of the Source pin!

Unraveling the Mystery of Transistors!
Semiconductors: The Secret Sauce

Transistors' magic is made possible by semiconductor materials, which we learned a little about in Chapter 7 with our FSR (the photoresistor, solar panels, and LEDs also use semiconductors!). As a refresher, semiconductors are somewhat conductive, acting as both an insulator and a conductor.

Semiconductor   A special type of material that can act as both an insulator and a conductor depending on the applied electrical signal.

A semiconductor acts as an insulator if an electrical signal is below a certain threshold and acts as a conductor above that threshold (the specific threshold depends on the semiconductor). For example, our 2N7000 transistor's Gate pin switches the transistor into a conductor above 1V – below this, it is an insulator. When our transistor's Gate pin was connected to the negative power rail, there was no voltage across it (or the voltage was undefined), so it acted like an insulator. Connecting the Gate pin to the 3V signal[4] of our coin cell converted our transistor into a conductor.

While the details of how a semiconductor works are beyond the scope of this book, it's helpful to know that there are two different types: P-type and N-type. By combining these two types together, we can create "PN" junctions where the two different semiconductor types meet. There are many different ways to build and sandwich these PN junctions together, which enables all sorts of different types of transistors!

---

[4] Again, simplifying here – the actual voltage across the transistor base pin isn't 3V because there are other components in our circuit.

So far, we've been using an N-Channel field-effect transistor. There are also P-Channel FETs!

🫤 **Question 3:** How do you think a PNP transistor works?

A P-Channel transistor functions in the opposite way of our N-Channel, where current flows into the Source pin and out of the Drain pin. We can see this illustrated via schematic symbols for N-Channel and P-Channel transistors like illustrated in Figure 8-9.

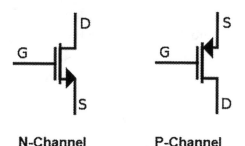

N-Channel   **P-Channel**

Figure 8-9. *Comparison of N-Channel and P-Channel field-effect transistors. Source: Wikimedia Commons*

Fortunately, the P- and N-Channel schematic symbols are super helpful in telling the two FETs apart. If you ever forget, come back to those symbols. (And you can always look these things up online.)

Wait! There's more! Transistors, that is. Onward to learn more!

Transistor Taxonomy

Thus far, we've only used one type of (N-Channel) field-effect transistor. Turns out there's a whole family of FETs with two main categories:

- Junction FETs (JFETs)

- Metal-oxide-semiconductor FETs (MOSFETs)

JFETs were the first transistors to be made successfully and are used as switches, amplifiers, and resistors. MOSFETs are the most widely used type of FETs, and they are also the ones that we've been using! MOSFETs are typically used to control conductivity, or how much electricity can flow through the transistor, particularly for high-power applications (e.g., switching a power supply).

Both JFETs and MOSFETs can be made in different combinations of PN junctions. For FETs, this is called "N-Channel" or "P-Channel" which, to simplify, tells us what semiconductor type is more prevalent (N-Channel means two semiconductor n-type materials and vice versa for P-Channel).

But wait! There's more! Transistors, that is. There's an entirely different type of transistor called "bipolar junction transistors" or BJTs for us lazy folks. BJTs are switched on/off using electric current. In other words, the control signal for a BJT is current, not voltage like for FETs.

BJTs also have three pins that function similarly to FETs:

- **C is the Collector pin**: This is where electric current goes into the transistor.

- **E is the Emitter pin**: This is where electric current comes out of, or is emitted by, the transistor.

- **B is the Base pin**: This is the pin that uses an electrical signal, specifically an electric current, that allows current to flow (or not flow) from the collector to the emitter.

There are two ways to make BJTs with PN sandwiches: NPN and PNP. NPN tends to be more common, and you may come across a 2N2222 NPN transistor – these work great as switches and amplifiers, just like what we've been building in this chapter!

Figure 8-10 gives a quick overview of the two main categories of transistors:

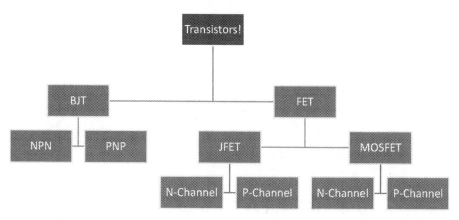

Figure 8-10. *Transistor "family tree"*

Too Many Letters!!

If all these letters and terms are confusing, that's okay! Be kind to yourself; this is a **lot** of technical jargon. The important point here is that there are lots of different transistors, so be wary if (when!) you're buying your own – I've purchased the wrong transistor(s) more than once.

The best way to get a feel for how to use different kinds of transistors is to find a project that uses them. You can do this by searching "MOSFET projects" or something similar in your favorite search engine.

Transistors As Amplifiers

Grab These Materials

- Half-size breadboard

- 1 9V battery

- 1 coin cell in battery case

- 2 alligator clips

- 3 jumper wires

- 1 (N-Channel MOSFET) transistor

- 2 100Ω resistors

- 1 motor

It turns out that transistors can do more than just switch electric signals: they can also amplify electric signals! This is one of my favorite use cases for transistors, probably because I'm always trying to find quick ways to control large motors with sensors.

Project 8-3: Make an Amplifier!

For this next project, your objective is to apply what you learned about transistors in Project 8-1 to build a circuit that uses a coin cell battery to switch on a motor.

As a bonus, we actually get to use the switch on our coin cell battery case for something useful, hooray!

We'll start by learning about what our circuit does, I'll walk you through the first steps, and then you get to use (and maybe challenge) your brain to figure out how to build the circuit.

Circuit Overview

- We're leveraging the special abilities of the transistor to control a power-hungry motor using a much lower-power battery.

- The 9V is used to power our motor. Our transistor acts as the switch for the motor. This means the transistor needs to be connected **between** the motor and the 9V (on one side of the circuit).

- Our resistor limits electrical flow from the 9V battery to our motor, which protects our motor.

- The smaller battery (our coin cell) is what switches on the circuit, which then switches on the motor.

- Since we're using two different power sources, we need to **connect the negative sides of both batteries together**.[5]

Written Starting Instructions

1. Connect the coin cell battery case wires to the breadboard power rails.

2. Connect an alligator clip to each of the 9V battery terminals (I'd recommend using colors to keep track of the terminal connections, e.g., red is positive, black is negative).

3. Connect the positive 9V battery terminal to one of the motor leads.

4. Insert the transistor into the breadboard so that its leads are in three different rows.

5. Connect the negative power rail to the transistor Collector pin (with its flat side facing you, this is the rightmost pin).

---

[5] Why?! This is both critical and confusing and is always true of circuits with two different power sources. A brief, hand-wavy explanation is that we have two different circuits that need to "talk" to each other. To do this, they have to know what the "common language" is or what the voltage reference point is. We'll learn more about why and what this is in Chapter 9. Hint: It is a concept called ground (or common)!

265

Try to build this circuit on your own for **at least ten minutes**. IF AND ONLY IF you get stuck (yes, I'm breaking out the caps here), *then* you can sneak a peek at the circuit diagram in Figure 8-11 and the written instructions.

Hint 1: Think of the transistor Drain and Source pins as two leads for a pushbutton switch (on the negative side of the circuit). Go back and look at the first switch circuit you built to help visualize this.

Hint 2: Connect the remaining motor lead to the transistor Drain pin (also use a resistor).

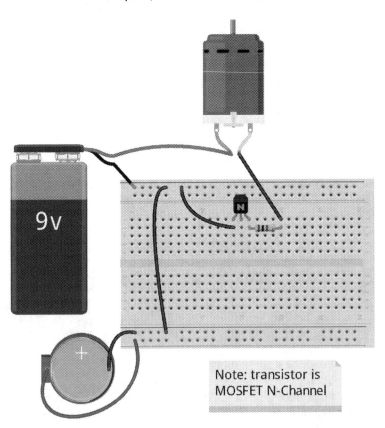

Note: transistor is
MOSFET N-Channel

Figure 8-11. *Circuit diagram for using a FET transistor as an amplifier*

Full Written Instructions

1. Connect the coin cell battery case wires to the breadboard power rails.
2. Connect an alligator clip to each of the 9V battery terminals (I'd recommend using colors to keep track of the terminal connections, e.g., red is positive, black is negative).
3. Connect the positive 9V battery terminal to one of the motor leads.
4. With the flat side facing you, insert the transistor into the breadboard so that its leads are in three different rows.
5. Connect a jumper wire between both breadboard negative power rails.
6. Connect the 9V negative power rail to the transistor Source pin (the left pin).
7. Connect a resistor to the transistor Drain pin (right pin) and an open row.
8. Connect the open motor lead to the resistor.

If it's not already on, flip the switch for the coin cell battery!

...

Now what?!

Well, what do YOU think?

Question 4: Which transistor pin acts as the switch pin?

Exactly! We haven't yet used the transistor Gate pin,
which acts as the switch pin. If you haven't done
so already, switch on the transistor. If you need
it, Figure 8-12 gives you the complete diagram:

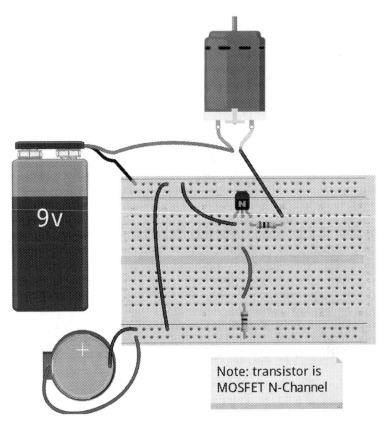

Figure 8-12. Complete diagram for the FET transistor amplifier circuit

Final Steps

9. Insert your second resistor so that it connects
    to the coin cell positive power rail and an open
    breadboard row.

10. Connect a jumper wire between the second resistor
    and the transistor Gate pin (middle pin).

And voila! Now that the transistor Gate pin has an electrical signal (above its trigger threshold), the transistor switches to "On" mode and completes the circuit for our 9V and motor!

Still not working? Check out the troubleshooting tips at the end of this section.

As I mentioned earlier, this is a super handy feature of transistors, especially if you're controlling motors. This is because we often want to control power-hungry motors with computers. Computers are useful for motor control because we can write instructions, via software code, to perform special functions, like moving a robotic arm or spinning when we press down on a pedal. A transistor enables us to "talk" to the motor with our software instructions while powering the motor with a large battery (that would fry our computer).

🔎 **Check it out**: Does it matter if the transistor switches the negative side of the circuit or the positive side? Explore different ways you can use the transistor as a switch between the 9V and the motor! And remember, for any different approach you try, **connect the negative side of the coin cell and the negative side of the 9V together.**

MY MOTOR WAS WORKING FINE FOR A WHILE AND THEN IT JUST… STOPPED??

If you're getting weird circuit behavior with the motor, it's likely because there is a buildup of energy due to the spinning motor. To simplify, when a motor is suddenly flipped off while running, it can cause a large negative voltage spike which may cause current to flow backward in the circuit and do funky things. To address this, you can **add a diode across the motor leads** to prevent current from flowing back into the power source. This is called a "flyback diode."

Want to learn more? Look up "flyback diode" in your favorite search engine!

TROUBLESHOOTING TIPS

1. Check the battery power switch and that the wires are in different power rails. Wiggle the wires to ensure they are making good electrical connection with the breadboard pins.

2. Check that all transistor pins leads are fully inserted into breadboard holes and are in different rows.

3. Wiggle the tiny motor wires to check that they are fully inserted into breadboard holes.

4. Check that the alligator clips are securely attached to the 9V battery terminals. Ensure that the metal parts of the two different alligator clips are not touching (i.e., shorting the battery).

5. **Check that the 9V negative power rail (i.e., the negative side of the 9V battery) is connected to the transistor Source pin.**

6. Check that the transistor **Gate pin** is connected to the **positive power rail** (i.e., the positive side of the coin cell battery) via a resistor.

7. Check that one of the motor leads is connected to the transistor Drain pin via a resistor.

8. Check that the other motor lead is connected to the positive 9V battery terminal.

9. Check that both resistor leads are fully inserted into the breadboard holes and that both resistors have their leads in different rows.

10. Check that the metal ends of the alligator clips make contact with the metal ends of the motor lead and the resistor (or the jumper wire if you chose that option).

11. Check that the jumper wires are fully inserted into the breadboard holes.

12. Check that the jumper wires are in the proper breadboard rows for each component.

13. Check for those rare faulty jumper wires by wiggling the wires or swapping out jumper wires.

14. Finally, check that the coin cell battery has energy by connecting it directly to an LED. Check that the 9V has enough energy by connecting it directly to the motor.

Still not working? Grab a friend, family member, or other humans to talk it out! As you do this, explain how the transistor works because this can often help you identify the problem.

(This is sometimes lovingly referred to as "rubber ducking" because having to verbalize the problem/challenge can help us resolve it, so even if we talk to a rubber ducky, it can be helpful!)

P-cause We Can: P-Channel FETs (Optional)

Earlier, we learned that there are two flavors of MOSFETs: N-Channel and P-Channel. We'll need both for the rad circuits we're building in Chapter 9. P-Channel MOSFETs behave in the opposite way that N-Channel MOSFETs do: current flows from the source to the drain.

Another cool opposite feature is that P-Channel MOSFETs are triggered on when the voltage across the Gate is 0V and are triggered off when the voltage is above a specified threshold (~3V for ours).

271

If you're curious to learn about P-Channel MOSFETs, grab one (er, well, a package because it's hard/expensive to buy just one transistor) and let's explore building with one!

(And if you're curious but not curious enough to get more parts, compare the build diagram for the P-Channel MOSFET with the N-Channel MOSFET!)

Grab These Materials

- Half-size breadboard

- Coin cell in battery case

- 5–6 jumper wires

- 1 P-Channel transistor (BS250 P-Channel MOSFET)

- 1 100Ω resistor[6]

- 1 pushbutton

- 1 LED

Project 8-4 (Optional): P-Channel Switch

As an introduction to P-Channel MOSFETs, we'll build the same switch circuit that we did with an N-Channel! Since this is less than obvious, we'll start with a circuit diagram shown in Figure 8-13.

---

[6] When we built our N-Channel transistor switch, we used a resistor to connect to the Gate pin. We can (and should) do the same thing here, but I wanted to simplify this circuit since transistors can be tricky and confusing. Going forward, I'd recommend using a resistor on the Gate pin of any transistor.

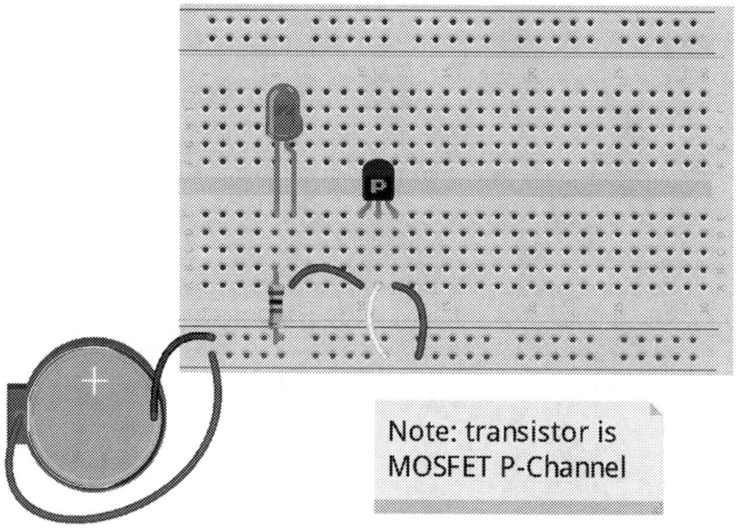

Note: transistor is
MOSFET P-Channel

Figure 8-13. *Circuit diagram for a P-channel FET transistor as a switch*

Written Instructions

1. Connect the coin cell battery to the breadboard power rails.

2. Insert the LED into the breadboard.

3. Connect a resistor between the negative LED leg and the negative breadboard power rail.

4. With the flat side facing you, insert the P-Channel MOSFET transistor into the breadboard so that its three leads are in three different rows.

5. Connect a jumper wire from the positive power rail to the transistor Drain pin (right pin).

6. Connect a jumper wire from the transistor Source pin (left pin) to the positive LED leg.

7. Connect a jumper wire from the transistor Gate pin (middle pin) to the positive power rail.

Voila!

Oh, wait... our LED is off??

😕 **Question 5:** How else might you connect the transistor Gate pin? Explore connecting it to different parts of the circuit and observing the behavior of the LED.

If you gave yourself enough time and pizazz to play around, you may have discovered that the LED is **off** when the transistor Gate pin is connected to the positive power rail. And the LED is **on** when the transistor Gate pin is connected to the negative power rail!

So cool!! We have a transistor that behaves like a "normally closed" (NC) switch!

And if you need it, Figure 8-14 shows the build diagram for when the LED is on:

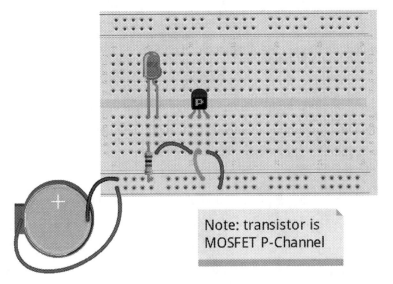

Note: transistor is MOSFET P-Channel

Figure 8-14. *Circuit diagram for a P-Channel FET transistor (powered on)*

Written Instructions

8. Move the jumper wire that connects to the transistor Gate pin (middle pin) so that it connects to the negative power rail.

   Huzzah! You did it!

   🔍 **Check it out**: Explore the behavior of the LED as you turn the transistor on and off by moving the Gate pin jumper wire between the positive and negative power rails. What do you observe? What is surprising? Share your circuit with a friend!

TROUBLESHOOTING TIPS

1. Check the battery power switch and that the wires are in different power rails. Wiggle the wires to ensure they are making good electrical connection with the breadboard pins.

2. Check that the LED leads are fully inserted into the breadboard holes and are in different rows.

3. Check that all transistor pins leads are fully inserted into breadboard holes and are in different rows.

4. Check that the transistor **Gate pin** is connected to the **negative power rail**.

5. Check that the positive LED pin is connected to the transistor Source pin.

6. Check that the transistor Drain pin is connected to the positive power rail.

7. Check that the jumper wires are fully inserted into the breadboard holes.

8. Check that the jumper wires are in the proper breadboard rows for each component.

9. Check that the negative LED lead is connected to the negative side of the battery via a resistor.

10. Check for those rare faulty jumper wires by wiggling the wires or swapping out jumper wires.

11. Finally, check that the battery has energy by connecting it directly to an LED.

Still not working? Grab a friend, family member, or other humans to talk it out!

Going Further: Transistor Time!

We can use transistors to make more complex circuits. Here are some ideas to get you started!

1. **Project 1: Dark detecting circuit**

   This circuit turns a light on when ambient light is low. This is the same basic circuit that turns on street lights and solar path lights! For this project, you'll need a **potentiometer** and a **photoresistor** (light sensor). As long as the combined in-series resistance of the potentiometer and photoresistor is less than 500kΩ, the circuit should work for different combinations.

Challenge yourself to build the circuit using your knowledge of circuits. If you need it, the schematic is below the reminders and hints.

Reminders:

- The resistance of the photoresistor decreases as more light shines on it.

- The potentiometer middle pin is the stationary contact. The resistance between the middle pin and the two outside pins changes as you rotate the potentiometer knob. (The resistance between the two outside pins stays the same.)

Circuit hints:

😜 **Hint 1:** *We want to make a circuit that turns on the light when the photoresistor is in darkness. This means our transistor switches on when the photoresistor is in darkness. Which transistor pin should we connect the photoresistor to so that the transistor state changes based on ambient light?*

😜 **Hint 2:** *Previously, we've used the potentiometer as a dimmer switch and volume knob. In this circuit, what is our potentiometer "tuning"? (It's not the LED!)*

😜 **Hint 3:** *Electricity is lazy. Let's think of our circuit in two extremes: a TON of light so that the photoresistor resistance is effectively zero (i.e., it behaves like a wire and allows all the current to flow) and ZERO light so that the photoresistor resistance is effectively infinite (i.e., it does not allow any current to flow). You can think about this like a switch: low ambient light means the switch is open and no* *current can flow through it; high ambient light means the switch is closed and current can flow through it.*

😵 *Hint 4: Think about the transistor Gate pin as your circuit load, like a light. If the photoresistor acts like a switch, how can you connect the Gate pin? (In series or in parallel with the photoresistor?)*

If you need a circuit diagram, look for "N-Channel MOSFET dark detecting circuit" (or a variation of this phrase) in your favorite search engine!

2. **Project 2: Robot upgrade**

    Use the transistor amplifier circuit with the 9V and the motor to build a more powerful (or sillier) robot!

    You could also harvest one or more small motors from an electronic toy and use the 9V to power those motors to build a vehicle, a mini merry-go-round or mini Ferris wheel, a spinning dart board, etc. What other rotating things can you conjure up?

3. **Project 3: Chain of transistors!**

    Connect the output of one transistor to the base pin of another. How many can you chain together like this?

What is something that surprised you in this chapter? Share it with a friend! What new questions do you have after learning about transistors? Look up concepts or questions using your favorite search engine, use Wikipedia to learn more about the building blocks of computers, and explore books on how computers work!

Summary

While transfixed by transistors, in this chapter we learned how these incredible components can switch and amplify electrical signals. We learned about the "family tree" of transistors and how this family of components has acronyms galore, like BJTs and FETs. We also learned more about semiconductor materials and how they are used in all sorts of electronics from photoresistors to solar panels to control the flow of electricity.

CHAPTER 9

Logic Gates Round 2!

The Truth About Physical Computing

Transistors are the building blocks of computers! In the "Going Further" section of Chapter 8, there is a delightful discovery to be made: transistors can trigger other transistors! We can use this incredible property and use transistors to build logic gates (the same kinds of logic gates that we learned about all way back in Chapter 6).

Logic gates do simple tasks in logic by blocking or allowing the flow of electricity. The fact that transistors can trigger other transistors means we can chain logic gates together. And this allows us to do calculations with electricity!

Calculations, like addition and subtraction, are the fundamental operations of computers. With a little hand waving, combining logic gates eventually gets us to a full-blown computer! In this chapter, we'll learn more about transistor logic gates. The circuits that you'll build are (larger versions of) the physical building blocks of all computers like your laptop, smartphone, and video game consoles.

WHAT'S IN A NAME: COMPUTERS?

A "computer" used to be a human who did mathematical calculations. The word itself is derived from Latin words *com*, which means "together," and *putare*, which means to think and to prune.

© Jennifer Fox 2023
J. Fox, *Beginning Breadboarding*, https://doi.org/10.1007/978-1-4842-9218-1_9

Human computer teams divided up large calculations into smaller chunks, then assembled the results and checked for errors. From the mid-1800s to the 1960s, computers were primarily women working for universities like Harvard, companies like American Telephone and Telegraph (AT&T), and government industries like NASA (Figure 9-1).

In addition to Ada Lovelace, the first person to publish a software program (or algorithm) for a computer machine, women computers made significant contributions to astronomy, ballistics (calculating the trajectory of missiles and other objects), space flight, and cryptography (encoding messages for secure transmission). By 1943, nearly all people employed as computers were women.

Figure 9-1. *Annie Easley worked at NASA doing calculations critical to space shuttle and satellite launches. Source: Wikimedia Commons*

Electronic computers started showing up in the 1940s. The programmers of these were women mathematicians like with the 1944 ENIAC computer. Grace Hopper was the first person to create a compiler for a programming language. Hopper is also credited with coining the term "bug" and "debugging" when a moth caused the Harvard Mark II computer machine to malfunction.

In the 1950s and 1960s, women continued to make significant contributions to computing, including Kathleen Booth who developed a low-level programming language called Assembly (still in use today), Frances Holberton who wrote code to enable keyboard inputs (and suggested computer housings should be beige), and Milly Koss who developed algorithms for graphics. (The list of women in computer history is way too long to list here! Check out Wikipedia or explore books on the topic! ☺)

Sources:

[1] Smith, Erika E. (2013). "Recognizing a Collective Inheritance through the History of Women in Computing." CLCWeb: Comparative Literature & Culture: A WWWeb Journal. 15 (1): 1–9 – via EBSCOhost.

[2] Frieze, Carol; Quesenberry, Jeria, eds. (2019). Cracking the Digital Ceiling: Women in Computing around the World. Cambridge University Press. ISBN 978-1-108-49742-8.

[3] Gürer, Denise (1995). "Pioneering Women in Computer Science" (PDF). Communications of the ACM. 38 (1): 45–54. doi:10.1145/204865.204875. S2CID 6626310.

Grab These Materials

- Half-size breadboard
- Coin cell in battery case
- 11 jumper wires

- 2 N-Channel transistors

- 2 pushbuttons

- 3 **10kΩ** resistors

- 1 LED

Projects 9-1 and 9-2: ANDs and ORs Galore

I'm combining our first two projects because I want to give you a choice to control your own destiny! And, well, because AND and OR transistor logic gates start with the same basic circuit, and I want to challenge you to deduce how to build them by thinking about how to connect circuit components.

Since we've got a lot of components to work with, we'll go step by step for this first part. Grab the battery, transistors, pushbuttons, and LED and insert them into the breadboard. You can choose to follow my approach and use the same breadboard rows and columns. If you are feeling confident and/or brave, try making your own layout!

Here's a high-level overview of this circuit to help you think about **why** you're connecting the components:

- The pushbuttons control the transistors – they turn the transistors on and off.

- The transistor states (on or off) determine if the LED turns on.

To start, we'll organize the pushbuttons, N-Channel transistors, and LED on the breadboard. For single logic gates, I prefer to group pushbutton-transistor pairs because it helps me see which pushbutton is controlling which transistor. You may prefer to organize your circuits in a different way – do that! Build them in a way that makes sense for you.

As a refresher, Figure 9-2 shows the N-Channel MOSFET pin labels (with the flat side marked with an "N"):

2N7000

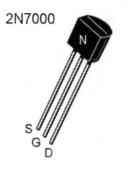

S
G
D

Figure 9-2. *Pinout for an N-Channel MOSFET*

Figure 9-3 is one way you can organize your transistor logic gate:

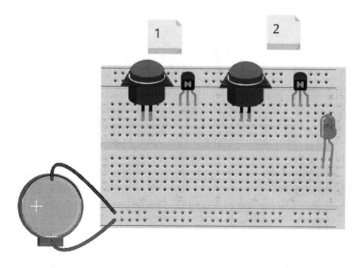

Figure 9-3. *Starting circuit diagram for a transistor logic gate*

Written Instructions (Part 1)

1. Insert the battery wires into the breadboard power rails.

2. Insert each N-Channel transistor so that its flat side faces you and its leads are in different rows.

285

3. With the breadboard facing horizontally, insert a
    pushbutton to the left of each transistor so that the
    two leads are in different rows.

4. Insert the LED into the breadboard to the right of
    the transistors and pushbuttons.

Next, we'll connect power to our pushbuttons (Figure 9-4). We also
need to connect the pushbutton to the negative power rail (because it
draws down the voltage when the pushbutton is open).[1] Fortunately, both
pushbuttons can be wired in the same way.

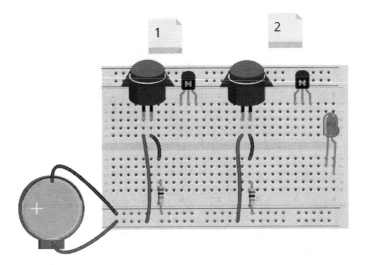

Figure 9-4. *Connecting the pushbuttons for our transistor logic gate*

---

[1] If this is weird and confusing, that's okay! We'll cover why this happens when we
learn about ground later in this chapter.

Written Instructions (Part 2)

1. With the breadboard facing horizontally, connect a jumper wire between the positive power rail and the left pushbutton lead.

2. Connect a resistor between the negative power rail and the right pushbutton lead. You may also need a jumper wire for this connection (see the black wire in the preceding diagram).

3. Repeat steps 1 and 2 for the second pushbutton.

The last stage of our starter circuit is to connect the pushbuttons to the transistor Gate pins (Figure 9-5). We'll also connect the LED to the positive power rail and to a resistor.

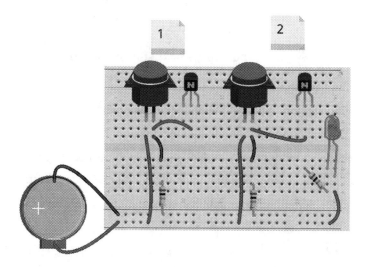

Figure 9-5. *Connecting the Gate pin of the transistors for the transistor logic gate*

Written Instructions (Part 3)

1. With the breadboard facing horizontally, connect a jumper wire between the pushbutton left lead and the transistor Gate pin (middle pin).

2. Repeat step 1 for the second pushbutton and transistor.

3. Connect a jumper wire between the positive power rail and the positive LED leg.

4. Connect a resistor between the negative LED leg and an open breadboard row.

Alright! Now you decide which logic gate you want to build first: an AND gate or an OR gate! (There are so many logic gate puns I can't decide which to bombard you with, so I'll also let you fill in those gaps.)

A refresher on AND and OR logic gates:

- **AND gates**: Both inputs must be on for the output to be on.

- **OR gates**: Either input can be on for the output to be on.

I highly encourage you to **try building one (or even better, both!) on your own** before looking at the diagrams or reading the written build instructions. You are absolutely capable of doing this!

Here are some hints to get you started:

- ***Hint 1***: *We need to complete the circuit! Trace the path of the electricity. How does it flow through each transistor? How can the electricity travel from the transistor(s) to the LED?*

- **Hint 2**: *The two different ways to connect circuit components are in series and in parallel. How can you apply this for the transistors?*

- **Hint 3**: *Think about the pushbutton logic gates we built. An AND gate output is only on if both inputs are on. An OR gate output is on if either inputs are on. How does this translate to the path(s) that the electric current can take? It might be helpful to go back to where you traced the path of the electricity through the AND and OR pushbutton logic gates!*

- **Hint 4**: *Rebuild the transistor switch circuit. The pushbutton sends the control signal (connects to the transistor Gate pin).*

WARNING: SOLUTIONS BELOW!!

AND Gate

Alright, now that you've tried on your own, let's look at how I built my AND logic gate with transistors! The full circuit diagram is given below in Figure 9-6.

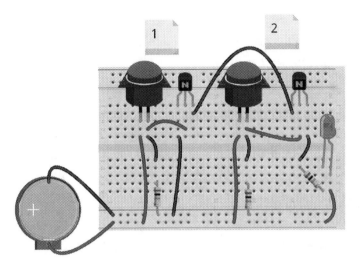

Figure 9-6. *Full circuit diagram for an N-channel MOSFET AND gate*

The AND gate output is on only when both inputs are on. This means that there is just **one path** for the electricity to flow. In other words, the transistors are connected **in series**. The output of one transistor (Drain pin) connects to the input (Source pin) of the second transistor. Figure 9-6: Full circuit diagram for an N-channel MOSFET AND gate.

Written Instructions

Since terminology can be confusing, I'll refer to the transistors based on the labels in the diagram: transistor 1 is the left-hand transistor, and transistor 2 is the right-hand transistor.

1. Connect transistor 1 Source pin (left pin) to the negative power rail.

2. Connect transistor 1 Drain pin (right pin) to transistor 2 Source pin (left pin).

3. Connect a jumper wire from transistor 2 Drain pin (right pin) to the LED resistor.

Test your logic gate! Check that the LED only turns on when both pushbuttons are pressed.

Not working as expected? To be honest, that's to be expected! These are **hard** *and have a lot of wires. Kudos on attempting. Give yourself a break if you need it. Otherwise, it can help to pull out the wires and start over. As frustrating and overwhelming as this sounds, this may be faster than trying to trace wires (at least until you've built these a few times!).*

Also, see the following for troubleshooting tips.

TROUBLESHOOTING TIPS: AND GATE

1. Check that the battery power switch is on and that the leads are in different power rails. Wiggle the wires to ensure they are making good electrical connection with the breadboard pins.

2. Check that you're using **10kΩ** resistors.

3. Check that the LED leads are fully inserted into the breadboard holes and are in different rows.

4. Check that the positive LED lead is connected to the positive power rail.

5. Check that all transistor leads are fully inserted into breadboard holes and are in different rows.

6. Check that the pushbutton pins are fully inserted into the breadboard holes and are in different rows.

7. For each pushbutton, check that one pushbutton pin connects to the positive power rail, and the other pin connects to the negative power rail via a resistor.

8. Go back to the diagram and double-check all the jumper wire connections one at a time. Trace from left to right, one wire at a time.

9. Check that transistor 1 Source pin (left pin) is connected to the negative power rail.

10. Check that the jumper wires are fully inserted into the breadboard holes.

11. Check that the jumper wires are in the proper breadboard rows for each component.

12. Check for those rare faulty jumper wires by wiggling the wires or swapping out jumper wires.

13. Finally, check that the battery has energy by connecting it directly to an LED.

Still not working? It's okay! Take a breather, and then show your circuit to a favorite human (or just ask someone nearby! For real, it's a great conversation starter!).

Refresher: AND Logic Gate Schematic Symbol and Truth Table

We learned about the AND logic gate schematic symbol and truth table in Chapter 6. That said, it's okay if you forgot or perhaps it's been a few weeks (or months) since you read that section. Here's a reminder for those of us who have a hard time remembering until we've had to put things in practice.

The AND logic gate schematic symbol is shown again in Figure 9-7:

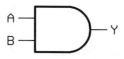

Figure 9-7. *Schematic symbol for AND logic gate*

where A and B are the inputs – in this case, our inputs to the transistor logic gate are the two pushbuttons. The output of the logic gate, Y, is connected to our LED so we can more easily visualize how the logic gate output changes.

The AND logic gate truth table is given in Table 9-1.

Table 9-1. *AND Gate Truth Table*

A	B	Output
0	0	0
1	0	0
0	1	0
1	1	1

As discussed in Chapter 6, we read the truth table as follows: if inputs A and B are 0 (or off), then the output is 0.

We'll build on this knowledge later in this chapter.

OR Gate

Figure 9-8 shows how I built an OR logic gate. Yours might look different and that's okay!

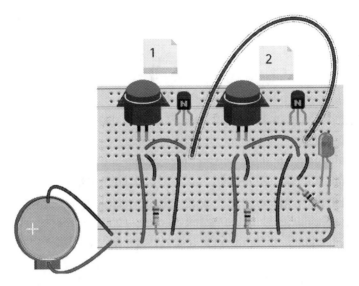

Figure 9-8. *Full circuit diagram for an N-Channel MOSFET logic gate*

For an OR gate, either input can be on for the output to be on. This translates to **two paths** for the electricity to flow. For two paths, the transistors are connected **in parallel**. We connect the output of both transistors (the Drain pins) to the LED.

Written Instructions

1. Connect a jumper wire between the negative power rail and transistor 1 Source pin.

2. Repeat step 1 for transistor 2.

3. Connect a jumper wire between transistor 1 Drain pin and transistor 2 Drain pin.

    a. *Note: This connects the two N-Channel transistor Drain pins.*

4. Connect a jumper wire from transistor 2 Drain pin to the LED resistor.

Test your OR gate!! Check that the LED turns on when either button is pressed.

Is your circuit behaving weirdly? See the following for some troubleshooting tips.

TROUBLESHOOTING TIPS: OR GATE

1. Check that the battery power switch is on and that the leads are in different power rails. Wiggle the wires to ensure they are making good electrical connection with the breadboard pins.

2. Check that you're using **10kΩ** resistors.

3. Check that the LED leads are fully inserted into the breadboard holes and are in different rows.

4. Check that the positive LED lead is connected to the positive power rail.

5. Check that all transistor leads are fully inserted into breadboard holes and are in different rows.

6. Check that the pushbutton pins are fully inserted into the breadboard holes and are in different rows.

7. For each pushbutton, check that one pushbutton pin connects to the positive power rail, and the other pin connects to the negative power rail via a resistor.

8. Go back to the diagram and double-check all the jumper wire connections one at a time. Trace from left to right, one wire at a time.

9. Check that transistor 1 Source pin (left pin) is connected to the negative power rail.

10. Check that transistor 2 Source pin (left pin) is connected to the negative power rail.

11. Check that both transistor 1 and 2 Drain pins are connected to the negative LED lead (via a resistor).

12. Check that the jumper wires are fully inserted into the breadboard holes.

13. Check that the jumper wires are in the proper breadboard rows for each component.

14. Check for those rare faulty jumper wires by wiggling the wires or swapping out jumper wires.

15. Finally, check that the battery has energy by connecting it directly to an LED.

Still not working? It's okay! Take a breather, and then show your circuit to a favorite human (or just ask someone nearby! For real, it's a great conversation starter!).

Refresher: OR Logic Gate Schematic Symbol and Truth Table

In case you need it, the OR logic gate schematic symbol is reproduced in Figure 9-9:

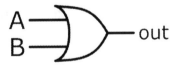

Figure 9-9. *Schematic symbol for an OR gate*

Similar to the AND logic gate, A and B are our pushbutton inputs to the OR transistor logic gate. The output again connects to our LED so we can visualize how the inputs change the logic gate output.

We can summarize the behavior of the OR logic gate with its associated truth table in Table 9-2.

Table 9-2. *OR Gate Truth Table*

A	B	Output
0	0	0
1	0	1
0	1	1
1	1	1

In this case, the truth table tells us that the output of the OR logic gate is 1 (or on) when either of the inputs are 1.

Project 9-3: NOT Gate with Transistors!

Our first NOT gate with pushbuttons used a short circuit to turn off an LED to when the button was pressed. With a transistor, we can build a better NOT gate that doesn't rely on a short circuit, yay!

For this logic gate, we'll need a subset of parts from what you've gathered for this section:

- Half-size breadboard

- Coin cell in battery case

- 6 jumper wires

- 1 N-Channel transistor

- 1 pushbutton

- 3 **10kΩ** resistors

- 1 LED

For the NOT gate, we want to turn on an LED when the transistor Gate pin is off (or low/0V). When the transistor Gate pin is on (or high/3V), the LED turns off.

To do this, we'll leverage the laziness of electricity! I'll get you started (if you'd like a helping hand; otherwise, have at it!). Again, since this is Chapter 9, I'm challenging you **to try this one on your own** before looking at the full diagram.

First, connect up the pushbutton like we did with the AND and OR gates (Figure 9-10):

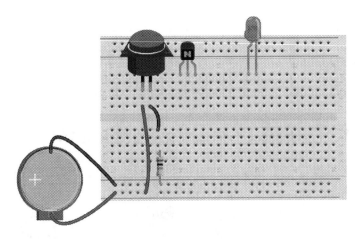

Figure 9-10. *Starting circuit for the N-channel MOSFET NOT gate*

Written Instructions (Beginning)

1. Insert the battery wires into the breadboard power rails.

2. Insert the N-Channel transistor so that the flat side is facing you and its leads are in different rows.

3. With the breadboard facing horizontally, insert the pushbutton to the left of the transistor.

4. Insert the LED.

5. Connect a jumper wire between the positive power rail and the left pushbutton pin.

6. Connect a resistor between the negative power rail and the right pushbutton pin.

   a. Note: You may need a jumper wire to make the full connection.

From here, think about how you could connect the transistor and the LED in parallel.

Hint: *You are giving the electrical current an easier path to flow when the transistor turns on.*

Need a lil' more help? Figure 9-11 shows how you start with the LED:

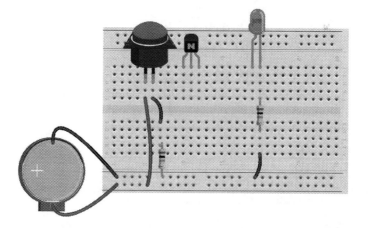

Figure 9-11. *Connecting the LED for the N-Channel MOSFET NOT gate*

WARNING: BUILD SOLUTIONS TO FOLLOW IN FIGURE 9-12!!

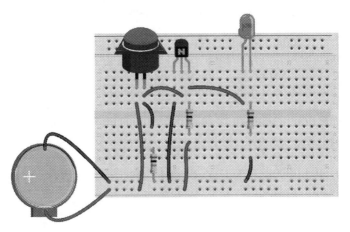

Figure 9-12. *Full circuit diagram for the N-Channel MOSFET NOT Gate*

Written Instructions (Remaining Circuit)

1. Connect the negative LED lead to the negative power rail via a resistor.

2. Connect the right pushbutton pin to the transistor Gate pin.

3. Connect the transistor Source pin to the negative power rail.

4. Insert a resistor between the transistor Drain pin and the positive power rail.

a. Note: You may need a jumper wire to complete the connection.

5. Connect a jumper wire between the transistor Drain pin and the positive LED lead.

Press the pushbutton to test your NOT gate!! *(See the troubleshooting tips at the end of the section.)*

WHAT. How in the Electric Universe Does This NOT Gate Work?!

Right!! Electricity is so weird and fun.

> 😵 **Question 1:** How many paths, or loops, are in our NOT gate circuit?

> 🔎 **Check it out:** Trace the path of the electricity! What do you notice about how the electricity flows when the pushbutton is open (and the transistor is off)? What do you notice when the pushbutton is closed (and the transistor is on)?

Wildly enough, there are three parallel loops in our circuit! The first loop is for the pushbutton: when the pushbutton is closed (i.e., pressed), electricity can flow through the pushbutton and back to the negative side of the circuit, like we see in Figure 9-13:

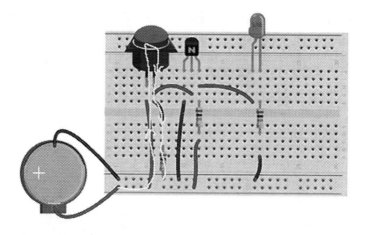

Figure 9-13. *Path of electric current flow through the pushbutton in the N-Channel MOSFET NOT gate*

301

When the pushbutton is pressed, it triggers the transistor to turn on because there is a voltage between the transistor Gate pin and the negative side of the circuit. (The negative side of the circuit is a reference point called **ground**... coming up soon!) Then electricity can flow through the transistor, like we see in Figure 9-14:

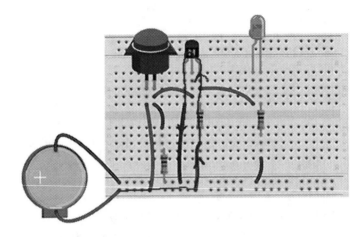

Figure 9-14. *Path of electric current through the transistor (when pushbutton is pressed) in the N-Channel MOSFET NOT gate*

If we release the pushbutton, electricity can also flow through the LED, like illustrated in Figure 9-15:

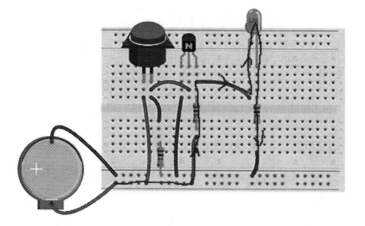

Figure 9-15. *Path of the electric current flow when the pushbutton is released in the N-Channel MOSFET NOT gate*

The NOT gate works because **electricity is always looking for the easiest path to flow from higher energy to lower energy**. In our circuit, the higher energy part is the positive side of our battery. The lower energy part is the negative side of the battery, or ground.

When the transistor is not conducting electricity (ohnologicgatepuns!), the current flows from high energy state (positive power rail) into the resistor. Then it flows from the resistor to the LED and to the low energy state (negative power rail). This makes the lil' charges happy because they can get from high energy to low energy via the LED!

When the transistor is conducting electricity, the charges can flow from high to low energy (i.e., from the positive side of the battery to the negative side) **without** traveling through the LED. They "want" to do this because it takes energy to flow through the LED. By skipping the LED, the charges can take the least energy-intensive path from high to low energy. Huzzah, lazy charges!

TROUBLESHOOTING TIPS: NOT GATE

1. Check that the battery power switch is on and that the leads are in different power rails. Wiggle the wires to ensure they are making good electrical connection with the breadboard pins.

2. Check that you're using **10kΩ** resistors.

3. Check that the LED leads are fully inserted into the breadboard holes and are in different rows.

4. Check that the negative LED lead is connected to the negative power rail via a resistor.

5. Check that all transistor leads are fully inserted into breadboard holes and are in different rows.

6. Check that the pushbutton pins are fully inserted into the breadboard holes and are in different rows.

7. Check that one pushbutton pin connects to the positive power rail, and the other pin connects to the negative power rail (ground) via a resistor.

8. Go back to the diagram and double-check all the jumper wire connections one at a time. Trace from left to right, one wire at a time.

9. Check that the jumper wires are fully inserted into the breadboard holes.

10. Check that the jumper wires are in the proper breadboard rows for each component.

11. Check for those rare faulty jumper wires by wiggling the wires or swapping out jumper wires.

12. Finally, check that the battery has energy by connecting it directly to an LED.

Still not working? It's okay! Take a breather; maybe talk it out to yourself or a pet. If you haven't cracked the mystery yet, show your circuit and the diagram to another human!

Refresher: NOT Logic Gate Schematic Symbol and Truth Table

Just in case you need it, Figure 9-16 shows what the NOT logic gate schematic symbol looks like:

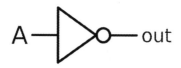

Figure 9-16. *Schematic symbol for NOT gate*

In this case, we only have one input (A) that we control with our pushbutton. Be careful though because the output is **not**[2] the Drain pin of the transistor!! In the AND and OR gate circuits, the Drain pin connected directly to our LED. With the NOT gate, the Drain pin connects to a resistor and to the positive power rail. The NOT gate output is **between** the resistor and the transistor Drain pin. This is where we connect our positive LED lead!

The behavior of the NOT logic gate can be summarized with its handy truth table in Table 9-3.

---

[2] No logic gate pun here, just trying to make sure you catch it; it's easy to miss!

Table 9-3. NOT Gate Truth Table

A	Output
0	1
1	0

Concept Break: Electric Ground!

Oh hey, we got to that thing I hinted at: Ground!

Electric ground   A reference point from which voltage is measured, a return path for current, and sometimes a connection to the earth.

So far in this book, we've referred to the two sides of an electric circuit: the positive side and the negative side. Sometimes, the negative side of our circuit is also called ground. **Ground is a reference point in an electronic circuit from which voltage is measured.**[3] Ground can also be a common return-to-the-source (like a battery) path for current or, quite literally, a connection into the earth.

Let's explore ground as a reference point because this is super important and (can be) super confusing.

Flashback to Voltage!

Voltage is measured between two points. For example, I can measure the voltage across an LED in a circuit. If I measure 3V with my voltmeter, this means that there is a 3V difference across the LED leads. This 3V difference

---

[3] Okay, okay, technically this is a "common" or COM point. But TBF, "ground" and "common" are used interchangeably at this point, so I'm going to be lazy and just use one term. ☺

across the LED pushes electric charges through the LED because they want to flow from higher energy to lower energy. If I reverse my voltmeter probes, I will measure negative 3V (or –3V). This means that the current flows in the opposite direction.

But... hold up! Can we measure the voltage of a single point?

No, we cannot! **Voltage is relative** – it is measured between two points, and its value depends on where we are measuring from.

As an example, imagine you want to measure how far the top of your head is from the earth. You're standing on the ground – no problem! You grab a tape measure, step on one end, and pull out the tape measure until you reach the top of your head (perhaps with the aid of a trusted friend). This measures how far your head is from the ground.

Now imagine you go visit a friend who lives in a tall apartment building. Your friend shows you the rooftop patio so you can watch the sunset. While you're standing up there, you realize: the height of your head from the ground is now much, much larger! If you repeated the measurement experiment, you (and your friend) would need a longer tape measure that could reach from the ground to the top of the apartment building and then to the top of your head. Ground stayed, well, at the ground, but the ending point for your measurement (the top of your head) has moved.

Voltage behaves similarly to our vertically moving head! By using ground as a common reference point, we can ensure that the components in our circuit don't get confused and think they are standing on a super tall apartment building (... something like that).

This is why we always have to connect the negative side of two power supplies, like a coin cell battery and a 9V battery. If we forget to do this, funky things happen and our circuit doesn't work as expected because there's no common reference point.

Ground As a Connection to Earth?

Heck yes, ground is also a literal connection to the earth! This is helpful for dissipating large amounts of (potentially unexpected) current – like when lightning strikes a building or an electric power line!

This is exactly what a lightning rod does: a conductive path allows the high-energy lightning charges an easy way to flow from the lightning rod to the earth. This prevents the lightning strike from damaging the building or the people inside, yay! Even if lightning strikes a building, like we see below in the impressively timed photo in Figure 9-17, it is safe to be inside.

Figure 9-17. Lightning striking the lightning rod at the top of the CN Tower in Toronto, Canada. Source: Wikimedia Commons

Connecting electrical circuits to the earth, as illustrated in Figure 9-18, also prevents us squishy humans from getting shocked if we touch an exposed metal part of a circuit or if internal insulation fails. Ground connections prevent the buildup of static electricity, and sometimes the ground itself can be used as one conductor of the circuit! If this blows your mind (it did for me when I first learned about it), this is actually how telegraph and power transmission circuits work! SO COOL!!

One more riveting "why connect this ish to ground" reason: The earth is a fairly constant reference point for measuring voltage because it is unfathomably large (especially in comparison to our teeny-tiny circuits). In electronic circuit theory, ground is often idealized as an infinite source or sink for charges that can also absorb an infinite amount of current without changing its reference point.

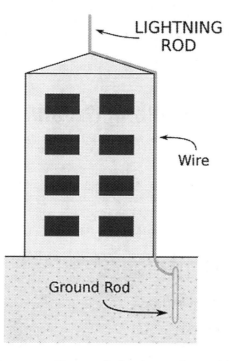

Figure 9-18. *A diagram of how a lightning rod provides a conductive path for electricity to flow into the earth. Source: Wikimedia Commons*

Schematic Symbol for Ground

Ground schematic symbols abound in electronics because it makes drawing circuits **way** easier and less confusing. Figure 9-19 shows what a ground symbol looks like:

Figure 9-19. *Schematic symbol for electric ground*

Instead of connecting up full circuit paths, we can show where components connect to the negative side of the circuit (or ground) by using the ground symbol.

Logic Gates: The More, the Merrier!

Aaand we're back to logic gates! Logic gates can be combined together to make more complex circuits, including binary adders! Getting to a binary adder requires a **lot** of transistors. Let's start with our friendly logic gate building blocks: AND, OR, and NOT gates!

Grab These Materials

- Half-size breadboard
- Coin cell in battery case
- 11 (or more) jumper wires
- 2 N-Channel MOSFET transistors

- 2 pushbuttons

- 3 **10kΩ** resistors

- 1 LED

Project 9-4: NOT Another Logic Gate! (Yes!)

For our next project, we'll take what we learned about the NOT gate and apply it to either an AND gate or an OR gate – your choice! You could also do both. ☺

With these projects, we'll create two new types of logic gates: NAND and NOR gates! As a refresher, NAND stands for "NOT AND" and NOR stands for "NOT OR." Just like the NOT gate reverses the input signal, NAND and NOR gates behave in the opposite way.

We'll check out the truth tables and schematic symbols for these logic gates at the end of the section. For now, let's dig in!

I encourage you to try these on your own! If you want a lil' guidance, here's what to consider:

1. You only need two transistors and two pushbuttons.

2. The LED is connected in a separate loop like we did with the NOT gate. The goal is to give the electricity an easy path to flow through the transistors when they are on. When the transistors are off, the electrical current should flow through the LED.

3. The NAND gate should have the transistors wired together.

4. The NOR gate should have the transistors wired separately.

If you get stuck or are just feeling brain-tired, diagrams and written instructions for both circuits are below in Figures 9-20 and 9-22, respectively.

NAND Gate

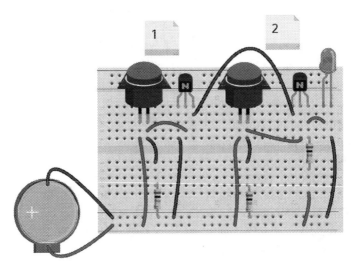

Figure 9-20. *Circuit diagram for an N-Channel MOSFET NAND gate*

Written Instructions

Note: There are many ways to organize this circuit on your breadboard. You might want to do something different than what is shown in my diagram and that's great! Explore how to best use the real estate on your breadboard.

1. Connect the battery to the breadboard power rails.

2. Insert the pushbuttons, transistors, and LED.

3. For each pushbutton

    a. Connect a jumper wire between the positive power rail and the left pin.

    b. Connect a resistor between the negative power rail (ground) and the right pin. (You may need a jumper wire to reach.)

    c. Connect a jumper wire between the right pin and the transistor Gate pin (middle pin).

4. Connect a jumper wire between the negative power rail (ground) and the negative LED lead.

5. Connect a resistor between the positive power rail and transistor 2 Drain pin (right pin). (You may need a jumper wire to complete the connection.)

6. Connect a jumper wire between transistor 2 Drain pin and the positive LED lead.

7. Connect a jumper wire between transistor 2 Source pin (left pin) and transistor 1 Drain pin.

8. Connect a jumper wire between transistor 1 Source pin and the negative power rail (ground).

Huzzah! 11 jumper wires later and we have a NAND gate! Press the pushbuttons and observe the behavior of your LED, then match it to the truth table at the end of this section.

(If it's not working as expected, walk through the following troubleshooting tips.)

TROUBLESHOOTING TIPS: NAND GATE

1. Check that the battery power switch is on and that the leads are in different power rails. Wiggle the wires to ensure they are making good electrical connection with the breadboard pins.

2. Check that you're using 10kΩ resistors.

3. Check that the LED leads are fully inserted into the breadboard holes and are in different rows.

4. Check that the LED orientation is correct (that its positive leg connects to the positive side of the circuit).

5. Check that the flat side of the transistor is facing you, then double-check the wire connections.

6. For each pushbutton, check that one pushbutton pin connects to the positive power rail, and the other pin connects to the negative power rail (ground) via a resistor. Check that its output (right pin) connects to the transistor Gate pin.

7. Check that there is a path for electricity to flow through the LED when the transistors are off.

8. Go back to the diagram and double-check all the jumper wire connections one at a time. Trace from left to right, one wire at a time.

9. Check that the jumper wires are fully inserted into the breadboard holes.

10. Check that the jumper wires are in the proper breadboard rows for each component.

11. Check for those rare faulty jumper wires by wiggling the wires or swapping out jumper wires.

12.   Finally, check that the battery has energy by connecting it directly to an LED.

Still not working? It's okay! Take a breather. Maybe try rebuilding it or talking it out. If you need more help, snag another human and go through the wiring together.

Refresher: NAND Logic Gate Schematic Symbol and Truth Table

The NAND gate schematic symbol is the AND gate with a circle on the output (Figure 9-21):

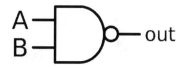

Figure 9-21. *NAND gate schematic symbol*

The circle tells us it's a "NOT" version of this gate or that the output is the opposite of an AND gate.

As we learned in Chapter 6, the truth table for our "NOT AND" gate output is opposite of the AND gate output. In other words, the output is true (or on) when any of the inputs are false (or off). When both inputs are true (on), the output is false (off). The truth table for the NAND gate looks like Table 9-4.

Table 9-4. *NAND Gate Truth Table*

A	B	Out
0	0	1
1	0	1
0	1	1
1	1	0

NOR Gate

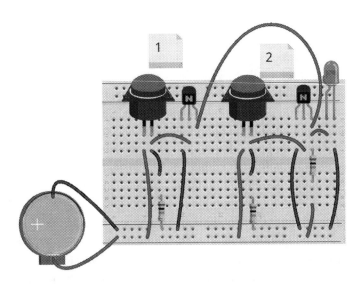

Figure 9-22. *Circuit diagram for an N-Channel MOSFET NOR gate*

Written Instructions

Note 1: Just like the NAND gate, there are lots of ways to organize this circuit on your breadboard! Do what makes the most sense for your brain.

Note 2: If you're starting from the NAND gate, you only need to change two wires: (1) connect a jumper wire between transistor 2 Source pin and ground (negative power rail), and (2) move the transistor 1 Drain pin jumper wire to connect between transistor 1 and 2 Drain pins.

1. Connect the battery to the breadboard power rails and insert the LED.

2. Insert both transistors into the breadboard. Leave some space for the pushbuttons and insert them to the left of the transistors. Speaking of...

3. For each pushbutton

    a. Connect a jumper wire between the positive power rail and the left pin.

    b. Connect a resistor between the negative power rail (ground) and the right pin. (You may need a jumper wire to reach.)

    c. Connect a jumper wire between the right pin and the transistor Gate pin (middle pin).

4. Connect a jumper wire between the negative power rail (ground) and the negative LED lead.

5. Connect a resistor between the positive power rail and transistor 2 Drain pin (right pin). (You may need a jumper wire to complete the connection.)

6. Connect a jumper wire between transistor 2 Drain pin and the positive LED lead.

7. Connect a jumper wire between transistor 2 Source pin (left pin) and ground (negative power rail).

8. Connect a jumper wire between transistor 1 Source pin and ground.

9. Connect a jumper wire between transistor 1 and 2 Drain pins.

You did it!! Test your NOR gate and compare its results to the following truth table.

(Or check the troubleshooting tips if it's behaving bizarrely.)

TROUBLESHOOTING TIPS: NAND GATE

1. Check that the battery power switch is on and that the leads are in different power rails. Wiggle the wires to ensure they are making good electrical connection with the breadboard pins.

2. Check that you're using 10kΩ resistors.

3. Check that the LED leads are fully inserted into the breadboard holes and are in different rows.

4. Check that the LED orientation is correct (that its positive leg connects to the positive side of the circuit).

5. Check the orientation of the transistors – make sure the flat side is facing you – and double-check the wire connections.

6. Check that all transistor pins are fully inserted into breadboard holes and are in different rows.

7. Check that the pushbutton pins are fully inserted into the breadboard holes and are in different rows.

8. For each pushbutton, check that one pushbutton pin connects to the positive power rail, and the other pin connects to the negative power rail (ground) via a resistor. Check that its output (right pin) connects to the transistor Gate pin.

9. Check that there is a path for electricity to flow through the LED when the transistors are off.

10. Go back to the diagram and double-check all the jumper wire connections one at a time. Trace from left to right, one wire at a time.

11. Check that the jumper wires are fully inserted into the breadboard holes.

12. Check that the jumper wires are in the proper breadboard rows for each component.

13. Check for those rare faulty jumper wires by wiggling the wires or swapping out jumper wires.

14. Finally, check that the battery has energy by connecting it directly to an LED.

Still not working? It's okay! Take a breather. Maybe try rebuilding it or talking it out. If you need more help, snag another human and go through the wiring together.

Refresher: NOR Logic Gate Schematic Symbol and Truth Table

To make a NOR gate schematic symbol, we take the OR gate symbol and add our cute lil' circle on the output! It looks like Figure 9-23:

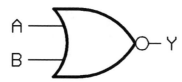

Figure 9-23. *NOR gate schematic symbol*

The truth table for our "NOT OR" gate is the opposite of our OR gate: the output is true (on) only when all inputs are false (off), and the output is false (off) when any input is true (on). The NOR truth table looks like Table 9-5.

Table 9-5. *NOR Gate Truth Table*

A	B	Out
0	0	1
1	0	0
0	1	0
1	1	0

Going Further!

We learned a ton in this chapter! And because this universe is big and beautiful, there are still more ways we can explore logic gates, yay!

1. **Project 1: Combine logic gates.**

   Using your knowledge of AND, OR, NOT, NAND, and NOR gates, explore how to combine logic gates together to get different outputs.

2. **Project 2: Decision maker!**

   Similar to the project you did in Chapter 6, use logic gates to make a decision tree that turns on a light or other output device when certain input conditions are met. Use conditionals to help you build this.

   For example, if you wanted to decide what kind of dinner to cook, you could set up the following conditionals:

a. If it's cold, then I will eat something spicy or something pumpkin flavored.

b. If it's cold and I don't have time to cook, then I will eat soup.

c. If it's cold or I don't have time to cook, then I will eat a sandwich.

Think about how to map the inputs to your conditions (cold and cooking time) and how to map the outputs to your decisions (spicy, pumpkin flavored, soup, and sandwich). You will need one light or output device per decision.

3. **Project 3: Logic gates with other kinds of inputs.**

What could you use instead of pushbuttons? Explore other types of input devices to trigger the logic gates. Try the sensors we played with or make your own input devices!

4. **Project 4: Add logic to a project!**

This rhymes **and** is a great way to make "smarter" circuit without any code. For example, if you want to turn on a light with either a switch or when it is dark, you can use an OR gate with a switch as one input and the dark detecting circuit as the second input.

5. *Project 5: Minecraft*: **Build logic gates!**

If you play *Minecraft*, use your knowledge to build AND, OR, and NOT logic gates with red stone! If you're feeling adventurous, you can also try NAND, NOR, and XOR gates!

What was your favorite discovery in this chapter? What was frustrating or surprising? What are some ways we could build computers instead of using logic gates (or even electricity!)? Share your questions, thought experiments, and ideas with a friend! Look up "wetware," "quantum computer," "chemical computer," or "mechanical computer" in your favorite search engine to learn more about different ways of building computers!

Summary

This chapter relied on our existing knowledge of logic gates and (N-Channel MOSFET) transistors to create the building blocks of computers: transistor logic gates! We built our familiar logic gates (AND, OR, and NOT gates) with transistors instead of (just) pushbuttons. We also extended our knowledge to more complex logic gates like NAND and NOR! We also took a concept detour through the wonderful world of electronic (and sometimes literal) ground to learn more about voltage and how the earth can dissipate large amounts of electrical energy (like lightning!).

In the next chapter, we'll build on what we learned in this chapter to connect multiple logic gates together. We'll also learn how we combine math with logic gates to get an electronic computer!! This will get us to your "capstone" project: a binary adder!

CHAPTER 10

A Simple Computer!

Cascading Logic Gates: A (Controlled) Electrical Waterfall!

The reason why we built transistor logic gates in Chapter 9 is because we need to connect multiple logic gates (our building blocks) together to build a computer – the output of one logic gate triggers the input of the next. When we connect multiple transistor logic gates, we can perform more complex operations than a single logic gate allows. In fact, we can create a circuit that can do (binary) addition! This is what all modern computers do: math with (binary) numbers! Lots and lots (and lots) of binary number math are what enables us to use electricity to type words, listen to music, and watch videos.

In our journey to build a simple adder, we'll also learn why we are using MOSFETs! Onward to building our final circuits!

*Side note: As we're learning to connect logic gates, I'd recommend **using one breadboard for each logic gate**. This helps keep the pieces separate and organized. It will also make it easier to connect multiple logic gates in different combinations.*

© Jennifer Fox 2023
J. Fox, *Beginning Breadboarding*, https://doi.org/10.1007/978-1-4842-9218-1_10

Grab These Materials

- 3 half-size breadboards
- Coin cell in battery case
- 28 jumper wires (lol, yes)
- 6 N-Channel transistors
- 2 pushbuttons
- 5 **10kΩ** resistors
- 1 LED

Project 10-1: NOT It!

Let's practice combining logic gates by adding a NOT gate to a NAND gate!

Why? … because we can!! For this first project, we'll only need a subset of the materials for this section (so when you end up with leftovers, you'll know why!).

You've already built both of these logic gates. Let's take your existing knowledge and use our critical thinking skills to explore how to connect a NAND gate to a NOT gate. Hooray for using our brains!

To start, let's look at a diagram of the NAND and NOT gate combo in Figure 10-1.

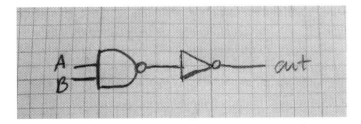

Figure 10-1. *Circuit schematic of a NAND and NOT gate*

For this logic gate waterfall, we have two inputs, A and B, and one output. The output of the NAND gate is connected to the (single) input for the NOT gate. The NOT gate output is the combined output of these two logic gates.

☺ **Question 1:** What will the truth table for this logic gate connection look like? Fill in your thoughts here in Table 10-1:

Table 10-1. *Truth table for NAND and NOT gate combo (for completion)*

A	B	OUT
0	0	
0	1	
1	0	
1	1	

To build this project, start by building a complete NAND gate. Then build a NOT gate and remove the pushbutton (and the rest of its circuit). When you have both gates completed, connect the output of the NAND gate to the input of the NOT gate. As mentioned earlier, I'd recommend using a separate breadboard for each logic gate.

Try this on your own for at least ten minutes before looking at the diagram in Figure 10-2 and written instructions below.

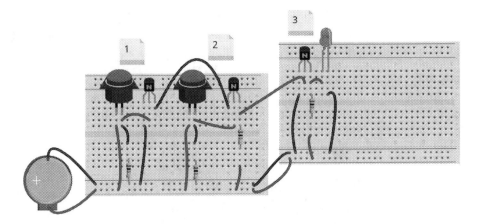

Figure 10-2. *Circuit diagram for a NAND and NOT gate combo*

WARNING!! BUILD SOLUTIONS FOLLOW.

Excellent effort trying on your own! Here is a build diagram for how I made my NAND-NOT gate combo. The NAND gate is on the left breadboard and the NOT gate is on the right breadboard.

Written Instructions

Starting from the NAND gate

1. Remove the NAND gate LED and the jumper wire connected to the negative power rail.

2. Grab a second breadboard and insert an N-Channel transistor and LED.

   a. Note: This is transistor 3.

3. Use two jumper wires to connect the power rails of the two breadboards (positive to positive and negative to negative).

4. Connect a resistor between the positive power rail of the second breadboard and transistor 3 Drain pin. (You may need a jumper wire to make this connection.)

5. Connect a jumper wire between the transistor 3 Drain pin and the positive LED leg.

6. Connect a jumper wire between the negative LED leg and the negative power rail (ground).

7. Connect a jumper wire between the NAND gate output (transistor 2 Drain pin) and transistor 3 Gate pin.

Test your cascading logic gate!! Press all the buttons to figure out when the LED turns on. The truth table for this logic gate combination acts like we see in Table 10-2.

Table 10-2. *Completed Truth Table for a NAND and NOT gate combo*

A	B	OUT
0	0	0
0	1	0
1	0	0
1	1	1

Wait a minute... this looks like our familiar AND gate truth table! Heck yes! Turns out the opposite of a NAND gate is, well, an AND gate! We can do the same with a NOR gate. (Bonus project perhaps??!)

(Troubleshooting tips for misbehaving circuits are provided at the end of this section.)

WHY ARE WE USING N-CHANNEL MOSFETS??

If you've worked with transistors before, you may have used BJTs to do things like build switches and amplifiers. BJTs are great fun! They can also be a simpler approach to learning transistors because they are turned on/off with a current instead of a voltage (which makes the trigger circuit simpler). It's even possible to build logic gates with BJTs!

There are two downsides for BJTs when it comes to building logic gates/ simple computers:

1. BJT logic gates cannot be connected together very easily because the input of one BJT is interacting with the output of the other. This means that as current flows through one logic gate to the other, the currents can become muddled (e.g., drop below the necessary threshold for triggering the BJT). It requires a more complex circuit to deal with how currents flow through BJT logic gates, which is beyond the scope of this book.

2. FETs only need a small amount of power to switch on.

Reason #2 is the primary reason that **computer chips** (i.e., computer processors) **are made using FETs**! While BJTs may be switched on with milliAmps of current, FETs can be switched on with nano-Amps of current (i.e., 1,000,000 times less current)! Computer chips are made of **billions** of transistors, so saving as much power consumption that you can is incredibly important!

TROUBLESHOOTING TIPS: NAND GATE PLUS NOT GATE

1. Check that the battery power switch is on and that the leads are in different power rails. Wiggle the wires to ensure they are making good electrical connection with the breadboard pins.

2. Check that you're using 10kΩ resistors.

3. If you're using two breadboards, check that the power rails of the breadboards are connected appropriately (positive to positive and negative to negative).

4. Check that the LED orientation is correct (that its positive leg connects to the positive side of the circuit).

5. Check the transistor orientation and make sure the flat side is facing you. Recheck the wire connections.

6. Check that the NAND gate output connects to the NOT gate transistor Gate pin (i.e., the NOT gate input).

7. For each pushbutton, check that one pushbutton pin connects to the positive power rail, and the other pin connects to the negative power rail (ground) via a resistor. Check that its output (right pin) connects to the transistor Gate pin.

8. Go back to the diagram and double-check all the jumper wire connections one at a time. Trace from left to right, one wire at a time.

    a. A common cause of error is jumper wires that snuck into the wrong rows. It's easy to make this mistake! It's okay – go slow and be patient with yourself. Take breaks as you need them.

9. Check that the jumper wires are fully inserted into the breadboard holes.

10. Check that the jumper wires are in the proper breadboard rows for each component.

11. Check for those rare faulty jumper wires by wiggling the wires or swapping out jumper wires.

12. Finally, check that the battery has energy by connecting it directly to an LED.

Still not working? Talk it out (with yourself, a pet, or another human), start over, or go back to your circuits in Chapter 9. If you need more help, ask another human and go through the wiring together.

Project 10-2: Our One and Only XOR Gate

For this next project, we'll cascade three logic gates together to get our last remaining logic gate building block: an XOR gate! This logic gate is super important for computers because we need it to build our binary adder. An XOR gate is made using a combination of AND, OR, and NOT gates.

XOR stands for "Exclusive OR," which means that its output is true (or on) if, and only if, one of the inputs is on. Since this is a bit confusing to put into words, Table 10-3 shows the truth table of the XOR logic gate.

Table 10-3. XOR Gate Truth Table

A	B	OUT
0	0	0
0	1	1
1	0	1
1	1	0

It's possible to build an XOR gate by combining the following logic gates illustrated in Figure 10-3:

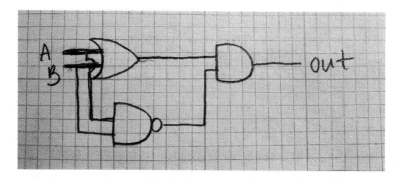

Figure 10-3. *Schematic diagram for XOR logic gate*

🤨 **Question 2:** Check the output of the XOR gate by following the binary digits (bits) through! If A and B are both 0, what is the output of the OR gate and the NAND gate? What goes into the AND gate and what is the output of that gate? Repeat this for A = 1 and B = 0, A = 0 and B = 1, and A = 1 and B = 1.[1]

Okay! We just combine the OR, NAND, and AND gates we've already made and... voila! An XOR gate!

Le sigh. Not quite. I have some good news and some bad news for our XOR gate. The bad news is that the AND and OR gates we've built don't cascade properly (something something we're cascading voltage and not current and the way I chose to have you build these was an attempt to keep things simple).

---

[1] If both A and B are 0, the OR gate outputs 0 and the NAND gate outputs 1. Inputs of 0 and 1 into the AND gate give a 0. If A is 1 and B is 0, the OR gate outputs 1 and the NAND outputs 1. Inputs of 1 and 1 into the AND gate give a 1 (same goes for if A is 0 and B is 1). If A is 1 and B is 1, the OR gate outputs 1 and the NAND gate outputs 0. Inputs of 1 and 0 into the AND gate give an output of 0! This gives us our XOR truth table.

The good news is that our knowledge of AND and NOT gates still comes in handy! Instead of building the circuit like that first diagram, we're building it like the diagram illustrated in Figure 10-4:

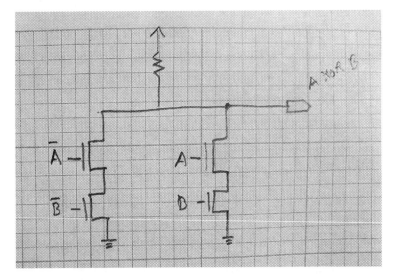

Figure 10-4. *Schematic diagram for an XOR gate made using N-Channel MOSFETs*

We read the diagram about in the following way:

1. We connect a resistor to positive voltage.

2. We have four signals: A, "NOT A" ($\overline{A}$), B, and "NOT B" ($\overline{B}$). We make $\overline{A}$ and $\overline{B}$ using two NOT gates (each NOT gate is made of one transistor).

3. We have two AND-like logic gates (each made of two N-Channel transistors). The inputs of one logic gate are A and B. The inputs of the second logic gate are $\overline{A}$ and $\overline{B}$.

4. The two AND-like logic gates are connected in an OR-like manner: if either logic gate #1 or logic gate #2 is on, the output is on. If both logic gates are off, the output is off. If both logic gates are on, the output is off.

Because this is weird and new, let's walk through it together. I'm using three breadboards to keep things organized: one breadboard for the pushbuttons and NOT gates, a second breadboard for the first "AND" gate, and the third breadboard for the second "AND" gate. (I'll also be using an "AND" gate in quotes to refer to each pair of N-Channel transistors in series because these aren't quite an AND gate.)

Okay!! Grab your components and let's get a-building! We'll start by inserting our components into the breadboard, an example of which is shown in Figure 10-5.

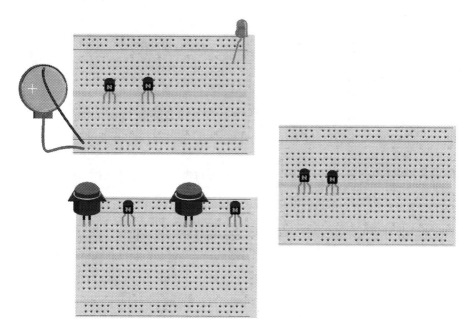

Figure 10-5. *Starting circuit for an XOR gate with N-Channel MOSFETs*

Step 1: Connect the coin cell battery to one of the breadboards.

Step 2: Insert all of the components into the breadboards. You can use my organizational system or devise your own.

Step 3: Connect the breadboard power rails together (Figure 10-6). (You can do this for only the power rails that you need, or you may choose to connect them all... just in case.)

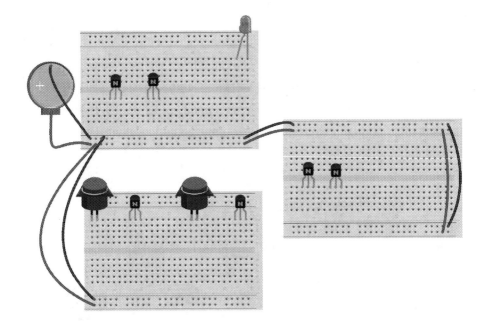

Figure 10-6. *Connecting the power rails for an XOR gate with N-Channel MOSFETs*

Be mindful of the positive and negative connections.

Step 4: Connect the LED! (Figure 10-7)

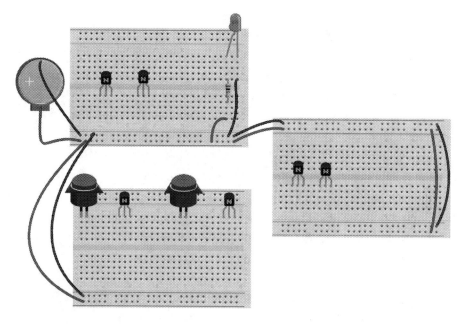

Figure 10-7. *Connecting the output device for an XOR gate with N-Channel MOSFETs*

a. Connect a resistor between the positive power rail and the positive LED leg. (You may need a jumper wire for this connection.)

b. Connect a jumper wire between ground (negative power rail) and the negative LED lead.

Step 5: Connect the pushbuttons! (Figure 10-8) For each pushbutton

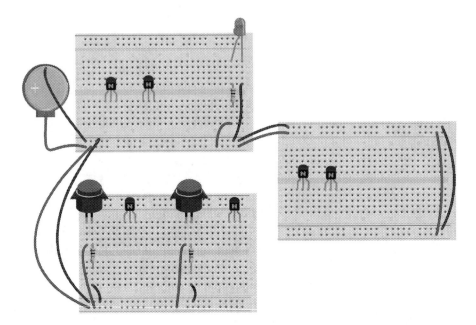

Figure 10-8. *Connecting the pushbuttons for an XOR gate with N-Channel MOSFETs*

   a.   Connect a jumper wire from the positive power rail
        to the left pushbutton pin.

   b.   Connect a resistor between ground (negative power
        rail) and the right pushbutton pin. (You may need a
        jumper wire for this connection.)

   Step 6: As shown in Figure 10-9, for each NOT gate transistor (bottom
breadboard), connect the pushbutton output (right pin) to the transistor
Gate pin.

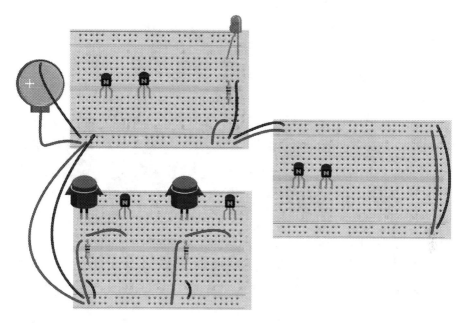

Figure 10-9. *Connecting the pushbutton outputs for an XOR gate with N-Channel MOSFETs*

Step 7: Wire up the rest of the NOT gate transistors (Figure 10-10)! For each NOT gate transistor

   a. Connect a resistor between the positive power rail and the transistor Drain pin (right pin). (You may need a jumper wire to complete this connection.)

   b. Connect a jumper wire between the transistor Source pin (left pin) and ground (negative power rail).

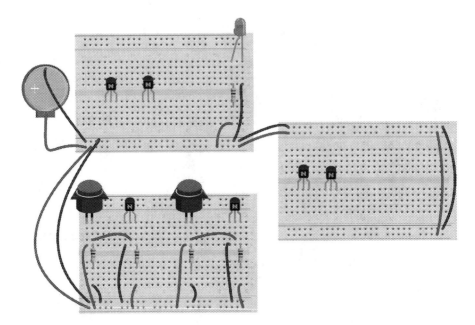

Figure 10-10. *Connecting the NOT gate transistors for an XOR gate with N-Channel MOSFETs*

Step 8: Connect the NOT gate output to the first set of "AND" gate inputs! These are the yellow wires on the diagram in Figure 10-11. For each NOT gate transistor

   a.   Connect a jumper wire between the NOT gate transistor Drain pin (right pin) and the "AND" gate transistor Gate pin.

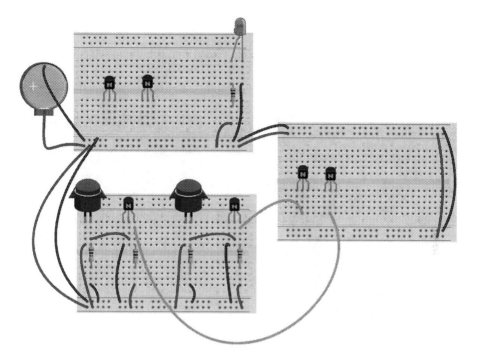

Figure 10-11. *Connect the NOT gate outputs for an XOR gate with N-Channel MOSFETs*

Step 9: Wire the first "AND" gate transistors (Figure 10-12)! These are the transistors on the **far-right breadboard**.

a. Connect a jumper wire between ground (negative power rail) and the left transistor Source pin (left pin).

b. Connect a jumper wire between the left transistor Drain pin (right pin) and the right transistor Source pin (left pin).

c. Connect a jumper wire from the right transistor Drain pin (right pin) and the positive LED leg. This is the orange jumper wire in the preceding diagram.

339

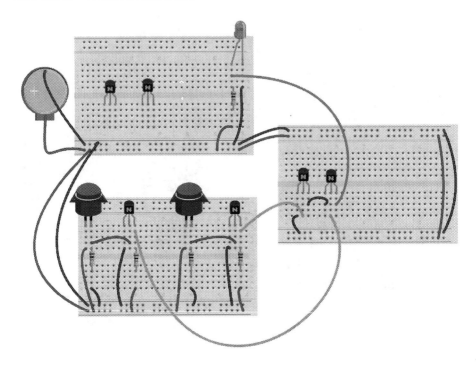

Figure 10-12. *Connecting the "AND" gate transistors for an XOR gate with N-Channel MOSFETs*

Step 10: We're on the second (and last) "AND" gate! We're almost done!! These transistors are on the top breadboard with the LED. Use Figure 10-13 below to help wire these transistors.

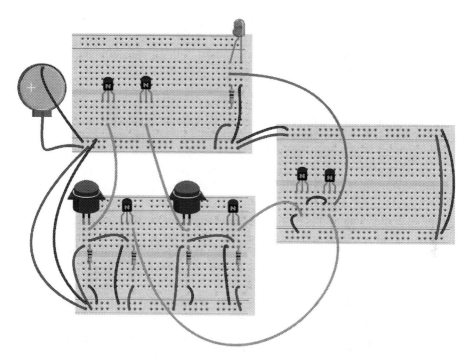

Figure 10-13. *Connecting the second "AND" gate transistors for an XOR gate with N-Channel MOSFETs*

Connect the pushbutton outputs to each transistor input (second set of yellow wires):

a. Connect the left pushbutton output (right pin) to the left transistor Gate pin (middle pin).

b. Connect the right pushbutton output (right pin) to the right transistor Gate pin.

341

Step 11: LAST STEP!!! YOU MADE IT! Okay, okay, now we just need to wire up the second "AND" gate (top breadboard with LED) so that our circuit matches what we see in Figure 10-14 below:

   a. Connect a jumper wire between ground (negative power rail) and the left transistor Source pin.

   b. Connect a jumper wire between the left transistor Drain pin and the right transistor Source pin.

   c. Connect a jumper wire between the right transistor Drain pin and the positive LED leg. This is the second orange wire in the preceding diagram.

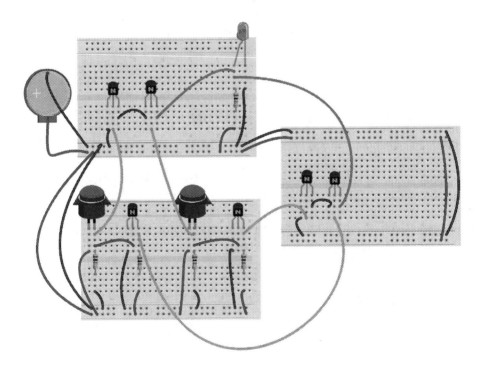

Figure 10-14. *Complete build diagram for an XOR gate with N-Channel MOSFETs*

YOU DID IT!!!

Press down on your pushbuttons! Your LED should light up if either of the pushbuttons is closed. Your LED should **not** turn on if both pushbuttons are closed.

Phew. Excellent effort and patience. **I'd recommend keeping this circuit intact because we'll need it later for our final project.**

(If your circuit isn't working as expected, there are troubleshooting tips at the end of this section.)

Uhhh, How Does This Give Us an XOR Gate?

This (complex) circuit has two inputs: our two pushbuttons. These are the logic gate inputs A and B.

The output of the circuit is the breadboard row connected to the positive LED leg. Technically, there are two output wires (from our two "AND" gates). But logic gates only have one output! To get a single output that is consistent with how a logic gate functions, we connect the two wires from the "AND" gates together.

And there we have it! A logic gate with two inputs and one output, yay!

WHY IS THE LED FLICKERING ON AND THEN TURNING OFF WHEN I PRESS BOTH PUSHBUTTONS?

Great question! There are two reasons why our LED might flicker. The first reason is that our fingers (and reflexes) are much, much slower than an electrical signal. When we push both buttons, we may not be pressing them both at precisely the same time. If this happens, there is a fraction of a second where one of the buttons is not pressed and the light turns on.

The second reason is called "**button debounce**." This is a fun phrase that describes how a mechanical pushbutton like ours bounces up and down when it is pressed. This is similar to dropping a soccer ball: the ball bounces a few times before settling on the floor. In our pushbutton, this happens super fast, so typically we don't notice it. Electricity is much faster than our eyes, so when we build a logic gate like an XOR gate, some of this bouncing may cause the LED to light up because the circuit doesn't yet "see" both buttons pressed.

Additional fun fact: When you're measuring the input of a mechanical button press with a computer or microcontroller (like a Raspberry Pi or Arduino board), you need a slight delay to only detect one press at a time because of this debouncing effect!

TROUBLESHOOTING TIPS: XOR GATE

1. Check that the battery power switch is on and that the leads are in different power rails. Wiggle the wires to ensure they are making good electrical connection with the breadboard pins.

2. Check that you're using 10kΩ resistors.

3. If you're using multiple breadboards, check that all the power rails are connected to each other. Check that negative goes to negative and positive to positive.

    a. It may be helpful to grab an extra LED and check that each power rail has power by quickly inserting an LED.

4. Check that the LED orientation is correct (that its positive leg connects to the positive side of the circuit).

5. Check the transistor orientation. All diagrams are shown with the flat side of the transistor facing you.

6. Just in case, check that you're using only N-Channel MOSFET transistors (2N7000).

7.   For each pushbutton, check that one pushbutton pin connects to the positive power rail, and the other pin connects to the negative power rail (ground) via a resistor. Check that its output (right pin) connects to the transistor Gate pin.

8.   Go back to the diagram and double-check all the jumper wire connections one at a time. Trace from left to right, one wire at a time. (If you've already done this, it may help to start over.)

9.   Using the diagrams, double-check positive and negative power rail connections.

10.   Check that the jumper wires are fully inserted into the breadboard holes.

11.   Check that the jumper wires are in the proper breadboard rows for each component.

12.   Check for those rare faulty jumper wires by wiggling the wires or swapping out jumper wires.

13.   Check that the battery has energy by connecting it directly to an LED.

14.   Finally, it may help to check individual parts of the circuit to ensure they are functioning as expected. For example, connect the output of a NOT gate to the LED (or to another LED). You can do this for the second NOT gate, the pushbuttons, and the "AND" gates.

Aaand if it's still broken, it's totally okay to take a break and/or start over. This is a **hard** circuit! It makes sense if you're feeling frustrated or overwhelmed. Maybe try rebuilding it or talking it out. If you need more help, conscript a fellow human for emotional support and/or assistance. You can do this!!

XOR Schematic Symbol

The symbol of the XOR gate is an OR gate with an extra line like we see in
Figure 10-15:

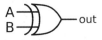

Figure 10-15. *XOR gate schematic symbol*

The way that I remember the functionality of an XOR gate is by saying,
"if one or the other but not both." Find a way that helps you remember!

NOT-ing the XOR

Logic gates being symmetric and all that goodness means that we can also
make an XNOR gate! The XNOR logic gate stands for "Exclusive NOT OR"
gate. This is a fancy phrase that means it is the opposite of the XOR gate:
the output is on only when both of the inputs are the same (weird and
fun, yay!).

Shown in Figure 10-16, the symbol of the XNOR gate is an XOR gate
with a little NOT gate symbol:

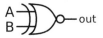

Figure 10-16. *XNOR schematic symbol*

The truth table for the XNOR gate looks like Table 10-4.

Table 10-4. *XNOR Gate Truth Table*

A	B	OUT
0	0	1
0	1	0
1	0	0
1	1	1

Don't worry, I won't ask you to build an XNOR gate! However, if you want to, you are 1000% encouraged to go for it!!

How to Build a (Simple) Computer

We almost have enough knowledge to build a simple computer! When I say a simple computer, I really mean an electronic device that can add numbers, just like the original human "computers" did in the early tech industry. At the end of the day, **an electronic computer is a binary electronics calculator**. That is to say, a computer counts and does operations using binary numbers, represented with 0s and 1s, or "on" and "off."

Our AND, OR, NOT, and XOR logic gates are a way to use binary numbers to represent information in the physical world. Transistor logic gates are special because we can cascade them indefinitely to build more complex logic gate functions, like our XOR gate. In other words, we can connect the inputs of one logic gate to the output of another.

This, my dear reader, is the actual, physical foundation of all modern computers! From the laptop that I am typing on to the smartphone where you take photos and search for the answers to all life's greatest mysteries (or sometimes to just play games because finding joy is also important). All of the circuits that make this possible boil down to four basic ingredients: AND, OR, NOT, and XOR logic gates made with (FET) transistors.

There are still a few missing pieces of information that we need to build a simple computer. Our old friends binary numbers reenter the stage for the finale!

Boolean Algebra and Binary Addition

The operations we can do with binary numbers are summarized with Boolean algebra. This is helpful for computers because digital circuits also only have two possibilities: on/off or, for ease of writing and doing mathematic calculations, 0/1.

We humans with our ten fingers are used to doing addition in base 10. We might as well make counting as easy as possible by using our fingers! Binary addition is like adding numbers if we were an alien species with only two fingers (one on each hand). In this situation, we can count the same amount using a different way to represent our numbers. Binary addition is also called base 2 counting, because we only have two numbers to represent our sums.

Compared to counting in decimal, counting from 1 to 15 in binary looks like Table 10-5.

Table 10-5. *Counting in Decimal and Binary Numbers*

Decimal (Base 10)	Binary (Base 2)
0	0
1	1
2	10
3	11
4	100
5	101
6	110
7	111
8	1000
8	1001
10	1010
11	1011
12	1100
13	1101
14	1110
15	1111

Binary numbers get very long very quick! Because of this, it's helpful to identify some traits. First, we use the term "**bit**" to talk about binary digits (BIT = BInary digiT). The farthest right number is called the **least significant bit (LSB)**. The farthest left number is called the **most significant bit** (**MSB**). For example, with the number **111**0, the LSB is 0 and the MSB is **1**.

349

Bit   An abbreviation for **bi**nary di**git**.

🤨 **Question 3:** What patterns do you notice about binary numbers?

Just as it's possible to convert between various units, like miles and kilometers, we can convert between decimal numbers, or base 10, and binary numbers, or base 2. Binary numbers are not exactly space efficient, but they are critical for a system where you can only store so many different types of information. This is what we're dealing with in digital electronics.

🤨 **Question 4:** Use the patterns you notice about binary numbers to convert decimal numbers 16 to 20 into binary numbers:

Table 10-6. *Decimal to binary conversion for numbers 16 - 20 (for completion)*

Decimal (Base 10)	Binary (Base 2)
16	
17	
18	
19	
20	

Counting by hand is all well and good, but how do we convert the decimal number 50, or 100, or 200 to binary? We need a faster method besides counting by hand.

Enter: Number conversion! Just like translating human languages, we can translate counting systems!

Translating Decimal Numbers into Binary (and Back Again)

The simplest way (but definitely not the fastest) to convert decimal numbers like 42 or 1077 into binary numbers is to continue dividing by 2. As you do this, you write down the remainder. **The remainders become the binary number**, with the first digit being the LSB (farthest right digit) and the last number being the MSB (farthest left digit).

Let's do a simple example using the number 14, covered in Table 10-7:

Table 10-7. *Example of converting decimal number 14 into binary*

1. Divide 14 by 2			
Result	7	Remainder	0 (LSB)
2. Divide 7 by 2			
Result	3	Remainder	1
3. Divide 3 by 2			
Result	1	Remainder	1
4. Divide 1 by 2			
Result	0	Remainder	1 (MSB)

We get that 14 is 1110 in binary!

😊 **Question 5:** How do you convert 21 into binary notation? Grab a piece of paper or fill out Table 10-8:

Table 10-8. *Converting decimal number 21 into binary notation (for completion)*

1. Divide 21 by 2	
Result	Remainder
2. Divide by 2	
Result	Remainder
3. Divide by 2	
Result	Remainder
4. Divide by 2	
Result	Remainder
5. Divide by 2	
Result	Remainder

You can check your answer by looking up "21 in binary" in your favorite search engine. ☺

There are multiple methods for converting a binary number into decimal. My personal preference is a technique called "positional notation." If you are not into this method, use a search engine to look up other conversion methods (or, honestly, you can find a lookup table that does it for you so... yea).

We'll use the binary number 11011001 as an example. **Positional notation** works like this:

1. Write down the binary number. Above it, write the powers of 2 from right to left so that they match up with the digits of the binary number, like we see in Table 10-9.

Table 10-9. *Using positional notation to convert binary numbers into decimal numbers (Step 1)*

Powers of 2	$2^7 = 128$	$2^6 = 64$	$2^5 = 32$	$2^4 = 16$	$2^3 = 8$	$2^2 = 4$	$2^1 = 2$	$2^0 = 1$
Binary Number	1	1	0	1	1	0	0	1

2. Multiply the binary number digit by the corresponding power of 2.

Table 10-10. *Using positional notation to convert binary numbers into decimal numbers (Step 2)*

Powers of 2	128	64	32	16	8	4	2	1
Binary Number	1	1	0	1	1	0	0	1
Multiplication Result	128	64	0	16	8	0	0	1

3. Add the resulting numbers up, and you've got your decimal number!

Table 10-11. *Using positional notation to convert binary numbers into decimal numbers (Step 3)*

Powers of 2	128	64	32	16	8	4	2	1
Binary Number	1	1	0	1	1	0	0	1
Multiplication Result	128	64	0	16	8	0	0	1
Add Digits	128 + 64 + 0 + 16 + 8 + 0 + 0 + 1 = 217							

Tada! Our binary number 1101101 translates to 217 in decimal. For longer binary numbers, continue calculating powers of 2 (e.g., $2^8 = 256$, $2^9 = 512$, $2^{10} = 1024$, etc.).

One More Thing: Adding Binary Numbers!

Counting and converting is all well and good, but we need math! Addition and subtraction with binary numbers is oodles of fun because it's new and different! Like most math, there are multiple ways of approaching binary addition (and subtraction). Again, I'll teach you my personal favorite, and you are welcome (and encouraged) to look up the other methods and find the one that most resonates with your brain.

Here we go!

We are adding binary numbers using **place value**. Here's how we do this using the numbers 11011001 and 110101:

1. **Write the binary numbers down so that the digits line up vertically.**

   If one binary number has more bits, add zeros to the left side of the number (i.e., to the left of the MSB). Our example would look like this, where the bolded zeros have been added to make both numbers the same length, like we see in Table 10-12:

Table 10-12. *Example of lining up bits and adding leading 0 bits to increase the length of a binary number*

1	1	0	1	1	0	0	1
0	0	1	1	0	1	0	1

2. **Sum the bits! Start from the LSB** (the far right).

   Since there are only two digits, the sum can be either 0, 1, or 2. If sum is 0 or 1, write the bit down in the appropriate digit column. If the sum is 2, this is the same as adding two numbers that equal 10: we write down a 0 and carry the 1 to the next column. Table 10-13 shows how to do this:

Table 10-13. *Summing binary digits*

Carried over	1	1	1	1			1	
Binary No. 1		1	1	0	1	1	0	0	1
Binary No. 2		0	0	1	1	0	1	0	1
Sum	1	0	0	0	0	1	1	1	0

Read the addition from right to left. Whenever we get a sum of 2, we put a 1 in the next left column and add that to both of the binary number columns.

I picked this example because it's a bit tricky – we end up with a longer number than we started with. (This also happens in decimal addition! And that is tricky at first, too.)

☺ **Question 6:** In Table 10-14, add the following binary numbers together: 0111 and 1011.

Table 10-14. Adding two binary numbers together (for completion)

Carried over				
Binary No. 1	0	1	1	1
Binary No. 2	1	0	1	1
Sum				

😊 **Question 7:** Another practice problem! In Table 10-15, add the following binary numbers together: 110010 and 11011.

Table 10-15. Adding two binary numbers together (for completion)

Carried over						
Binary No. 1	1	1	0	0	1	0
Binary No. 2	0	1	1	0	1	1
Sum						

😊 **Question 8:** One more! In Table 10-16, add the following binary numbers together:

Table 10-16. Adding two binary numbers together (for completion)

Carried over						
Binary No. 1	1	1	0	1	0	1	1
Binary No. 2	0	1	0	1	0	1	0
Sum						

If you want to check your answers, check this footnote[2] ☺ (and you can also look up binary calculators online!).

Hooray! You have math powers in an entirely new number system! But... Aren't we learning about computers? How does this apply to computers?!

How Does This Translate to Computers??

If you've dabbled in computer memory before, the term bits or the numbers 256 and 1024 may look familiar! All computers are digital electronics, which means that they use electrical signals that are binary, either on or off. We can represent digital signals with 1s and 0s because this makes it easier to do calculations.

Computer processors are made of transistors formed into logic gates. For the sake of simplicity, let's focus on computer memory. The function of memory is to store information. There are a few different physical ways to do this with electricity, like with magnetization (this is how a hard disk drive, or HDD, works). An electrical signal applies a current to the magnet to store 0s and 1s as tiny magnetic North or South. When we need to retrieve that information, we go back and measure the magnetization of each of those spots and can get back our 0s and 1s!

Okay, so far, so good. We can store binary number digits, or bits, using electricity and magnets. By grouping bits, we can get more complex data. The standard across the entire world is to store data in groups of 8 bits, which is called a **byte**. (Hilariously, a byte is made of two nibbles of 4 bits each – I swear, I cannot make this ish up! Humans can be delightfully silly sometimes.)

---

[2] Question 6: 10010 (if we end up with a decimal sum of 3, that means we have 1 + 2, so we pull down a bit of 1 and carry forward the 2 [which is 1 bit in the next column left]). Question 7: 1001101. Question 8: 10010101.

Byte   A group of 8 bits.

A byte of memory is used to store codes that represent different characters, like a decimal number, a letter, or a symbol like # or @. A byte (8 bits) can store as many as 256 codes! In the first computers, engineers and computer scientists were like, "Cool, 256 is good enough!" and came up with a translation code for the 10 decimal digits, 26 lowercase letters plus 26 uppercase letters, and some symbols (probably $ was in there because, you know, economics).

One of the most common translation codes that stuck around is called **ASCII**. This stands for American Standard Code for Information Interchange – a fancy name that means "this is how we translate human-readable language into computer-readable bits!" Figure 10-17 illustrates what the ASCII code looks like:

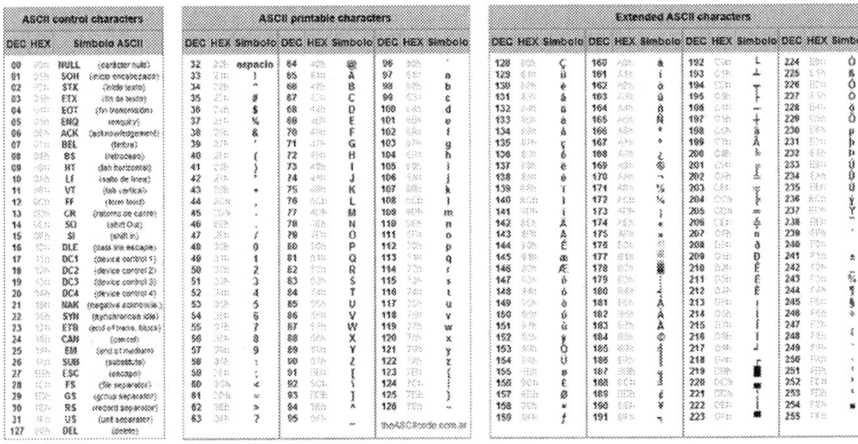

Figure 10-17.   *The ASCII code! Source: Wikimedia Commons*

Another code system is called Unicode – this is **way** larger than ASCII and allows for 1,112,064 different characters! It does this by using between 1 and 4 bytes (between 8 and 32 bits). This enables the beautiful spectrum of the world's languages to be translated, stored, and processed with computers, yay!

Coming back to computers as a whole: We use computers to extend our memories and also to amplify our processing capabilities. I **love** being lazy, and that means that I often use my computer to do calculations for me (most of the time, it's also a LOT faster). As we learned, we can do math calculations with binary numbers. We'll need to temporarily store the binary numbers like we did with memory and then add in some logic via circuits (oh heyyy you see where this is going) to do the math parts. Read on and let's build some logic gates!!

To summarize (because this was long and epically in depth): Human-readable language, numbers, and other symbols can be stored in digital computers by representing digital signals with binary digits, or bits. We can store more meaningful information using strings of bits called bytes (8 bits). We can also do math with bits just like we can with decimal numbers!

Bringing Bits Along for the Ride: Binary Adders!

Single-Bit Adder

Enough theory!!! Let's get to practical applications. How do we actually add (binary) numbers with logic gates?

Let's start with our new friend, the XOR gate. An XOR gate makes it WAY easier to build a binary adder because its truth table is very similar to how binary addition works. Table 10-17 shows the XOR gate truth table again now that you know about binary addition:

Table 10-17. *XOR Logic Gate Truth Table*

A	B	OUT
0	0	0
0	1	1
1	0	1
1	1	0

Oh hey! **Technically, you've already built a (very) simple computer: an XOR gate is an adder for single bits!**

So that's awesome.

Imagine we forgot how to add binary digits (understandable) or that we wanted to check our work (reasonable). We could use the XOR gate to help us by doing the following:

1. We send in the two bits[3] we want to check, for example, 0 + 1, using the two inputs, A and B.

   a. If we were using our pushbutton circuit, this would mean pressing one button and leaving the other one open.

2. If the answer is 1, the XOR gate output turns on the LED. If the answer is 0, the LED does not light up.

3. We can keep using the inputs to check different combinations of binary digits. The LED tells us what the answer is (on is an answer of 1; off is an answer of 0).

---

[3] I'll be using "binary digits" and "bits" interchangeably in this section. They mean the same thing, but sometimes using one can help comprehension (or at least, it does so for my brain, and I hope that it helps you, too).

4. But wait! What happens if we have 1 + 1 = 0 with
    a remainder of 1?? Our single LED will be off, and
    there's no indication that there's a remainder.
    Sad panda.

This last part is the limitation of our XOR gate in binary addition: our
XOR gate cannot handle remainders!

Well, foo. For a fully functional binary digit adder, we need a way of
keeping track of binary addition remainders. In other words, we need to
bring the remainders along for the (electric) current ride! Is there another
logic gate we could add to get a second LED that lights up if there is a
remainder? This logic gate would output 1 if and only if both inputs are 1.

🙂 **Question 9:** What logic gate could we use to carry
forward the remainder?

_____ !

Look at that, our trusty ol' friend the AND gate has just the output we
need! Connecting the AND gate to the XOR inputs lets us keep track of
remainders, like we see in Figure 10-18:

Figure 10-18. *Schematic diagram for connecting an XOR and an*
AND gate

Also, congratulations! You've exceeded the electronic circuit threshold
where experimenting/trial and error is waaay slower (and much harder
to get what we want) than theorizing. Before we build this (or honestly
instead of building this... for now ☺), let's work through the different

inputs and outputs to make sure the preceding circuit gives us what we want: binary digit addition that keeps track of remainders.

First, inputs of 0 and 0 (i.e., binary addition of 0 + 0) like we see in Figure 10-19:

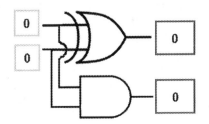

Figure 10-19. *Example input and output bits for the XOR and AND* gate combo

Okay! So far, so good: both the XOR gate and the AND gate output 0 if both inputs are 0. This means our bit sum is 0 and the remainder is 0.

What about 0 and 1? Let's check Figure 10-20:

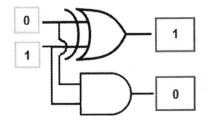

Figure 10-20. *Example input and output bits for the XOR and AND gate combo*

In this case, the XOR gate outputs 1 because one of its inputs is 1. The AND gate outputs 0 because... it's an AND gate and both inputs must be 1 for it to be 1! In this instance, the sum of the bits is 1 and the remainder is 0.

What about 1 and 0? (You do this one! Fill out Figure 10-21 below.)

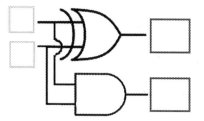

Figure 10-21. *Example input and output bits for the XOR and AND gate combo (for completion)*

And finally, inputs of 1 and 1 (do this one too by filling in Figure 10-22!!):

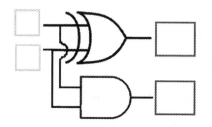

Figure 10-22. *Example input and output bits for the XOR and AND gate combo (for completion)*

Huzzah!! The XOR outputs 0 because both inputs are the same. The AND gate finally has its moment and outputs a 1 because both inputs are 1! This means we have a binary digit sum of 0 with a remainder of 1, which would give us the binary number of 10 (i.e., 2 in decimal numbers!).

We now have a complete circuit for (single) binary digit addition! And that means... drumroll!

We're ready to tackle building adders for longer binary numbers!!!

2-Bit Adder

Per usual, let's build our binary adder piece by piece: How do we take our XOR/AND gate combo and build a 2-bit adder?

We can figure this out by breaking down a 2-bit adder into **inputs and outputs**. How many bits do we need to send and how many bits do we need to receive?

2-bit numbers are two digits each, like 10 or 11. We need to add each column of bits together, like we see in Table 10-18:

Table 10-18. 2-Bit binary addition

Carried over	1		
Binary No. 1		1	0
Binary No. 2		1	1
Sum	1	0	1

😊 **Question 10:** How many **inputs** do we need for a 2-bit adder? _____

😊 **Question 11:** How many **outputs** do we need for a 2-bit adder? _____

Since we need to add two sets of binary digits together, we need to send in 4 bits! This means we need **four inputs**. For our 2-bit adder circuit, this looks like four pushbuttons as inputs into two XOR gates.

When we add 2-bit numbers together, we either get a result that's the same size (2 bits) or we get an answer that's one bit longer (literally 1 bit longer: 3 bits!). This means we need **three outputs**: this circuit has three LEDs! (Yesss, more lights!)

Next, let's think about remainders!

😵 **Question 12:** How many remainders do we need to bring along? _____

I like to think in terms of scenarios. For the first input, there is one scenario where we need a remainder: when both inputs are 1. This means our first input needs an AND gate to carry this remainder forward! The second input also has one scenario where we need a remainder (again, where both inputs are 1). Another AND gate for the second input!

To recap, we need two of the single-bit adder circuits, like we see in Figure 10-23:

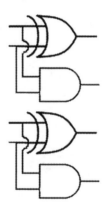

Figure 10-23. *Two single-bit binary adders*

😵 **Question 13:** If we were to just use these two pieces as is, what works for what we've figured out so far for our 2-bit adder? What does not work?

Let's work through this. What's working so far:

- With two sets of the XOR/AND gate combo, we now have four inputs for the binary digits (the first pair of bits goes into the first XOR/AND gate combo; the second pair of bits goes into the second XOR/AND gate combo).

- Each piece on its own gives us a correct answer for binary digit addition.

- The first XOR gate is sufficient to give us the correct result for the first set of binary digits. This is our first output for a 2-bit adder!

Hooray! We are completing the 2-bit adder puzzle!

Buuuut what's also apparent is that there are four outputs... one more output than we need. There's also currently no way to carry the first remainder forward. This remainder gets lost and forgotten. So sad! Like a younger sibling, we need a way to honor our remainder and bring it along!

To carry the remainder forward, we connect the first AND gate output and the second XOR gate output together (Figure 10-24).

🫤 **Question 14:** What happens if we connect the first AND gate directly to the second XOR gate? How would LEDs connected to each output behave?

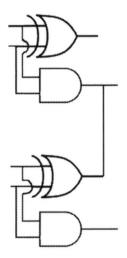

Figure 10-24. *Connecting two single-bit binary adders (Step 1)*

If only our adder circuit were this simple! If we connect our AND and XOR gate outputs together, we lose the information outputted by both logic gates. For example, if there is no current flowing out of the XOR gate (i.e., a bit of 0) and there is current flowing out of the AND gate (i.e., a bit of 1), the combined output will have current flowing through it (i.e., a bit of 1). The problem is that we have no way of knowing which gate caused the current flow (which we interpret as a bit of 1). (The same problem happens if both gates output current (i.e., both bits are 1) because our output will be a current (i.e., a bit of 1). This is not a correct result for binary digit addition.)

To put it another way: If we connect an LED to the second output and it lights up, we don't know **why** it lit up. This fails to achieve our quest to build a 2-bit binary adder!

But we are smart and determined, and we keep on questing! To help us, **we need some more logic (gates)**. Before I give you the answer, use your knowledge of logic gates to think through how you could do this!

> 😊 **Question 15:** What logic gate do we need to connect the first AND gate and the second XOR gate?
>
> *Hint: What logic gate gives us the correct answer for binary digit addition?*

Quest onward! Now that you combined your new knowledge with your existing brain power, let's walk through our next connection.

To carry forward the remainder from the first binary digit addition, we connect the first AND gate output and the second XOR gate output into another XOR gate! We can see this in Figure 10-25:

Are we done??

You decide!

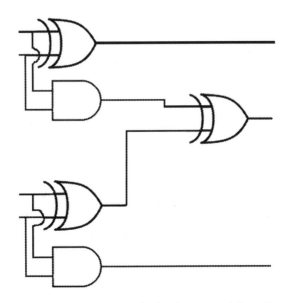

Figure 10-25. *Connecting two single-bit binary adders (Step 2)*

😕 **Question 16:** Test the 2-bit adder circuit! Use
Figure 10-26 below to see how it handles adding the
following binary numbers: 01 and 10, 10 and 11, and
11 and 01. (Test other combinations, too!!)

*If you're still getting comfy with binary addition, I
recommend writing the numbers vertically so that the
digits line up in columns. This will make it easier to
see what to input into the XOR gates!*

What we discover when we test our 2-bit adder is that it works as
expected for adding 01 and 10: 011 (if we had LEDs connected to these
outputs, we would see the first two LEDs light up). It also gives us the
correct answer for adding 10 and 11: 101 (the first and third LEDs would
light up).

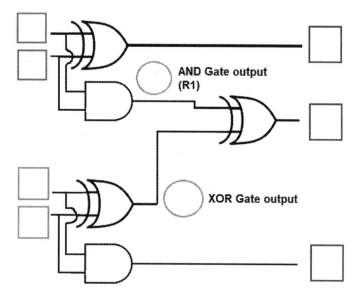

Figure 10-26. *Analyzing inputs and outputs of a two-bit adder circuit*

But when we add 11 and 01, we get an answer of 000! None of our LEDs lights up. Figure 10-27 shows what our test circuit looks like for this scenario (for those of you who may be reading/perusing quickly, I included a red X so it's more obvious that it doesn't work):

Well, foo again! We're so close but aren't quite there yet.

😵 **Question 17:** Why did this 2-bit adder fail? Where did we lose information?

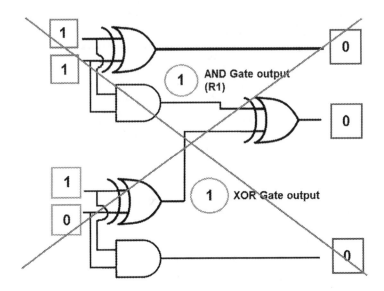

Figure 10-27. *Incorrect two-bit binary adder circuit*

The scenario that our current 2-bit adder fails is when the first AND gate and the second XOR gate outputs are both 1. This sounds like another challenge for our trusty friend the AND gate!

This means that we need **another** XOR/AND gate combo for our second output, like we see in Figure 10-28:

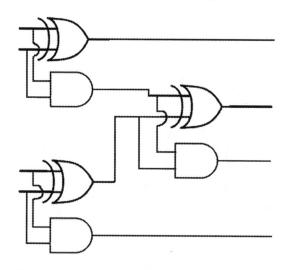

Figure 10-28. *Re-doing the two-bit binary adder*

... but now we have four outputs again?! Gahhh. What do we do??

🙂 **Question 18:** How can we combine the AND gate outputs without losing any information??

Hint: Think through some scenarios. Are there any scenarios where the second and third AND gates would both be 1?

The final piece of a 2-bit adder puzzle is... (drumroll please!) An OR gate!! Figure 10-29 shows what the schematic looks like:

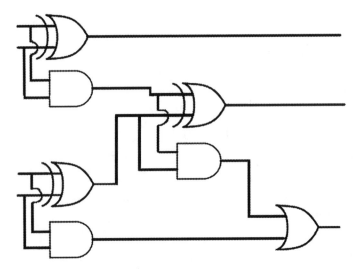

Figure 10-29. *Full schematic for a two-bit binary adder!*

Huzzah!! We did it! We achieved our quest to build a 2-bit adder with (transistor) logic gates!!

Because we are diligent engineers, let's test our 2-bit adder to make sure that it works as expected.

I'll do one example for you, and then you get to test the rest because I want you to learn to apply your knowledge and check the work of your teachers! (Even educators make mistakes. ☺)

Figure 10-30 demonstrates how our adder behaves when we add the numbers 11 and 01 (the combo that our first circuit didn't work for):

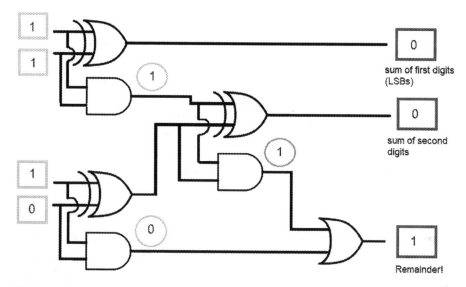

Figure 10-30. *Mapping inputs to outputs for our two-bit binary adder*

Your turn!

😳 **Question 19:** Use Figure 10-31 to test how the circuit adds the following binary numbers: 01 and 10, 10 and 01, 01 and 11, 10 and 11, and 11 and 11.

Note: If you want to check the 2-bit adder output and you're still unsure if your binary addition is correct, use a binary calculator online! (Search for "binary calculator" in your favorite search engine.)

373

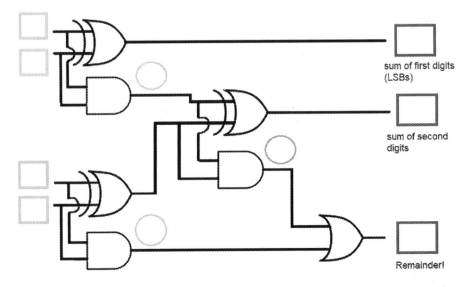

sum of first digits
(LSBs)

sum of second
digits

Remainder!

Figure 10-31. *Mapping inputs to outputs for the two-bit binary adder (for completion)*

It works as expected!! Holy stars, that's a LOT of logic gates just to add two 2-digit binary numbers! This is a hilariously challenging circuit to build with transistors because we need 6 transistors per XOR gate, 2 transistors per AND gate, and 2 transistors for the OR gate. That's (counts on fingers) **26 transistors!!** (This is a laugh-cry project for me. Yes, I've done it. It's satisfying and, inevitably, frustrating.)

I wholeheartedly encourage you to build the 2-bit adder with (N-Channel MOSFET) transistors if you're inspired. That said, a circuit with 26 transistors is a hilarious number of connections to keep track of, so I will not ask that you build this circuit. What I DO want you to build is the XOR/AND gate combo! Then you can decide if you want to build two more of those, connect them together, and add an OR gate.

Besides, these kinds of quests are best tackled in a group. Wrangle some friends and ask each of them to build an XOR/AND gate combo. Then connect those pieces, build an OR gate, and wire up the LEDs! Much easier and faster (and way more fun) than doing this on your own. Yay for friends!

Onward to your final project!!

Adding It All Together: Single-Digit Binary Adder!

Grab These Materials

- 3 half-size breadboards

- Coin cell in battery case

- 34 jumper wires

- 8 N-Channel transistors

- 2 pushbuttons

- 5 10kΩ resistors

- 1 100Ω resistor

- 2 LEDs

For this project, start with the XOR gate that we built earlier in this chapter. If that feels like eons ago, Figure 10-32 gives you the wiring diagram for our XOR gate:

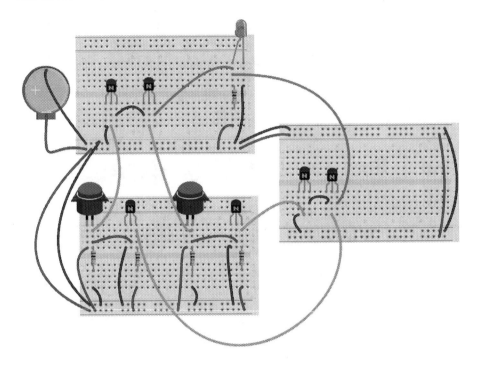

Figure 10-32. *Circuit diagram for an XOR Gate*

I chose to build the AND gate on the far-right breadboard. You can organize your single-digit adder however it makes sense to you. You may even choose to use a fourth breadboard for the AND gate if you have a spare!

Whatever way you choose to organize your circuit, build the same AND logic gate that you made in Chapter 9. Connect the AND gate output to the second LED.

Try this on your own for at least 15 minutes. This is the final project, so try to build as much of it on your own as possible! (You are totally capable!!) If, or when, you need help, the full build diagram is given below in Figure 10-33.

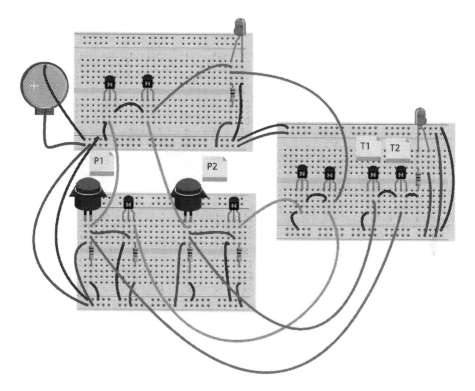

Figure 10-33. *Circuit diagram for a full single-bit binary adder with remainders*

Written Instructions

Starting from the XOR gate

1. Insert the two additional transistors into the far-right breadboard so that the flat side is facing you. These are labeled "T1" and "T2."

2. Insert the second LED above these transistors.

3. Connect a jumper wire between the positive power rail and the (positive) LED leg.

377

4. Connect the **100Ω resistor** between the negative LED leg and an open row on the breadboard.

5. Connect the left pushbutton (P1) to T1's Gate pin.

6. Connect the right pushbutton (P2) to T2's Gate pin.

7. Connect a jumper wire between ground (negative power rail) and T1's Source pin (left pin).

8. Connect a jumper wire between T1's Drain pin (right pin) to T2's Source pin.

9. Connect a jumper wire between T2's Drain pin and the second LED's resistor.

Test your single-bit adder!! The XOR gate LED should light up when either of the pushbuttons are pressed and off when both pushbuttons are pressed (a brief LED flicker is okay and expected). The AND gate LED should light up only when both pushbuttons are pressed – this LED represents the remainder of our single-bit addition!

As a reminder, an LED that's on represents a binary digit of 1, and an LED that's off represents a binary digit of 0 (assuming your battery is turned on and has power... ☺).

(Circuit not working as expected? It's okay; it happens to me all the time. Check the troubleshooting tips at the end of this section.)

TROUBLESHOOTING TIPS: SINGLE-BIT ADDER

These tips are specific to adding on the AND gate to an existing (functional) XOR gate. If your XOR gate isn't behaving as expected, walk through the troubleshooting tips for that circuit.

1. Check that the battery power switch is on and that the leads are in different power rails. Wiggle the wires to ensure they are making good electrical connection with the breadboard pins.

2. Check that you're using 10kΩ resistors for the transistors.

3. Check that you're using a 100Ω resistor for the second LED.

4. The second LED may be dim and hard to see. Turn off ambient lighting and test your circuit again. I'd also highly recommend using red LEDs because they need the least amount of power.

5. Check that all of the breadboard power rails are connected together – positive to positive and negative to negative.

6. Check the orientation of the transistors. The flat side should be facing you.

7. Check the orientation of the LED. Make sure that the positive lead is connected to the positive power rail.

8. Check that the Gate pins of the AND gate transistors are connected to the pushbutton outputs.

9. Go back to the diagram and double-check all the jumper wire connections one at a time. Trace from left to right, one wire at a time.

10. Check that the jumper wires are fully inserted into the breadboard holes.

11. Check that the jumper wires are in the proper breadboard rows for each component.

12. Check for those rare faulty jumper wires by wiggling the wires or swapping out jumper wires.

13. Finally, check that the battery has energy by connecting it directly to an LED.

If your final project is failing to cooperate, take a breather. Maybe try rebuilding it or talking it out with yourself (for real, this helps!) or another person. If you need more help, snag another human and go through the wiring together.

Where Do We Go from Here?

Holy stars, you did it!! You built a simple computer! That is so awesome. Now what?!

There's no "official" schematic symbol for a single bitwise adder (i.e., the circuit we made that adds two binary digits together). This is because we are getting into computer chip territory. Computer chips, also called integrated circuits, or ICs, have their own special schematic symbols. (These computer chips are the black squares often covered with black blobs you discovered in the take apart bonus chapter!)

Let's learn more about ICs!

I Hear You and I See (IC) You: An Easier and Faster Way to Build "Smart" Circuits

It would be hilariously tedious and difficult to build computers and other complex electronics if we always had to start with transistors. At some point, a lazy human was like, "Um, can we just package logic gates together and start with those instead of transistors?!"

And the answer is yes! Introducing integrated circuits (ICs), dun dun dun!!!

Figure 10-34. *An integrated circuit (IC)! Source: Wikimedia Commons*

An **integrated circuit (Figure 10-34)** is made of one or more circuits on a tiny, flat piece of semiconductor material (a chip!). Most ICs are made of super tiny MOSFETs wired into logic gates. For example, you can purchase an IC with multiple XOR gates inside, like the Texas Instruments' SN74HCS86 IC which has four (yes, 4!!) XOR gates in one package. You'll never need six transistors to build an XOR gate again!

There are specialized ICs to perform all sorts of computations, from binary calculators to timer circuits to counters and beyond! There are also ICs for tons of common applications, like controlling motors, reading sensors, and connecting to WiFi. Figure 10-35 below gives you a peek inside one type of IC used for memory.

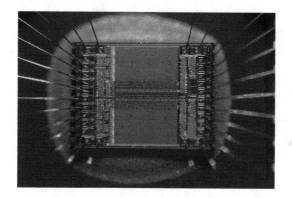

Figure 10-35. *Inside an integrated circuit (IC) from an EPROM memory microchip. Source: Zephyrus from Wikimedia Commons*

... So why did I make you build an XOR gate and a binary adder with transistors?!

Because knowledge. ☺

Computers can seem like a daunting mystery because they are made of many different parts and can do many complex tasks. By having you build (up to) a simple adder, you now understand the fundamental building blocks of computers. This is great for sharing knowledge with others (yay computer facts!), understanding computer vocabulary (e.g., bits, bytes, and chips) and concepts (e.g., 256 ASCII symbols or programming terms like "if-then," "and," "or," "not," etc.), and knowing how to connect and debug new components and circuits. Plus, if you're feeling ambitious or stoked on electronics, knowing how the first computers were built can help you design new types of devices using electricity!

Going Further: Logic Gate Circuits and Beyond!

It is with bittersweet fondness that I present to you this last "Going Further" section. There are so many things to explore that I can't include them all, but I'll give you some recommendations based on what I have discovered from my adventures in teaching these subjects to folks of all ages.

Further Exploration with Logic Gates!

Here are some of my suggestions for extending your knowledge of logic gates and binary numbers:

1. **Project 1: XNOR gate**

   Using your knowledge of NOT and XOR gates, build an XNOR gate!

2. **Project 2: Design a 3-bit adder! Then a 4-bit adder! Maybe even a 5-bit adder!!**

   Use your knowledge of the 2-bit adder circuit to design (i.e., draw out) a 3-bit adder circuit! Here are some hints to get you started:

- A 3-bit adder circuit needs three inputs and four outputs.

- Start with three of the XOR/AND gate combo circuits (our bitwise adder).

- Build a 2-bit adder between the first and second bitwise adders.

- The output of the 2-bit adder OR gate handles the remainder of the 2-bit adder. This needs to be carried forward to the third and final binary digit addition (i.e., the XOR gate output in our third bitwise adder).

- Remember to carry forward the other remainders!

When you've designed your 3-bit adder, check your work by testing out all possible combinations of adding 3-bit binary numbers!

If you want to check your work, there's a schematic at the very end of this chapter.

3. **Project 3: Cascade logic gates in different ways!**

In what other ways can you combine logic gates? How can you increase the number of inputs with the same number of outputs or vice versa?

How might you use logic gates to add "intelligence" to circuits from earlier in this book?

4. **Project 4: Explore other types of transistor and logic gate circuits!**

It's possible to build TONS of useful circuits like a touch switch, audio mixer or amplifier, and light flasher (or alarm) by combining transistors and/or logic gates with other components like resistors and capacitors. Look up "transistor circuits" in your favorite search engine or poke around on your own (or with a friend)!

Other types of circuits to look up: Timer, flip-flop, dual LED flasher, tone generator, radio transmitter, bounceless switch, frequency generator, and theremin.

5. **Project 5: Take apart IC exploration!**

   For your next take apart exploration, search for ICs and look up their part numbers online. See if you can find a datasheet to figure out what it does and what the pins do (or take in). Use your multimeter to measure the voltage, resistance, and polarity of the tiny pins.

   Note: If you're careful and the electronic device does not have any large capacitors, it may be useful to reinstall the batteries while you explore the IC with your multimeter.

6. ***Project 6: Minecraft: Build a computer!***

   If you play *Minecraft*, use your knowledge of binary numbers, binary math, and logic gates to build a 2-bit adder!

Beyond Logic Gates!

The next logical step (it's still my book, and I will make terrible puns at every possible chance) is to start exploring ICs and/or to learn how to use a beginner-friendly microcontroller like an Arduino board or an Adafruit board.

If you choose to explore with microcontrollers, here are some of my favorites:

1. **Adafruit Circuit Playground Express (CPX)**: You can program this board with block-based coding using Microsoft MakeCode (`www.makecode.org`). It comes with all sorts of fun onboard inputs, like buttons and touch-sensitive pads, and outputs, like color-changing LEDs and a buzzer!

2. **Arduino Uno**: This is the de facto beginner breadboard. It's a great choice for beginners because there are lots of protection circuits which make it difficult to break the board. While there are no onboard inputs, it does have one built-in LED for testing or status/alerts. This board is programmed using the free Arduino IDE in a language that resembles C/C++.

   a. Note: There are TONS of free online resources both from Arduino (the company) and from folks passionate about making things with electronics. Some of my favorite websites to find projects are Instructables, Hackster IO, and Adafruit Learn.

3. **BBC micro:bit**: Another board that can be programmed with block-based code via Microsoft MakeCode. This is similar to the Adafruit CPX in that it has lots of onboard inputs, like buttons and touch-sensitive pads, and outputs like an LED matrix and Bluetooth signals.

We've come to the end of the content in this book! What was something that delighted you? What was something that frustrated you? What are you newly curious about?

There are lots of great books on electronics that you are now ready for! Some of my favorites include any and everything from Forrest M. Mims III, Code by Charles Petzold, and Make magazine projects. And finally, for those curious about how more complex adders work, Figure 10-36 illustrates how to build a 3-bit adder:

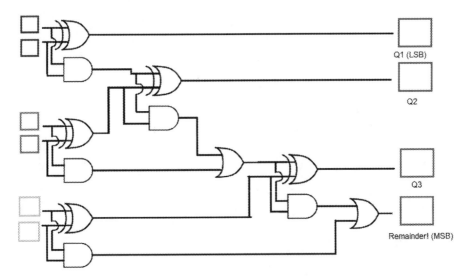

Figure 10-36. *Circuit design for a 3-bit adder!*

Summary

Congratulations!!! You read through and built all the projects in this book! Even if you didn't get *every* project to work as expected, I'm proud of your effort and determination in getting this far. I hope you are proud of yourself, too!

In our final chapter, we learned how to connect multiple logic gates together using N-Channel MOSFETs. We built an XOR gate which means you've officially built an advanced circuit![4] We took a deep dive into binary

---

[4]Who gets to decide that a transistor XOR gate is an advanced circuit? Me! At least in this book.

numbers. Our exploration of binary numbers included learning how to count with binary numbers, add binary numbers, and using electricity to represent these calculations (by using a bit of 0 to represent no current and a bit of 1 to represent current).

With this knowledge of binary numbers in our heads, we culminated our exploration of circuit components with an XOR gate, using that to piece together a 2-bit adder, and finally by actually building a single-bit adder! We wrapped up our learnings with a quick introduction to integrated circuits, or ICs (a.k.a. why you never have to build a logic gate again if you don't want to).

My goal in having you build an XOR gate and, ideally, a bitwise adder (XOR/AND gate combo) was to give you direct experience building a small piece of a computer. I did this because I wanted to show you that you are capable of (1) understanding computers, (2) learning how to wield the power of electricity with circuits and computers, and (3) building electronic projects that you are passionate about.

I hope you found joy and delight as you went through this book. I also hope that you're inspired to keep learning and exploring!!

Thank you so much for going on this electronic journey with me. I'd love to hear from you about what worked well, what could be improved, and what you were most excited to learn and build!

You can find me on most of the social media (Instagram, YouTube, TikTok, LinkedIn): @jenfoxbot.

Applied Project 1: Using a Multimeter!

In this chapter, we learn how to use a multimeter, an invaluable tool in electronics for measuring all sorts of information about our circuit, including voltage, current, and resistance.

What Is a Multimeter?

Grab These Materials

- 9V battery

- Coin cell battery

- 1 LED

- 2 alligator clips

Overview

Checking your car battery life, debugging circuits, and finding that pesky short are all super useful functions that can be done with just one awesome tool: the multimeter! Some different types of multimeters, both digital and analog, are shown in Figure A1-1.

© Jennifer Fox 2023

J. Fox, *Beginning Breadboarding*, https://doi.org/10.1007/978-1-4842-9218-1

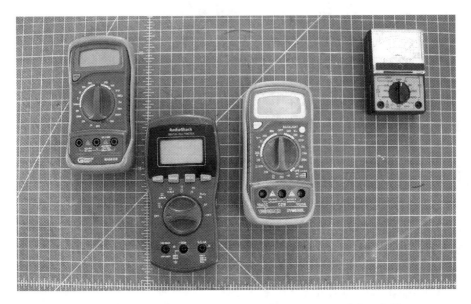

Figure A1-1. *Multimeters abound! Here are some of the different multimeter choices*

First of all, what the heck is a multimeter?? Excellent setup question, dear reader! It's a handheld device with a bunch of different electrical meters – hence, multimeter!

Measuring voltage, current, resistance, and continuity (a.k.a. electrical connection) is the most common use of a multimeter. Read on (and/or check out the videos) to learn what this means, how to do it yourself, and how to choose your very own multimeter!

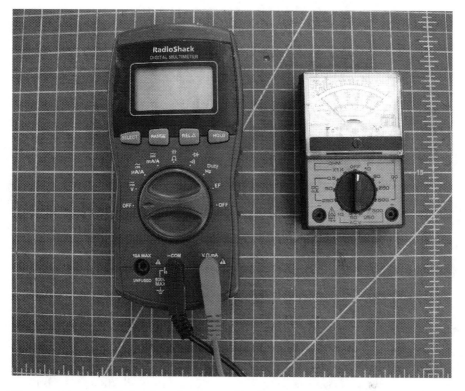

Figure A1-2. *A digital multimeter (left) and an analog multimeter (right)*

There are a few key differences between multimeters, the main one being analog vs. digital. In Figure A1-2, an analog multimeter is pictured on the right and a digital multimeter on the left.

Analog multimeters show real-time changes in voltage and current, but can be difficult to read and log data.

Digital multimeters are easier to read, but may take some time to stabilize.

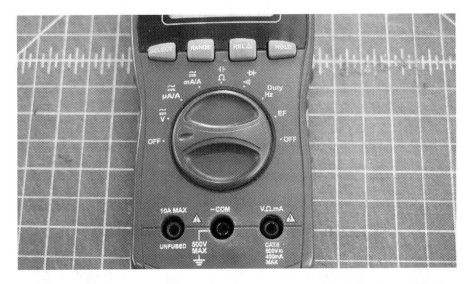

Figure A1-3. *An autoranging multimeter with separate ports for current and voltage measurement*

There are also **autoranging multimeters**, like shown in Figure A1-3, that automatically detect the measurement range and **manual ranging multimeters** where you have to choose a range yourself (or start with the highest setting and work down).

Other than those two main differences, **you'll want a multimeter that has separate ports for current and voltage measurements** (this is a safety issue, both for the meter and for yourself).

Next comes the fun part: **features**! All multimeters have voltage and current meters (otherwise, they'd just be called voltmeters and ammeters!), and most also measure resistance. There are a variety of other "extra" features depending on the manufacturer and cost (e.g., continuity, capacitance, frequency, etc.).

Second to lastly, there are a ton of different types of **probe leads**, including alligator clips, IC hooks, and test probes. Can't decide? Here's a kit that has four different types!

Lastly, **always check the multimeter maximum voltage and current ratings** to be sure that it can handle what you want to use it for.

Measuring Voltage

An example of setting up your multimeter to measure voltage is shown in
Figure A1-4.

Figure A1-4. How to set up the probes and dial selection to measure
voltage on a digital, autoranging multimeter

A voltage measurement tells us about the electrical potential **across** a
particular component.

Voltage is basically the "oomph" in our circuit, so we want to avoid drawing any power from the circuit when we take a voltage measurement. This means we need to **measure voltage in parallel** with a particular component using infinite (or really, really high) resistance. Figure A1-5 shows a mock-up of where to place the multimeter probes in a circuit to measure voltage across an LED.

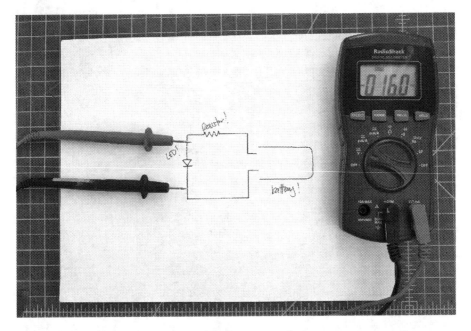

Figure A1-5. *Placement of multimeter probes to measure voltage*

How to use a multimeter to measure voltage across a component (or battery):

1) The black multimeter probe goes into the COM port and the red probe into the port marked with a "V."

2) Switch the dial to the "voltage" setting (choose the highest setting if you have a manual ranging multimeter).

3) Place the black probe on the negative side of the component and the red probe on the positive side (across or in parallel with the component). If you get a negative reading, switch the leads (or just note the magnitude of the voltage reading).

Read the meter output and you're done! Not too bad. ☺

Project A1-1: Measure Battery Voltage!

Your turn! **Measure the voltage of the 9V and coin cell batteries.**

Set up the multimeter as shown earlier. Place the probes on the metal terminals on the 9V battery. Record the reading as follows.

Next, place the multimeter probes on either side of the coin cell battery. Record the reading as follows. Remember to include units! (Voltage is measured in Volts; read the multimeter to see if it's mV or V.)

9V Battery Voltage: _____

Coin Cell Battery Voltage: _____

Are these what you expected?

More to explore: Measure the battery voltage of a battery that's inside a remote or flashlight. What do you notice? If you have one handy, measure the battery voltage of a dead battery. Again, what do you notice? Look up any mysteries you discover!

Measuring Current

Setting up a digital multimeter to measure current is pictured in Figure A1-6.

Figure A1-6. *How to set up the probes and dial selection to measure current on a digital, autoranging multimeter*

Taking a current measurement tells us the amount of electricity flowing **through** a given component or part of a circuit.

To measure current, we want to measure all of the electrons flowing in our circuit. This means we **measure current in series** with a component using zero (or negligible) resistance. Figure A1-7 shows how to use the multimeter probes to measure current in a circuit (our circuit is "pretend" to more clearly show how to do this).

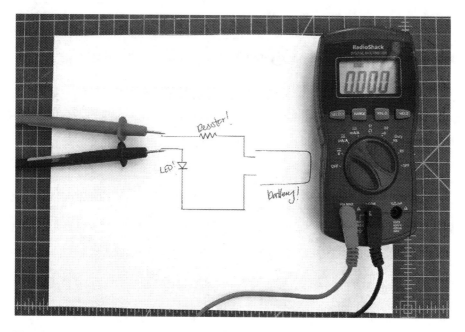

Figure A1-7. *How to place multimeter probes to measure current*

How to use a multimeter to measure current through a component:

1. The black multimeter probe goes into the COM port and the red probe into the port marked with an "I" or an "A" (or "Amp").

2. Switch dial to the current setting (choose the highest setting if you have a manual ranging multimeter).

3. Connect the red probe to the current source and the black probe to the input of the component, so that the current flows from the source, through the meter, to the component (in series with the component).

Read the meter output! If you're not getting a reading, switch to a lower setting.

Measuring Resistance

We can also use our multimeter to measure resistance! Figure A1-8 shows how to set up a digital multimeter to measure resistance of a component in a circuit.

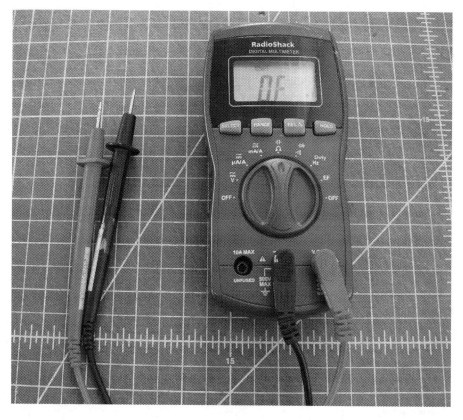

Figure A1-8. *How to set up the probes and dial selection to measure resistance on a digital, autoranging multimeter*

Measuring resistance, which is how much an object resists the flow of electricity, is like measuring voltage. The biggest difference is that you must disconnect the component from the circuit (otherwise, the other circuit components interfere with your measurement). Check out Figure A1-9 to see an example of where to place the multimeter probes to measure the resistance of a component.

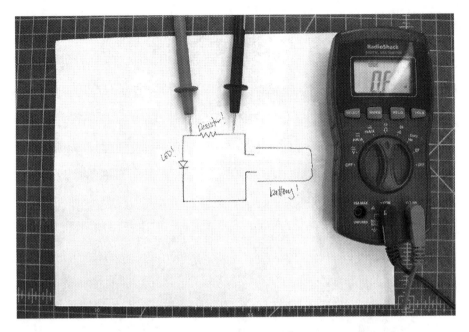

Figure A1-9. *How to place multimeter probes to measure the resistance of a circuit component*

How to use the multimeter to measure the resistance of a component:

1. Put the black probe in the COM port and the red probe in the port marked with a "Ω" or "Ohm" – it should be the same port as the voltage port.

2. Switch dial to the setting marked with a "Ω" (may have to choose an approximate range for manual ranging multimeter).

3. Place probes on either side of the component (orientation doesn't matter).

Read the meter output, and you have conquered resistance!

Project A1-2: Measure the Resistance of Your Skin!

All objects and materials have some resistance to the flow of electricity, including our skin! It's one of the many ways our body keeps us safe. Let's find out how much our skin resists the flow of electricity!

Set up the multimeter as shown earlier. Place the probes about an inch (2cm) apart on your skin. Record the reading as follows.

Explore what happens when you change the distance between the probes. Record the readings as follows. Remember to include units! (Resistance is measured in Ohms, or Ω. Read the multimeter screen to see if it's MΩ, kΩ, mΩ, etc.

Skin Resistance 1: _____

Skin Resistance 2: _____

Skin Resistance 3: _____

Are these what you expected?

More to explore: What other objects are you curious about? Measure the resistance of various things around your house, car, work, and outside! Look for objects made of different kinds of materials and include some metal objects in your exploration. Do you discover anything surprising?

Measuring Continuity!

The continuity measurement checks if two points in a circuit are electrically connected, otherwise known as a conductance test. **Before measuring continuity, be sure that the circuit power is OFF.** Figure A1-10 shows how to set a (digital) multimeter to measure continuity.

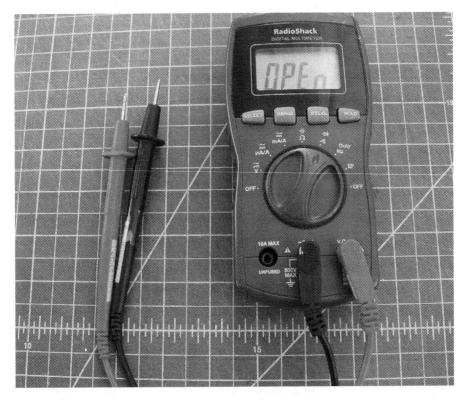

Figure A1-10. *How to set up the probes and dial selection to measure continuity on a digital, autoranging multimeter*

When the probes are electrically connected, there will be an audible "Beep!" and the multimeter screen will indicate a short, like shown in Figure A1-11.

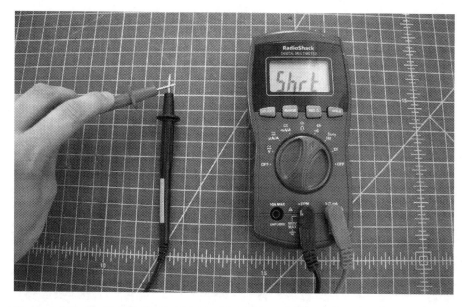

Figure A1-11. *Multimeter detecting an electrical short*

Measuring continuity is similar to measuring current. Set up the multimeter probes like pictured in Figure A1-12.

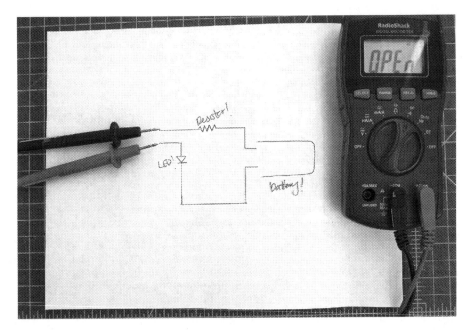

Figure A1-12. *How to place multimeter probes to measure an electrical short in a circuit*

How to use the multimeter to measure continuity:

1. Place the black probe in the COM port and the red probe in the voltage port.

2. Switch dial to the setting marked with an audio symbol.

3. Place probes at points you want to check – if the meter makes a beep sound, it means the two points are connected.

La fin!

Project A1-3: Does It Conduct?

A quick way to figure out if a material conducts electricity is to use the continuity setting on your multimeter. Let's explore some everyday materials and discover if we could use them in our circuits!

Set up the multimeter as shown earlier. Gather some (or all) of the following materials (or walk around and measure them where they live in your house... probably the junk drawer): pencil, paper, spoon, water bottle, thermos, water (in a cup), pencil lead, rubber band, paperclip, cardboard.

Measure the continuity of the object by placing the multimeter probes about 1 inch (2cm) apart on the object. Make sure the probes are not directly touching. Record your findings as follows, including what the object is (no need for units this time).

Does it conduct?

Object 1: _____Does it conduct (circle one)?   Yes / No

Object 2: _____Does it conduct (circle one)?   Yes / No

Object 3: _____Does it conduct (circle one)?   Yes / No

Object 4: _____Does it conduct (circle one)?   Yes / No

Object 5: _____Does it conduct (circle one)?   Yes / No

Object 6: _____Does it conduct (circle one)?   Yes / No

Object 7: _____Does it conduct (circle one)?   Yes / No

Object 8: _____Does it conduct (circle one)?   Yes / No

Object 9: _____Does it conduct (circle one)?   Yes / No

Object 10: _____Does it conduct (circle one)?   Yes / No

What surprised you the most?

More to explore: What patterns do you notice? What other objects could you measure to test those patterns?

Summary

This first applied project chapter employed your skills as a citizen science to teach you how to use a multimeter. We conducted experiments to measure current, voltage, resistance, and continuity to learn how to use the tool and to better understand the behavior of electricity. I encourage you to apply what you've learned and done in this chapter to your circuits going forward! My multimeter has helped me troubleshoot circuits that don't work as expected more times than I can count. You can also use your multimeter to troubleshoot broken electronics at home!

In the next applied project chapter, we will learn about the super handy circuit building tool that this book is named for: breadboards!

APPENDIX 2

Applied Project 2: Ohm's Law!

In this chapter, we will take a different look at electricity using the beautiful language of mathematics! This chapter is optional, so if you're nervous or uninterested, you can skip it and still be okay with the rest of the content in this book.

BUT!!

I would highly recommend challenging yourself to work through this chapter because (1) it's not graded and no one will judge your performance (there are only positive learning opportunities here, and you are 100% capable), and (2) it will expand and deepen your understanding of this weird and wild phenomenon called electricity. This knowledge gives you skills to solve problems and build cooler projects more easily.

Some pretty great reasons to learn about Ohm's Law. ☺

Ohm's Law: How to Math Electricity!

First, what is Ohm's Law?? Ohm's Law is an equation, or a math sentence, that shows us how current, voltage, and resistance are related.

© Jennifer Fox 2023
J. Fox, *Beginning Breadboarding*, https://doi.org/10.1007/978-1-4842-9218-1

If we were to read the equation (because math is just a language), we would read that **the current flowing[1] from one point to another is directly proportional to the voltage across those two points. The scaling factor, or the constant of proportionality, is the resistance between those two points.** (It's okay if you need to read those last two sentences a few times for it to sink in.)

Since equations sum up words way more succinctly (like pictures!), Eqn. A2-1 shows the relationship expressed in handy math symbols:

$$V = I \times R \hspace{3cm} \textit{Eqn. A2-1}$$

where *V* is the voltage across the component (in Volts), *I* is the current through the component (in Amps), and *R* is the resistance of the component (in Ω). If there are prefixes like kilo, milli, etc., on the units that you're using, be sure to convert them into regular ol' units, for example, convert 1mA into 0.001A.

Let's consider a specific example. If we have a circuit with a resistor, the current flowing through a resistor is proportional to the voltage across the resistor leads. If we were to divide the voltage across the resistor legs by the current, we would calculate the resistance of the resistor!

Alternatively, if we wanted to calculate the current through the resistor but we didn't have our handy-dandy multimeter, we could use Ohm's Law! This is because we will usually know the voltage of a battery and the resistance of the resistor in our circuit, so we can plug that into Ohm's Law and solve for current, like this:

If R = 100Ω and V = 3V, then

1. I = V / R

2. I = 3V / 100Ω

3. I = 0.03A (or 30mA)

---

[1] More specifically, the current flowing in a conductive material.

What if we had a bigger resistor, like 10kΩ?

1. $I = V / R$

2. $I = 3V / 10,000\Omega$

3. $I = 0.0003A$ (or 0.3mA)

Hey... wait a minute! We used Ohm's Law to figure out that **a higher resistance reduces the amount of current flowing through the resistor!**

😵 **Question 1:** What sorts of things could we use this knowledge to do in our circuits??

All sorts of things!! Ohm's Law gives us a mathematical way to make predictions about our circuit before needing to build anything, like how bright an LED will be with different resistors or the smallest value resistor we could safely use for an LED if we had a 9V battery.

This is the power of theory and mathematics: we can use these tools to make plans and figure out what to expect before we build (and possibly destroy) anything. If our circuit isn't behaving as expected, we can also use theory and math to debug.

Naturally, this is easier said than done. Despite being a relatively straightforward equation, Ohm's Law is sneakily complicated. Applying it to a circuit can get messy and confusing real quick. This is because circuits have lots of components, so there are many points where the current and voltage vary. The trick is to figure out *what* two points you are looking at and to **be consistent**.

Let's work through some circuits to get a better handle on what is meant by those precise words "current between two points" and "voltage across two points."

Grab These Materials

- Multimeter

- Half-size breadboard

- Coin cell in battery case

- 2–3 jumper wires

- 3 resistors of different resistances (e.g., 100Ω, 1kΩ, and 10kΩ)

- 1 LED

For this first project, we'll learn how to calculate current using Ohm's Law. To do this, we'll use an LED and resistor circuit to measure voltage across each of the three components: the battery, the LED, and the resistor. We'll repeat the same experimental procedure for two other resistors so that we can compare and extend our findings!

First, build the LED and resistor circuit. Since you've already built this same circuit in Chapter 4, **try on your own for at least five minutes** before looking at the circuit diagram in Figure A2-1 and reading through the build instructions.

Once you've built the circuit, flip to the "Calculating Current" section. (If you get super stuck, return to the resistor section in Chapter 4, "Resistance: Limiting Electricity," for troubleshooting tips.)

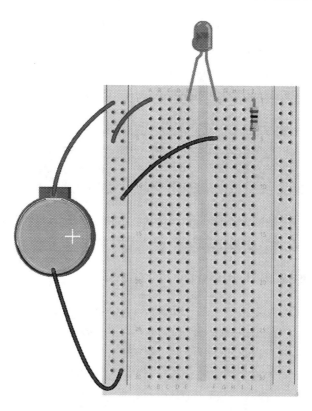

Figure A2-1. Sample LED-resistor circuit for applying Ohm's Law

Written Procedure

1. Insert the coin cell battery into its case and move the switch to the "On" position. Plug the red wire of the battery case into the positive breadboard power rail. Plug the black wire into the negative breadboard power rail.

2. Insert the LED into the top row. Its positive (longer) leg is plugged into the left-hand row 1. Its negative (shorter) leg is plugged into the right-hand row 1.

411

3. Connect your first jumper wire between the positive breadboard power rail and longer LED leg (the red wire going into left-hand row 1).

4. Grab a resistor (e.g., 100Ω) and connect it between the negative LED leg and row 5 on the right side.

5. Connect your second jumper wire between the resistor (right-hand row 5) and the negative power rail (the black wire).

Project A2-1: Calculating Current

Trial 1: Resistor Value = _____ Ω

Step 1: Using the (digital) voltmeter setting on your multimeter, measure the voltage across all the components in your circuit.

Once you've got the circuit built and the LED is on, put your multimeter on the voltage setting. Measure the voltage across the coin cell battery, LED, and resistor. Record your findings in Table A2-1.

Table A2-1. *Voltage Measurements for Circuit 1*

Component	Voltage Measurement
LED (Color =)	
Resistor (Value =)	
Coin Cell Battery (total circuit voltage)	

For this first circuit, let's compare findings. Table A2-2 gives my measurements for a 100 Ω resistor.

Table A2-2. *Example Voltmeter Measurements for an LED and Resistor Circuit*

Component	Measurement
LED (Color = red)	1.9V
Resistor (Value = 100 Ω)	0.6V
Coin Cell Battery (total circuit voltage)	2.5V

🔍 **Check it out:** What do you notice about your measurements? What was surprising? What mysteries did you discover?

WHY ARE MY MEASUREMENTS DIFFERENT THAN WHAT DATASHEETS SAY THEY SHOULD BE??

Real-world measurements are almost always different than theory (e.g., datasheet specifications). For example, the voltage across my coin cell is only 2.5V – not 3V!

This suggests two things: first, that measurements are likely to be different than theory and datasheets and, second, that my coin cell battery has likely lost energy (probably because I've been using it to power so many circuits!).

Getting different results is common for physical projects. This is a major reason why experiments are useful despite us having a wealth of theory to draw from.

😵 **Question 2:** Sum the voltage across the LED and the resistor. What do you notice??

Sum of the LED and resistor voltages:

_____

When we sum the voltage across the LED and the resistor, we find that those voltages (1.9V and 0.6V in my example, respectively) equal the total voltage of the circuit (2.5V)! **This should always be true** and in fact forms the basis of another super helpful circuit equation: **Kirchhoff's Voltage Law**!

Kirchhoff's Voltage Law (KVL)   The sum of the voltages around any closed loop is zero.

Kirchhoff's Voltage Law (KVL) states that **the sum of the voltages around any closed loop is zero**. The phrasing is a bit confusing because voltage can be both positive and negative depending on how we measure it. The gist of KVL is that the voltage across a loop, for example, the battery voltage across our whole circuit, must be used by the parts in that loop, for example, our LED and resistor. There can't be any "leftover" voltage – the components will use all the energy that's available to them.

With that knowledge tucked into our bag of tricks, let's move on to the next step in our experimental procedure!

Step 2: Use your voltage measurements to calculate the current flowing through our circuit.

Okay! This is where we get into the complexity of Ohm's Law. We now have to combine Ohm's Law with our other knowledge of current and voltage.

As a reminder

1.   Current is the same in series.

2.   Voltage is the same in parallel.

This means that **in a single circuit loop, the current flowing through all of the components is the same**. Our LED-resistor circuit has just one loop, so the current flowing through the LED and the current flowing through the resistor are the same.

But wait! All of the components have different voltages across them! How could the current be the same if $V = I \times R$?!

Heck yes, you're paying attention!

We need some subscripts in our equation so that we can tell the different values apart.

Every circuit has a total circuit voltage, total circuit current, and total circuit resistance, like shown in Eqn. A2-2:

$$V_{total} = I_{total} \times R_{total} \qquad \textit{Eqn. A2-2}$$

Since our circuit only has one loop, the total circuit current is the same through every component. This means we can drop the subscript on the I, like we see in Eqn. A2-3:

$$V_{total} = I \times R_{total} \qquad \textit{Eqn. A2-3}$$

The total circuit voltage is the voltage across our battery! Eqn. A2-4 expresses this in the language of math:

$$V_{total} = V_{battery} \qquad \textit{Eqn. A2-4}$$

So now we can just calculate the current using the total circuit resistance, right? Well, let's see...

🤓 **Question 3:** What is the total circuit resistance?

...

Wait a second!

We're missing some information.

The total circuit resistance isn't necessarily the value of the resistor in our circuit. This is because the battery has some internal resistance, the wires add some resistance, and our LED also has some resistance.

We can also apply Ohm's Law to the LED and to the resistor, updating the subscripts like given in Eqn. A2-5 and Eqn. A2-6:

$$V_{LED} = I \times R_{LED} \qquad\qquad \textit{Eqn. A2-5}$$

$$V_{resistor} = I \times R_{resistor} \qquad\qquad \textit{Eqn. A2-6}$$

☺ **Question 4:** Which preceding equation could we use to calculate the circuit current?

Yes! We know the resistance of the resistor, *and* we just measured the voltage across the resistor! That application of Ohm's Law enables us to calculate the circuit current. Do this and record your calculations in Table A2-3!

Table A2-3. *Current Calculation Using Ohm's Law for the Resistor*

Component	Voltage Measurement	Current Calculation
Resistor (Value =)		

Reminder: I = V / R

For my example, Table A2-4 shows how I would apply Ohm's Law.

Table A2-4. *Example Current Calculation Using Ohm's Law for a Resistor*

Component	Voltage Measurement	Current Calculation
Resistor (Value = 100Ω)	0.6V	I = 0.6V / 100Ω = **0.006A**

Step 3: Use the current flowing through the circuit to calculate the internal resistance of the battery and LED.

Now that we know the current flowing through our circuit, we can use that value to calculate the internal resistance of both the battery and the LED. Use Ohm's Law and record your answers in Table A2-5.

Table A2-5. *Resistance Calculation Using Ohm's Law and Calculated Current*

Component	Voltage Measurement	Resistance Calculation
LED (Color =)		
Coin Cell Battery		

Reminder: R = V / I

And if you need an example, Table A2-6 shows you how I plugged in my calculated current into Ohm's Law.

Table A2-6. *Example Resistance Calculation Using Ohm's Law and Calculated Current*

Component	Voltage Measurement	Resistance Calculation
LED (Color = red)	1.9V	R = 1.9V / 0.006A = **316.67 Ω**
Coin Cell Battery	2.5V	R = 2.5V / 0.006A = **416.67 Ω**

And that's it! To summarize, here is what we discovered:

1. The voltage across the battery equals the voltage (drop) across the LED and the resistor.

   a. This led us to Kirchhoff's Voltage Law!

2. Ohm's Law can be applied to the circuit as a whole, to individual components, or to circuit loops within a larger circuit.

3. We can make measurements using a voltmeter to get missing information. We can use this information to make calculations about our circuit.

Alright!! We have now learned and applied two of the most important circuit laws: Ohm's Law and KVL!

But we're not done yet!!

Good scientists are skeptical. At a minimum, we double- and triple-check our findings because we want to make sure we didn't make a mistake, that we are not basing our results on faulty equipment, or that something weird and unexpected (and hidden) didn't happen during our experiment. This means to test and extend our discoveries from this first experiment, **repeat the Trial 1 procedure for at least two more resistors of different values!**

Trial 2: Resistor Value = _____ Ω

Step 1: Measure the voltage across all the components in your circuit. Record your measurements in Table A2-7.

Table A2-7. *Voltage Measurements for Circuit 1*

Component	Voltage Measurement
LED (Color =)	
Resistor (Value =)	
Coin Cell Battery	

Step 2: Use your voltage measurements to calculate the total circuit current, the current through the LED, and the current through the resistor. Record your findings in Table A2-8.

Table A2-8. *Current Calculation Using Ohm's Law for the Resistor*

Component	Voltage Measurement	Current Calculation
Resistor (Value =)		

Reminder: I = V / R

Step 3: Use the current flowing through the circuit to calculate the internal resistance of the battery and LED. Use Table A2-9 to log your calculations.

Table A2-9. *Resistance Calculation Using Ohm's Law and Calculated Current*

Component	Voltage Measurement	Resistance Calculation
LED (Color =)		
Coin Cell Battery		

Trial 3: Resistor Value = _____ Ω

Step 1: Measure the voltage across all the components in your circuit. Use Table A2-10 to record your measurements.

Table A2-10. *Voltage Measurements for Circuit 1*

Component	Voltage Measurement
LED (Color =)	
Resistor (Value =)	
Coin Cell Battery	

Step 2: Use your voltage measurements to calculate the total circuit current, the current through the LED, and the current through the resistor. Write your findings in Table A2-11.

Table A2-11. *Current Calculation Using Ohm's Law for the Resistor*

Component	Voltage Measurement	Current Calculation
Resistor (Value =)		

Reminder: $I = V / R$

Step 3: Use the current flowing through the circuit to calculate the internal resistance of the battery and LED. Log your calculations in Table A2-12.

Table A2-12. *Resistance Calculation Using Ohm's Law and Calculated Current*

Component	Voltage Measurement	Resistance Calculation
LED (Color =)		
Coin Cell Battery		

Project A2-2: Measuring Current

In our first experiment, we measured voltage to calculate current using Ohm's Law. Along the way, we discovered that measurements may be different than theory. This leads us to our next experiment: we will measure current and compare that with our calculations!

We'll use the same LED and resistor circuit that we did in Experiment 1 with three trials using three different resistor values. We'll change our experiment by using the ammeter setting on our multimeter to measure, rather than calculate, current!

Trial 1: Resistor Value = _____ Ω

Step 1: Using the (digital) ammeter setting on your multimeter, measure the current going through the LED.

To do this, unplug one end of the red jumper wire that connects the positive power rail and the positive LED leg. Unplug the end of the jumper wire **closest** to the LED.

Then connect one ammeter probe to the jumper wire lead and the other to the positive LED leg. Record your measurement in Table A2-13.

Table A2-13. *Current Measurement Through the Resistor*

Component	Current Measurement
LED (Color =)	

As an example, I measured the current through the LED in a circuit with a 100 Ω resistor. My measurement is shown in Table A2-14.

Table A2-14. *Example Current Measurement Through the Resistor*

Component	Current Measurement
LED (Color = red)	0.007A

Step 2: Measure the current going through the resistor.

Do this by unplugging one end of the black jumper wire (the end closest to the resistor). Then connect one ammeter probe to the jumper wire lead and the other to the closest resistor lead. Record your measurement in Table A2-15.

Table A2-15. *Current Measurement Through the LED*

Component	Current Measurement
Resistor (Value =)	

My example current measurement through a 100 Ω resistor is given in Table A2-16.

Table A2-16. *Example Current Measurement Through the LED*

Component	Current Measurement
Resistor (Value = 100Ω)	0.007A

Step 3: Measure the current coming out of the battery.

To do this, unplug one end of the red jumper wire (the end closest to the power rails). Connect one ammeter probe to the jumper wire lead and the other to the positive battery wire. Record your measurement in Table A2-17.

Table A2-17. *Current Measurement Out of the Battery*

Component	Current Measurement
Coin Cell Battery	

Finally, if you need to compare, my measurements are shown in Table A2-18.

Table A2-18. *Example Current Measurement Out of the Battery*

Component	Current Measurement
Coin Cell Battery	0.007A

That's it! We've successfully used our ammeter to measure the current flowing through our circuit!

😵 **Question 5:** Does this support our findings in Experiment 1??

Although my ammeter measurement was slightly different than what I calculated using Ohm's Law, the two values are close enough to be acceptable. More important, we confirmed that **the current through each component in the circuit is the same**.

This should always be true (just like the voltage pattern we discovered). You may have guessed that this hints at another circuit law: **Kirchhoff's Current Law!!**

Kirchhoff's Current Law (KCL) states that **for any node, or intersection, in an electric circuit, the sum of currents flowing into that node is equal to the sum of the currents flowing out of that node**. In other words, the current flowing into a part of the circuit must equal the current flowing out of that circuit. Another way to look at this is that there is only so much current in a circuit, and it all has to go somewhere!

Kirchhoff's Circuit Law (KCL)   The sum of the currents in a network of conductors meeting at a point is zero. In other words, for any node in a circuit, the sum of currents flowing into that node is equal to the sum of currents flowing out of that node.

Just as we did for Experiment 1, repeat this experiment for two more trials! Use the same resistors as you did for Experiment 1 Trial 2 and Experiment 1 Trial 3.

Trial 2: Resistor Value = _____ Ω

Step 1: Measure the current going through the LED. Use Table A2-19 to record your measurements.

Table A2-19. *Current Measurement Through the Resistor*

Component	Current Measurement
LED (Color =)	

Step 2: Measure the current going through the resistor. Log your measurement in Table A2-20.

Table A2-20. *Current Measurement Through the LED*

Component	Current Measurement
Resistor (Value =)	

Step 3: Measure the current coming out of the battery and record it in Table A2-21.

Table A2-21. *Current Measurement Out of the Battery*

Component	Current Measurement
Coin Cell Battery	

Trial 3: Resistor Value = _____ Ω

Step 1: Measure the current going through the LED and record it in Table A2-22.

Table A2-22. *Current Measurement Through the Resistor*

Component	Current Measurement
LED (Color =)	

Step 2: Measure the current going through the resistor and record it in Table A2-23.

Table A2-23. *Current Measurement Through the LED*

Component	Current Measurement
Resistor (Value =)	

Step 3: Measure the current coming out of the battery and log it in Table A2-24.

Table A2-24. *Current Measurement Out of the Battery*

Component	Current Measurement
Coin Cell Battery	

Going Further

Kirchhoff's Voltage and Current Laws are incredibly useful if (when!) you start using Ohm's Law to analyze more complex circuits. This is because these two laws allow us to break apart different parts of circuits and analyze them piece by piece. They also allow us to check out work by making sure that voltages sum to zero and currents are all accounted for. To learn more about KVL and KCL, a thorough overview can be found at Wikipedia: https://en.wikipedia.org/wiki/Kirchhoff%27s_circuit_laws.

Another useful equation is the **Power Law**, which allows us to calculate the power provided by, or consumed by, a circuit component. The Power Law is given by Eqn. A2-7:

$$P = V \times I$$

Eqn. A2-7

where V is the voltage across the component and I is the current through the component. Power is given in units of Watts (W), which are Joules (J) per second (J/s). This law is particularly important as it is critical to use components with a suitable power rating to avoid risk of overheating and failure.

Finally, I'll leave you with a tip for analyzing more complex circuits.

DRAW A DIAGRAM. Yes, really, it's super helpful! And then label the voltages, currents, and resistances. Figure A2-2 illustrates an example for our LED-resistor circuit.

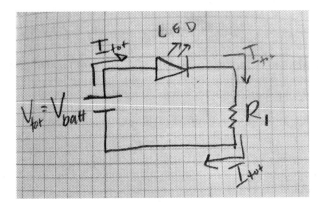

Figure A2-2. *Example of a circuit diagram for identifying current, voltage, and resistance*

Since multiple loops can be tricky, Figure A2-3 shows you how you can draw and label a circuit with three resistors in parallel.

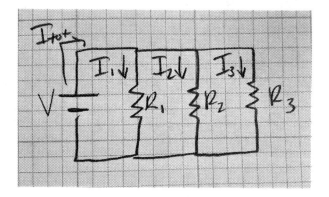

Figure A2-3. *Example schematic drawing of a parallel circuit for identifying current, voltage, and resistance*

Doing this helps you visualize where current is the same (in series) and where voltage is the same (in parallel). By labeling the different electric currents and voltages in your circuit, you can apply Ohm's Law more easily!

Note that this is still just an introduction to Ohm's Law – if you end up needing more ways to simplify circuits, check out more advanced texts on the subject as can be found in electronics textbooks. I love *Basic Electronics for Scientists and Engineers* by Dennis L. Eggleston!

Summary

In this bonus chapter, we learned about one of the most important equations in electronics: Ohm's Law! We practiced how to use this equation and then combined our knowledge of Ohm's Law with a multimeter to make experimental measurements and compare our findings with theory.

Along the way, we learned two new circuit laws: Kirchhoff's Voltage Law (KVL), which states that the sum of the voltages around any closed loop is zero, and Kirchhoff's Current Law (KCL), which tells us that the current flowing out of a node must equal the current flowing into that node. With these three circuit laws, we can analyze all sorts of circuits!

Applied Project 3: PCB Identification

Welcome to your third and final applied project! In this chapter, we'll discover the wonders of Printed Circuit Boards (PCBs) and how we can explore, observe, and harvest parts from PCBs in all sorts of electronic devices. Along the way, we'll learn more about circuits and how to get new parts to explore and build with!

Look Inside: An Overview of Harvesting Parts

Before we go treasure hunting, there are a few helpful topics to cover. We'll start with an overview of PCBs because they are awesome and fascinating! We'll also go over safety guidelines for using tools and harvesting parts, the types of tools I'd recommend (and some places where you can purchase them), and where and how we can get more information about the parts and pieces we find (a.k.a. datasheets).

Printed Circuit Boards: Tiny Cities for Electronic Components

Like shown in Figure A3-1, Printed Circuit Boards, or PCBs for short, are found inside every (modern consumer) electronic device. They are used to connect electronic parts efficiently and effectively. PCBs are typically flat, or two-dimensional, and come in all shapes and sizes. PCBs can be designed to fit inside any type of external case you might need, from an electronic car key (i.e., a key fob) to a toaster to a clothes washer. Each of these electronics is a different size and has different amounts of space for its circuits.

Figure A3-1. *An example of a Printed Circuit Board! Source: Wikimedia Commons*

Smaller electronics may have simple circuits that can be easily sized to fit within the device case. Others may require more clever PCB engineering – some may use both sides of a PCB or even have additional layers. These days, electronic components like transistors, resistors, and capacitors can be manufactured so small that they are almost invisible to the human eye! The electronic parts that we have been working with throughout this book are "artificially" larger in the sense that they are designed for our fingers and eyesight.

When you open up older electronics, you'll find parts that are nearly identical to the parts you've worked with throughout this book. When you open newer electronics, you will likely find much smaller parts, like pictured in Figure A3-2. There are some key exceptions often due to human interaction. For us to be able to interact with electronic devices, we need switches, buttons, knobs, etc., that are friendly and comfortable for our finger sizes.

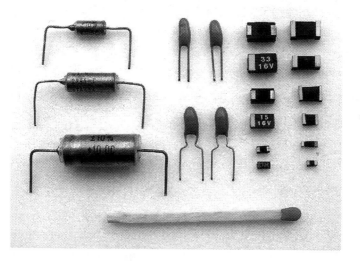

Figure A3-2. *Different sizes of electrolytic capacitors! The capacitors on the right are surface mount, which means they are meant only for PCBs. Source: Wikimedia Commons*

Other components that will be familiar to you when you look inside electronic devices are parts that are difficult to miniaturize due to limitations in the laws of physics and sensory needs, like speakers, motors, and lights. As we'll learn later in this chapter, these types of components are often the easiest and most useful to harvest from PCBs.

PCBs are a delightfully clever design of both conductive and insulating material. The conductive material forms paths called **traces** that function like roads and electrically connect components. Traces are typically formed out of copper. The insulating material prevents short circuits, forces the electrical current to travel the desired path, and enables engineers to put multiple separate circuits in the same board.

Traces   Paths of conductive material on a PCB that connects electronic components.

Electronic components are **soldered** to the PCB traces, a process of melting metal that connects the parts to the board both electrically and mechanically.[1] If you enjoy building circuits on breadboards, I'd highly recommend you explore soldering! It is a fairly low-cost, accessible, and practical skill that makes you feel powerful because it gives you the ability to repair electronics. Anyway, back to PCBs!

Soldering   A process of melting metal to electrically connect wires and electronic components.

PCBs are designed by humans, most often by electrical engineers, who design circuits for functionality, energy and space efficiency, and safety. Once a PCB has been designed, it can be assembled automatically by special machines that etch the copper traces and solder the components to the board. For boards that use both sides of the PCB or have multiple

---

[1] While soldering does help adhere parts to the PCB, solder is not super strong. If solder joints are stressed or flexed too much, the joint will break! This is a common mode of failure for electronics. It is also why parts in our electronics that get a lot of wear often have more robust interface mechanisms and why circuits are hidden behind sturdy cases.

layers, other machines can also drill holes into the PCB called **vias** – these are coated with conductive material so that the electricity can flow from the copper traces on one side of the board, "via" the hole, to the copper traces on the other side of the board.

Via   An electrical connection made "via" a hole between layers of a PCB.

As with all product design, initial designs of PCBs are tested before they are made en masse because the real world is complicated, circuits can behave strangely (even for experts), and insights often come from observing and experimenting with physical designs. Most PCBs will be tested and modified multiple times before being manufactured for final products that we use. Once a design is ready, PCBs can be manufactured in sheets, which means many of the same PCB can be made at once. This makes PCBs much cheaper and faster than other wiring methods.

Figure A3-3. *Point-to-point wiring as is common in older and small batch electronics*

In older electronics, PCBs were hand-soldered like in Figure A3-3. In much older electronics, like before the 1950s or 1960s, you might find wire-wrapped components. You may also discover these methods in custom or small batch electronics or in electronics where the circuit is part of the aesthetic. Art and design do not always need to be economical to be functional!

Safety Guidelines

Yay, safety! Harvesting parts from PCBs is super fun and, in general, quite safe. That said, anytime we work with tools or new electronic parts, we need to be aware of safety protocols. First, let's cover tool safety, and then we'll learn more about safety rules for opening electronics, PCBs, and working with new or different electronic components that you may come across.

Tools: Using Them Safely and Effectively

1. **Wear safety goggles.**

   It may seem silly and overly cautious, but our eyes are fragile and important, so let's protect them! When opening electronics and harvesting parts, we may (accidentally or intentionally) break cases, clip off small pieces of metal, or fling parts. So, please, wear safety goggles because your eyes matter.

2. **Use the right tool for the job.**

   The next guideline for tool safety (which, let's be honest, we all break from time to time) is to use the right tool for the right job. Sometimes, our screwdriver is out of reach, so we opt for a knife to pry open a can of paint or to open the case of an electronic device like a computer monitor.

Most of the time, this is harmless. However, occasionally a tool will slip, break, or dull. When this happens, we put both our tools and our bodies at risk. When I've been lazy and used the wrong tool, I've wound up with scraps, cuts, bruises, and more. So please, learn from my mistakes and be smarter and more diligent. If you need to pry open a case, use a screwdriver or, better yet, a pry bar or opening pick which are designed specifically for opening electronics!

The same goes for any task you need to perform when harvesting parts from PCBs: use the right tool(s) to undo screws and bolts, cut wires, pull out cables, etc.

3. **Leave electronics unplugged for at least two weeks.**

As we'll learn later, some electronics have large capacitors which can be dangerous if charged. Capacitors can hold charge for up to two weeks. To err on the side of caution, leave any electronics unplugged for a minimum of two weeks before opening them up and/or taking them apart.

4. **Listen to mechanical failures.**

Most electronics are designed to be opened. And even if they are not (or are only designed to be opened by a highly specialized tool or person with super secret training), the device had to be closed at some point. This means that it is possible to open all electronics without breaking things. If you

435

hear cracking, snapping, crunching, etc., stop what you're doing and observe the part to see where it is breaking.

Why does this matter? When things break, we risk irreversible damage to the device. Even if you're okay with this (and if you're new to taking things apart, I'd highly recommend that you're okay breaking the thing you're opening up/taking apart), breaking things can risk damage to ourselves because sharp edges can be dangerous.

5. **Leave PCBs intact** (i.e., avoid cutting/sawing/ otherwise breaking them).

PCBs are fine to touch and handle. However, if you saw or cut or break them, the particulates that come off them are not great for our lungs. Not as bad for us as, say, asbestos, but for the sake of keeping our bodies safe, avoid extra contamination by keeping PCBs intact.

If, for some reason, you absolutely have to cut a PCB, wear an appropriate respiratory mask and use an air filtration device.

6. **Don't smash it.**

While this feels a bit redundant with #3 and #4, I'm often surprised at the determination and eagerness some of my students display when taking apart electronics! It really can feel like treasure hunting, and that excitement may translate into poor decision making or not thinking through potential consequences.

Smashing parts causes things to break which, as mentioned earlier, creates sharp edges. Some electronics, like smartphones, also use glass for touchscreens or other purposes which can shatter.

This guideline is a reminder that **safety requires patience**. If you find yourself frustrated that a device won't open, it can help to take a few deep breaths or walk away for a few minutes (or hours or maybe days). Come back to it when you're feeling calm to keep yourself safe. Because, I promise, you're worth it!

7. **Wash your hands when you're done.**

Like with most projects, it's important to wash our hands afterward to remove any materials that may be hazardous to ingest.

DO I NEED TO WORRY ABOUT LEAD IN ELECTRONICS??

By law, most electronics cannot have lead in them. This is a standard that has been in place for over a decade. As a result, a good rule of thumb is that newer electronics are safe to take apart and repurpose in a variety of ways, including modification or destruction of internal components.

If there is a concern about lead, wash your hands and keep food and drink away from the materials.

Tools! (Besides Your Hands ☺)

Figure A3-4. *Students grabbing tools for a take apart workshop!*

This is the chapter where you get to break out tools that you've used before! To take apart most electronics, many of the tools in your standard toolbox, like shown in Figure A3-4, will suffice:

- **Driver set** and/or **screwdriver assortment** (both Phillips and flathead)

- **Pliers**, especially slip-joint and needle-nose pliers

- **Tweezers**

- **Scissors**

- **Tape**

- **Magnifying glass**

    - If you have one, it's a great way to observe and identify parts more easily. If you don't have one, I'd highly recommend purchasing a kid's magnifying glass because they are relatively inexpensive

(typically less than $10) and can be used for getting
a closer look at all sorts of weird and wonderful
things in this world! ... And yes, I'm talking about
things beyond electronics, like bugs and plants!

Hopefully, this means that you can start opening most electronics
without needing to purchase a whole new set of tools, yay! I have two
general guidelines for starting out:

1. Larger electronics, like desktop computers, are
    easier to open than smaller electronics, like
    smartphones.

2. "Less smart" electronics, like toasters and
    hairdryers, are easier to open than "smart"
    electronics, like laptops.

Some types and brands of electronics are much more difficult,
meaning that they may be prone to breaking, have unique types of screw
heads, or use adhesives instead of screws (I'm looking at you, brand-that-
is-the-name-of-a-fruit). As you start to explore opening up electronics,
you'll notice which brands are friendly to your tools and hands and which
brands are, well, frustrating. You'll also start to get a feel for where to look
for screws (hint: always check under labels and stickers).

For electronics with touchscreens and smaller electronics, I'd
recommend the following tools in addition to the preceding list (these are
given, in my opinion, from **most to least important** for getting started):

1. **Full driver kit**: A manual (not electric) driver kit
    with screwdriver bits, including Pentalobe, Torx and
    Torx Security, Hex, and Tri-Point.

2. **Wire strippers/cutters**: For removing the plastic
    insulation from wires and cutting wires.

3. **Magnets**: For keeping track of tiny screws! Fridge magnets work great. If you get really into opening and/or repairing electronics, I'd highly recommend a magnetic dish.

4. **Precision tweezers**: For pulling off lil' parts.

5. **Jimmy**: A general-purpose opening tool for cutting, prying, and sliding open electronic device cases, screens, and cables. Note that a **precision knife** also works, but a Jimmy is a safer approach.

6. **Spudger**: For separating pressure-fit plastics.

7. **Reverse tweezers**: Spring-action tweezers for holding cables and other parts.

8. **Heat gun**: If you really get into harvesting parts, a heat gun is indispensable for quickly melting solder and removing parts with the least amount of damage.

Where to buy?!

Some of these tools are super specific, and you will not find them at your local (or national) hardware store. My personal favorite toolkits are sold by **iFixit** (ifixit.com) because these kits are designed for opening and repairing electronics. As a bonus, this company is a huge proponent of Right to Repair laws, which benefit all sorts of folks from electronics consumers who want to be able to open and fix their electronics to farmers who want to repair their tractors and other farm machinery.

You can also find electronics toolkits from companies that sell electronic parts, like Adafruit Industries (United States), SparkFun Electronics (United States), Pimoroni (UK), and Seeed Studio (China).

Datasheets: All the Information Your Heart (and Brain) Could Desire

Datasheets are like the encyclopedia for parts. Most manufacturers publish datasheets for the parts and pieces they make, which gives detailed information about the physical design (i.e., physical measurements and specifications), operating requirements like max and min voltage and current or the functional temperature range, electrical specifications like schematics and wiring diagrams, and operating behaviors like the component's output voltage.

A datasheet can answer your most pressing questions. The lack of a datasheet can make using a part incredibly challenging. Datasheets for common parts, like the ones that we've been using, can be found using your favorite search engine – even if you cannot find a datasheet from the specific manufacturer that you purchased from, most of the time a datasheet from another source will suffice.[2]

Learning to read datasheets is an incredibly useful skill because it is often the difference between getting indefinitely stuck with a part and being able to troubleshoot it to make something useful. And, as this book is hands-on, to learn how to read a datasheet, let's actually look at one!

Figure A3-5 shows a datasheet for a coin cell battery, specifically a CR2032 from Energizer.

The first thing you might notice is that there's a lot of information contained on a single page! Most of the time, there is more information than you'll need. That said, if you're an engineer who's aiming to design

---

[2] This is because, for common parts, manufacturers typically use the same chemistries and manufacturing processes. However, this is not always the case. If you end up with strange, unexpected behavior from components like batteries or sensors, it may be because a manufacturer changed something in the process (or sometimes manufacturing processes go awry and parts don't function as expected).

products with the part, having all this information is vital. For example, if you want to fit the coin cell into a product, you'll need to know how big it is and what shape it is – this is where the dimensional drawings, volume, and weight are helpful.

Many engineers learn how to read datasheets on the job, which means that you too can learn how to identify and pull out the information that you need. To help you get started and reduce some of the cognitive load, I've added arrows that point to information that will likely be useful as you go forward with electronics.

Here's a quick written list of key information that I've called out with a brief explanation as to why it's helpful:

1. **Nominal voltage**: This is the voltage that the battery puts out. Note that this is the ideal or theoretical voltage and, as we've learned, the real world is messy and complicated, so the actual operational voltage will be slightly different (typically less) than this.

2. **Typical capacity**: The capacity of a battery is how much electric current it can provide over time. A higher battery capacity for the same kind of load, like an LED, means that the battery can power the load (the LED) for a longer amount of time.

3. **Operating temp**: This is the temperature range within which the battery can function as expected. It is also often the safe operating range. For hobbyist projects, it's unlikely that you'll find yourself outside of this range. That said, it is always helpful to note because some parts need to be kept cooler than expected.

4. **Self-discharge**: This is one of my favorite pieces
    of information! If we leave a battery unused in a
    drawer (or if it's sitting unused in an electronic
    device), the self-discharge rate is how much energy
    the battery loses over time. 1% per year is incredibly
    low! This is why coin cell batteries are often used as
    power sources for hard-to-reach places or as backup
    power for alerts and feedback.

5. **Continuous discharge characteristics**: This is how
    the battery voltage changes over time under use,
    like when it's powering a light or motor. When the
    battery voltage gets too low, for example, 2.0V for a
    3V coin cell, it is effectively dead because it cannot
    provide sufficient power to a circuit. The discharge
    curve, as shown under the Continuous Discharge
    Characteristics section, tells us how long it takes to
    drain the battery at a constant load at 15K Ohms
    and 0.19mA.

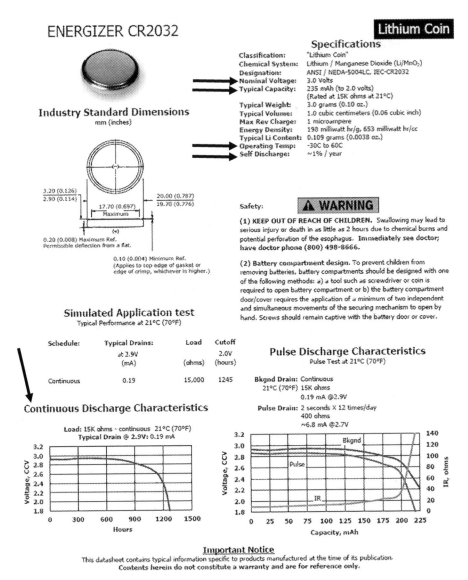

Figure A3-5. An Energizer CR2032 datasheet

Although I pointed out the minimum information that I believe is useful for you to know, I encourage you to read through the datasheet to see what else is there! Other things that you may want to note for different types of batteries include weight (batteries can get super heavy super quickly), chemistry (batteries made with lithium have strict transportation limitations), and the dimensions (buying things online can obfuscate the size/shape of batteries and sometimes what might look like a standard battery in a photo can be entirely unexpected when it arrives in person!).

Having looked at a specific datasheet will, hopefully, help you feel more confident when you look at a datasheet on your own. Of course, a battery datasheet has different information than, say, a photoresistor datasheet or a motor datasheet. Each category of electronic components has its own jargon, key specifications, communication signals, and more. If we were to look at an example of every type of datasheet you may come across, you would (1) probably get bored and (2) wonder when we were getting back to building things.

So! Here we are. After seeing an example, I believe you'll be okay going forward because you now know that you don't have to look at everything on the datasheet. The key is to identify the crucial pieces of information, such as

- Minimum and maximum operating voltage

- Current and/or power consumption

- Operational temperate range

- Output characteristics (e.g., voltage and/or current output)

- Resistance

- Communication signal(s)

- Physical size (if that matters for your needs)

You are quite capable of learning how to read different types of datasheets! Seeing an example will help you more quickly identify what information to look out for and what information you can skip.

As a final overview of datasheets, the following are some tips for finding accurate and relevant datasheets for all the parts you wish to learn about.

Tips for finding datasheets

1. Be as specific as possible.

    Include as much precise information about the part as you can. For example, if you're searching for the datasheet for a coin cell battery, look at the writing on the battery and identify its part number. Try this with the coin cells that you've been using throughout this book!

    If you purchased the parts from the materials list in the beginning of the book, you'll find that the coin cell is a CR2032. This is the same type of coin cell battery that we looked at in our example datasheet. These types of coin cell batteries are common in electronics and have a high battery capacity (i.e., they can last a long time). If you are using a different type of coin cell battery, locate the part number on the battery, look it up in your preferred search engine with the addition of "datasheet," and look for a link that has a PDF of the datasheet.

    Avoid clicking on search results that are ads, as these may not be what you're looking for and can sometimes be spam and/or malicious links.

2. Avoid clicking on ads.

    Oh hey! We just touched on this. While folks running websites need to make a living, ads don't always have the information that we're looking for. Occasionally, ads may have malicious links or downloads that are harmful to our computers. When using search engines, blogs, or other types of websites, avoid clicking on popup ads, targeted ads, and other links marked as "ad."

Even if a website is legitimate, some websites aim to surface their content whether or not it is relevant to our needs. This is surprisingly common with datasheets because we are searching for specific components. Manufacturers would prefer that we buy that part from them instead of their competitors, so if you search for a part, the company will pay to have their website surface even if they do not provide a datasheet. A discerning eye and a healthy amount of skepticism when searching for datasheets can help us identify what websites actually have what we need.

To summarize, when using a search engine, just because a website is the first result doesn't mean it will help you find what you need!

(P.S. This is a recommendation even beyond datasheets. Searching for super specific information, like datasheets, can help us build skills for finding accurate and trustworthy sources because we start to learn how and what to look for when learning new things. Yay for learning to identify reliable, trustworthy, and reputable sources of information!)

3. Read the website description and look for keywords, like "datasheet" or part specifications (e.g., "nominal voltage").

A website description surfaced by a search engine is super helpful for quickly identifying whether or not that site may have what you're seeking. When looking for datasheets, if a website provides a link, a download, or a text form of the datasheet, the site will have some sort of description that lets you know what you'll find. Here are some examples of text that indicates you will find a datasheet:

- "This datasheet contains information for the CR2032 lithium ion battery…"

- "Battery type and ratings… 2.1 Battery Type: CR2032. 2.2 Nominal Voltage: 3.0V…"

- "Details, datasheet… Voltage: Rated 3.0V…"

Datasheets may also be offered in a PDF format, so keep an eye out for that.

4. Be willing to look at a few different sites.

When you're first getting started, you might not find the part datasheet on the first go. That's totally okay! I often look at two to three websites before I find the right datasheet. Sometimes, we end up on a manufacturer's site where the datasheet is obfuscated or nonexistent, sometimes we find a datasheet in a language that we can't read, or sometimes we end up on a totally random site.

Finding the right datasheet can be an art form in patience and wordsmithing. Be patient and forgiving (to yourself and to site owners) – it's a skill to be learned, and it's okay if it takes you a few tries.

Where and What to Look for When Taking Apart Electronics

Destruction feeds creation! By looking inside electronics, we can find inspiration, knowledge, *and* useful parts. This section gives you some tips on where and what to look for when opening up all sorts of electronics!

Locating Electronics for Take Apart Shenanigans

Start your search for electronics to open by looking around your home! Most of us have a bin (or a box or a garage) full of electronics that we've been meaning to fix or give away. So many useful educational gadgets in there!

But, electronics are sensitive lil' creatures and cannot withstand the slings and arrows that life throws at them – hence why they are enclosed in airtight containers away from sticky fingers and mechanical stresses. I thoroughly believe that breaking things is a great educational experience, which is why I included this chapter and why I'm serious when I say that you should absolutely, 100%, open up some electronics.

If you're starting out, I recommend **only taking apart electronics that you don't care about**. It's likely that the first few (dozen) times you take an electronic device apart, you may not be able to reassemble it. Or, you may accidentally (on purpose?) break it.

So, when it comes to take apart shenanigans, start with the things that you are okay with breaking. If you happen to fix them, wonderful! Use it or gift it to a friend.

Hold on... what if there are no electronics to destroy (ahem, take apart) in my home?

Great question! Another place to look for inexpensive electronics is at **thrift stores** like Goodwill or Salvation Army. You also can **ask friends, family, and colleagues** if they have old electronics that they don't want – although be careful in this case because you may become "that friend" that folks seek to pawn their old stuff on. (... I have been that friend before. At first, it's delightful and fun. And then you have a garage full of dusty and sticky voicemail machines.)

Another option is to **ask local companies for old electronics**. If they give you computers, make sure they wipe or remove hard drives because you'll want to avoid any potential issue of accessing sensitive information.

WHAT DO I DO WITH THE ELECTRONICS WHEN I'M DONE DISMANTLING THEM??

Electronics that we don't want anymore should be properly disposed of. Most electronics should go to ewaste recycling facilities where they will harvest materials and safely discard any potentially hazardous materials.

You can take any electronics that you take apart to a government-run hazardous waste facility. Some companies, like Best Buy, will recycle electronics for you, and many nonprofits will readily accept donations of electronics that are intact (i.e., before you take them apart or if you are able to piece them back together).

Types of Electronics for Take Apart

Not all electronics are created equal for taking apart. Some are way more fun, way less messy, and way safer than other types of electronics. In general, aim for electronics that have parts that are visible, harvestable, and safe to touch. Older electronics can be super fun because parts are larger and there's an historical aspect that is illuminating and tickles your brain.

The following are my recommendations for the types of electronic devices to seek out and the ones to avoid for take apart adventures.

Safe Electronics

- Small electronics like solar path lights, remote controls, night lights, etc.

- Computers (desktop and laptop)

- Computer accessories (e.g., keyboards, mouse, external hard drive, etc.)

- Electronic toys and cars

- Smartphones and cellphones

- Voicemail machines

- Speakers and headphones

- MP3/CD/tape players

- Inkjet printers

Electronics to Avoid

- Microwaves

- Old TVs with cathode ray tubes (TVs with depth – flat screens are fine)

- Large appliances (e.g., refrigerators, washer/dryers, dishwashers, etc.)

- Toner printers

WHY DO WE WANT TO AVOID CERTAIN ELECTRONICS??

Some electronics are simply messy, and other electronics have components that can be dangerous when opened up. The most dangerous components that you may come across are large capacitors. I use a "thumb rule" when identifying potentially dangerous capacitors: **a capacitor that is as big or larger than your thumb is dangerous.**

It is possible to discharge a capacitor with a **plastic**-handled screwdriver.

HOWEVER.

I recommend that you leave this to the professionals because: safety! Instead, if you open up a device and see a capacitor that is as big or larger than your thumb, close up the device (avoid touching the PCB) and leave the device unplugged for two weeks or more.

Capacitors can hold charge for a long time. Most of the time, this is exactly why we want to use them! Occasionally, this is hazardous. Like when we want to open up and poke around electronics for educational and curiosity purposes. By leaving an electronic device unplugged for two weeks, we give the capacitor time to discharge, or lose, any amount of electrical energy it has stored.

Harvesting Parts

Once you've found some rad electronics to open up, you may want to look for parts that are hard to find or expensive. There are also parts that you can more easily harvest than others. My recommendation is, in general, look for parts that are about the same size as the ones we've worked with on breadboards because these are easier to remove and use in future projects without totally destroying them.

Easily harvestable parts

- Switches and pushbuttons

- Speakers

- Motors

- Connectors and holders

- Photoresistors

- Relays and solenoids

HOW DO YOU ACTUALLY GET PARTS OFF OF PCBS AND OUT OF ELECTRONICS?!

If you're comfortable with a soldering iron, or open to learning how to use one (do itttt, it's such a fun and useful skill!), heating the solder joints that connect an electronic component to a PCB is one way to get a part off of a PCB. To do this, you'll also need some tweezers or needle-nose pliers.

Look Inside: Let's Take Some Things Apart!

Finally! If you've made it this far without breaking open the nearest electronic device, congratulations, you have more patience than me! For this next section, we put our learnings into practice and look inside an electronic toy. I encourage you to follow along and take something apart with me!

Going through this with me will help you figure out how to take things apart in a way that makes it more likely you'll be able to put it back together and less likely that you'll break something or get frustrated.

Before we start, a couple more things to note:

1. **Remove all batteries.** Leave the device without any power for at least two weeks.

2. **Go slow.** Make lots of observations before you take any actions.

3. **Be flexible with your tools.** The first tool you try may not work. When that happens, set it aside and try a different tool.

4. **You'll probably get a little messy.** Wear appropriate clothing, protect surfaces, and wipe/wash your hands as needed.

Grab These Materials

Tools

- Fridge magnet (or two)

- Driver set (also recommended to have standard Phillips and regular screwdrivers on hand)

- Tweezers

- Wire cutters

- Needle-nose pliers

- Multimeter

- Rag

Electronic Parts (for Exploration)

- Breadboard

- Coin cell battery in case

- 5–10 jumper wires

- 2 or more pushbuttons

- 2 or more LEDs

Electronic Toy

Electronic toys, like the one pictured in Figure A3-6, are one of my most favorite things to take apart! This is because they typically have fun outputs like motors, speakers, and lights. Bonus: These parts are often easy to harvest and play with!

Figure A3-6. A toy for taking apart!

Taking things apart is super educational because you get to see how designers create interactive parts, how mechanical engineers use motors to make things move, and how electrical engineers design robust circuits!

Grab your screwdriver and let's goooo!

General Procedure

You can apply this general procedure to (most) electronic devices that you'll take apart.

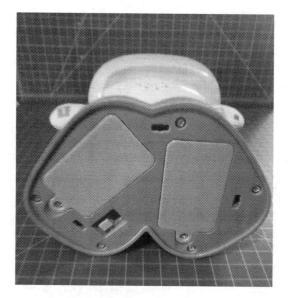

Figure A3-7. *Checking for batteries*

1. **Double-check that the batteries are removed.**
   Most of the time, batteries are installed on the
   bottom of a device, like shown in Figure A3-7.

Figure A3-8. *Remove as many screws as you can find*

2. **Look for and remove all the screws you can find.**
   Like shown in Figure A3-8, use a fridge magnet to
   keep track of screws. (I like to use multiple magnets
   to keep the screws organized, e.g., one magnet to
   hold external screws and another to hold internal
   screws.)

   Most of the time, the screws are on the bottom and/
   or back of the device. That said, hidden screws are
   common. Check under labels and other stickers
   (including squishy pads used for gripping surfaces).

   Tool tip: Feel for the screwdriver tip latching
   onto the screw head. You may need to apply
   more pressure onto the screw and slowly turn the
   screwdriver to get this useful tactile sensation.

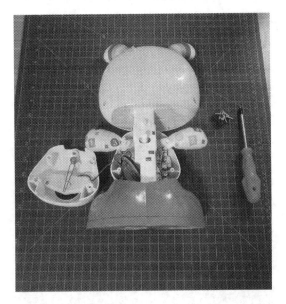

Figure A3-9. Removing the first pieces for our toy take apart

3. **Gently tug at the case to pull the pieces apart.**
    Notice if the pieces are resistant to you tugging
    on them – if so, stop and look for stuck or hidden
    screws. It's also important to be gentle and go slow
    because there may be wires connected between
    pieces on the inside of the device. Figure A3-9
    illustrates an example of removing the first pieces
    for our take apart.

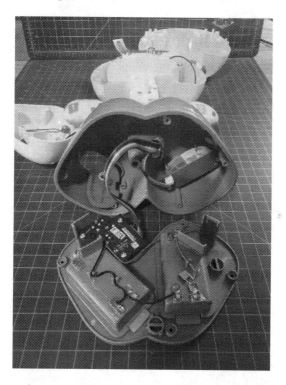

Figure A3-10. Observe the electronics on the inside!

4. Once you've got some pieces open, like shown
    in Figure A3-10, **observe first while keeping
    hands still**.

Use your observations to answer the following questions:

- Where are screws on the inside? What do these connect to?

- Where are electronic connectors? What do these connect to and how do they get there?

- How do things on the inside connect physically? Electrically?

- What is being held in and what is doing the holding?

5. **Make a loose plan for how you'll explore the inside.** Avoid cutting anything at this early stage.

   Think about the following:

   - What's the easiest/fastest way to disconnect things?

   - What parts do you want to (and can you) harvest? What parts and pieces do you need t

   - o unscrew/open/remove to safely get access to these?

6. Have at it! **It's likely that you'll need to repeat steps 1–4** a few times because most electronic devices have a few layers of parts on the inside. Super fun!

Next, we'll walk through how I fully took apart the toy and harvested parts.

Harvesting Parts

How far you go taking something apart depends on your goals and
interests. You do not have to harvest parts or get at everything on the
inside. Observing what's inside and how it's put together is totally
acceptable!

If you do want to see all the details and/or harvest parts, here's how
I approached this toy. Hopefully, it gives you some guidance on what to
tackle first and how to best use your tools.

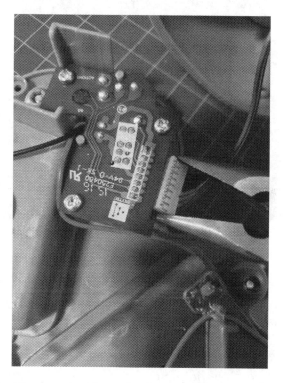

Figure A3-11. *Demonstration of using needle-nose pliers to remove
electronic connectors*

1. **Look for and unplug any accessible connectors.**
   This is important to avoid damaging wires and other parts inside.

   Use needle-nose pliers to gently unplug electronic connectors like demonstrated in Figure A3-11. Observe closely to find all the connectors. I found connectors in the base and in the body.

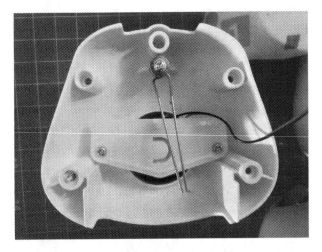

Figure A3-12. Electronic speaker inside of a toy

2. **Remove the most accessible parts first.** For my toy, this was a speaker!

   As we see in Figure A3-12, I discovered a speaker on the inside of the toy's torso. It was held in place by a piece of plastic and two screws. I removed the screws, took out the plastic bit, and was then able to take out the speaker!

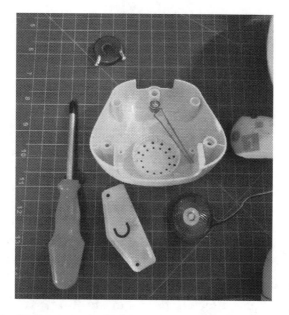

Figure A3-13. *Fully removed electronic speaker with all parts shown*

𝒫 **Check it out:** Look at Figure A3-13. What do you notice about how the speaker is physically installed in the toy? How does a person playing with the toy hear the speaker? When you find components like this, what do you notice about how they are installed electrically? Trace the path of the wires!

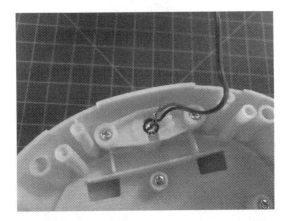

Figure A3-14. *Harvesting another electronic component*

3. **Observe your handiwork to see how removing the first part affected the rest of the device. Then identify the next most accessible part to remove.** For me, this was a microphone in the toy's head! This part is shown in Figure A3-14.

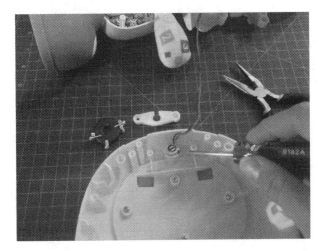

Figure A3-15. *Gently removing the microphone from the toy*

Like the speaker, the mic was held in place by a plastic bit secured with two screws. After removing the plastic part, I tried to use pliers to pull out the mic and was utterly unsuccessful! Setting aside the pliers, I opted for a thin screwdriver to pry out the mic and its squishy casing – this approach is shown in Figure A3-15.

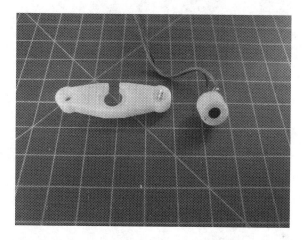

Figure A3-16. *A fully harvested electronic microphone!*

Huzzah! Microphone successfully harvested (Figure A3-16). I'm unsure how this mic was used in the toy, but I'm totally going to add it to my sensor collection!

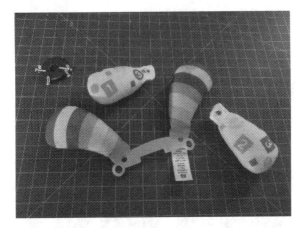

Figure A3-17. *Assorted soft parts that came off of the electronic toy*

4. **Continue identifying easy parts and pieces to remove, including nonelectronic bits.** After removing the speaker and mic, I noticed that there were some cute fabric pieces that easily came off their holders. All of these fabric pieces are shown in Figure A3-17. Saving those ears for sure!

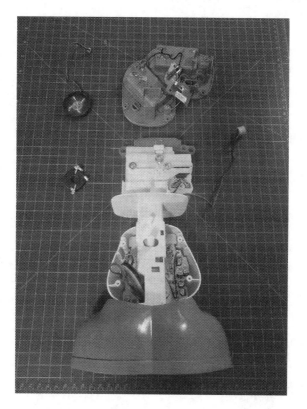

Figure A3-18. *Continuing to remove larger pieces of the electronic toy*

5. **Take stock of your progress! Remove large pieces
    that are still attached** like shown in Figure A3-18.
    It's helpful at this stage to check for any missed
    wire connectors, screws, or other pieces that can be
    (gently) pried off.

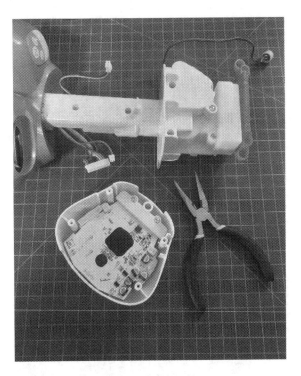

Figure A3-19. *Removing wire connectors*

At this point, I pulled off the front of the toy's
body and discovered more wire connectors! I
used needle-nose pliers to carefully remove these
(Figure A3-19).

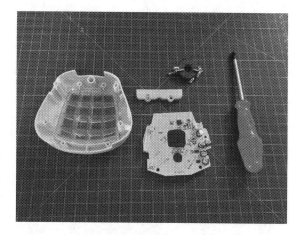

Figure A3-20. *A fully removed PCB*

6. ***Remove accessible PCBs*** (Figure A3-20). With the
   wire connectors unplugged, we can remove the
   PCB(s) inside our device!

Figure A3-21. *A close-up of the PCB inside my electronic toy*

As we see in Figure A3-21, one side of this PCB
has some black splotches – this is a common
manufacturing technique to obscure proprietary
designs and prevent folks who open up devices (like
us!) from seeing the code instructions that make the
device function.

Under these splotches are special circuit
components called integrated circuits (ICs) that
have been programmed by the company that makes
the device. Manufacturers hide these ICs because

if we could get at the ICs, or chips, it's possible that we could use electronic equipment to read the instructions on the chip and see how the device was made. We'll learn a bit about ICs at the end of Chapter 10!

Figure A3-22. *A close-up of the second side of the PCB inside the electronic toy*

Shown in Figure A3-22, on the other side of the PCB is a matrix of LEDs and two squishy (soooo satisfying) pushbuttons. These are LEDs designed for PCBs called "surface-mount LEDs."

What I love about discovering these kinds of designs is that I can see how the designers and engineers diffused the light from the LEDs. In other words, how they took the point source of light that LEDs give off and used material to spread the light more uniformly behind a surface. Diffusing light can be super tricky. Taking apart electronics helps us learn how to do this for our own projects!

🔍 **Check it out:** What else do you notice about the electrical and mechanical designs on this PCB? When you find a PCB in your device, look closely at the writing on it! You can look up parts and other writing on the PCB in your favorite search engine to learn more.

While this PCB was super fun to observe and learn from, there isn't much we can harvest from it. (Although I'll show you how to play with the LEDs in the next section!)

Figure A3-23. *Close-up of the PCB for the batteries*

This toy had a second, smaller PCB at the bottom by the battery holders which we can see in Figure A3-23. I'm super excited about this PCB because it has two large switches on it! I could harvest these later using wire cutters (and probably a small screwdriver) to remove them from the PCB.

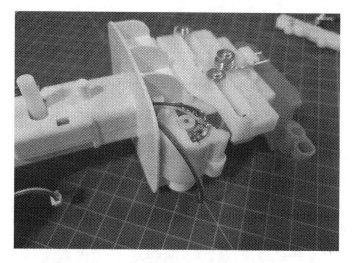

Figure A3-24. *Beginning to harvest a motor!*

7. ***Remove any remaining parts that you want to explore and/or harvest.*** Motors, like in Figure A3-24, will typically be near the end because they are connected to gears and other moving parts.

Motors are messy! Moving parts need to be lubricated to keep pieces from getting stuck. As soon as you start to get at the motor, you'll get covered in greasy stuff. Keep a rag handy and wash your hands when you're done.

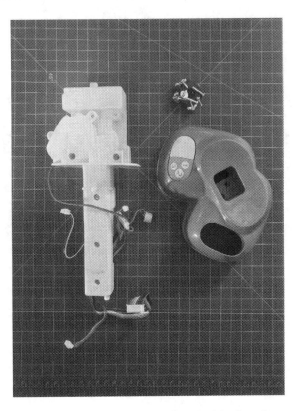

Figure A3-25. *More disassembly was needed before harvesting the motor*

Motors can also be tricky to remove because of all the moving part shenanigans. Take your time and observe how the pieces fit together. You may need to remove seemingly unrelated pieces to get at the motor. For example, like shown in Figure A3-25, in my toy I discovered that I had to completely remove the toy's feet so that I could pull apart the white "spine" that held in the motor.

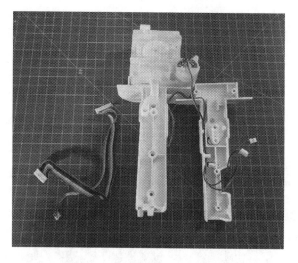

Figure A3-26. *Wires hidden inside disassembled parts*

As a bonus for getting at the motor, the "spine" part allowed me to harvest wire connectors (Figure A3-26)!

Figure A3-27. Continuing to harvest a motor

Leverage (yay tool puns ☺) your assortment of tools! The last plastic part holding in the motor was impossible to get at with my hands. Instead, I grabbed my handy-dandy screwdriver and gently pried it open as demonstrated in Figure A3-27.

Aha! Like we see in Figure A3-28, the motor compartment popped open! And all its gears fell out. Womp womp. Classic challenge when getting at motors. It's possible to put this gear system back together if you pay attention to what parts go where.

Motor gears and moving mechanisms can also be reused for other projects! Harvesting gears is way easier than building your own. You may also want to keep the motor compartment intact so that you can more easily repurpose it for another project.

Figure A3-28. *Disassembled motor gears*

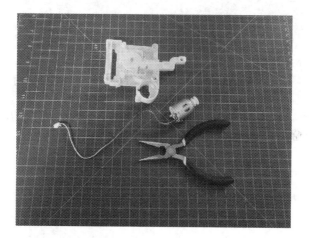

Figure A3-29. *Harvested motor*

If you just want the motor, needle-nose pliers may be useful to gently pry it out (Figure A3-29).

And there we have it!! We opened up the entire electronic toy and found some rad parts! Here are the treasures I discovered that I'm adding to my electronics collection.

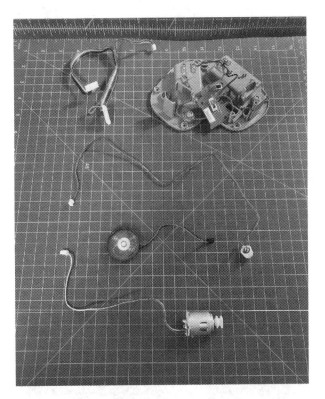

Figure A3-30. *Harvested parts from my electronic toy (that I plan to keep, the rest I will bring to an ewaste facility)*

The parts I opted to keep are shown in Figure A3-30. I decided to keep the toy's feet and the power switch circuit intact because it gives me some fun battery holders to play with and use for other projects!

Speaking of... let's explore how we can play with and use some of these finds!

Playing with and Using Harvested Parts

What parts did you discover? What parts did you harvest? Grab your electronic parts and let's explore our treasures! You'll need a breadboard, some jumper wires, and a couple coin cell batteries. A multimeter will also be super helpful.

First up: **The speaker!**

Explore connecting the speaker directly to a battery. I recommend turning off any music or other background sounds and listening closely to the speaker (literally put your ear close to it) as you connect it to the battery.

Figure A3-31 gives an example circuit that you can use to explore how the speaker works in a more controlled manner.

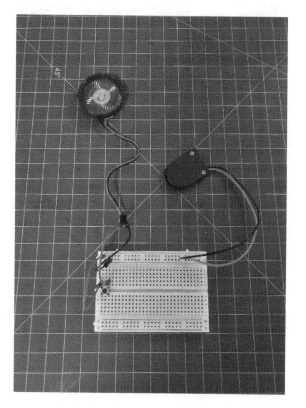

Figure A3-31. *A sample circuit for powering the speaker*

Connect a pushbutton (or other switches) between the battery and the speaker. Explore what happens when you close and open the circuit!

Next: **The PCB LEDs!**

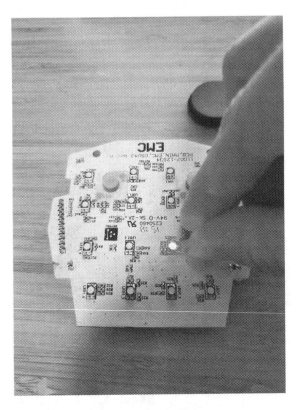

Figure A3-32. *Light up LEDs on the PCB!*

Grab your coin cell battery holder and connect the battery leads to the exposed LED leads on the PCB like demonstrated in Figure A3-32. It may take a few tries to get it right. If you try for a few minutes and nothing happens, try reversing the battery leads or using a multimeter to measure the LED polarity. A magnifying glass may also help to get a better look at what you're doing.

I'll leave it to you to **explore the motor on your own** because it behaves similarly to the small breadboard-friendly motor we've been using. (Except, of course, this one is much larger and more power hungry, so use your 9V or grab some AA batteries for this motor friend.)

The wire connectors are useful for working with complex circuits and/ or microcontrollers. And that's it!

...

Wait!! What about the mic??

Ah, yes, that lil' friend! Once I pulled off the squishy case on the mic, I looked up the part number written on the metal canister. The mic that I found in this toy is an analog microphone which is fairly typical. This means that it's way easier to use with a microcontroller, or a simple computer, where I can write instructions to read in the signal from the mic. (I mention microcontrollers in Chapter 10 and give you some suggestions on where and how to start learning to use them.) If you find parts like this, I recommend saving them for explorations with microcontrollers.

That reminds me of my final tip for you in this bonus chapter: **look for information written on the component and on PCBs.** Then use your favorite search engine to find more information about that part! You can learn to recognize all sorts of new components this way.

Going Further

Huzzah! I hope you found taking apart electronics as fun and satisfying as I do! For me, it always feels exhilarating and powerful to know that I am capable of recognizing parts and, in some cases, repairing my electronics.

Here are some thoughts for how you can leverage this power further.

Project 1: Repair Electronics

With great power comes great responsibility! Once you understand that electronics are an accessible realm of exploration, you can learn to repair them. For this, you'll likely need to learn how to solder as this is the most effective and reliable way to repair most electronics. However, it is possible to use wire wrapping to fix broken connections (a common mode of failure for electronics).

I hope that you become that friend your community comes to for aid when their favorite electronics break. It is truly gratifying to provide this kind of act of service for loved ones.

Project 2: Toy Mashup

Take apart one or more electronic toys and modify the parts! Swap in and out different speakers, motors, resistors, or whatever else you want to explore. Can you take pieces of electronics and smoosh them together? What electronics could you harvest parts from and incorporate into the toy (or vice versa)?

Project 3: Electronic Instruments

When you come across electronics that make sounds, open them up! How might you add inputs to control or change how the device makes sound? Making instruments can be like making art – there are infinite ways to get sounds, including repurposing electronics!

Project 4: DIY Robotic or Motorized Toy

Harvest motors from electric toothbrushes, electronic toys, and other things that move. Use them to make new kinetic creatures! Cardboard, plastic cups, berry cartons, and packaging foam make great bases for all types of beings!

What other projects are you inspired to make? What did you discover in the electronics that you took apart that brought you joy? What is something that you did not expect to see? Share your learnings and discoveries and mysteries with your friends and family! Even better, do a take apart craft night with all your favorite people!

Summary

In this chapter, we learned more about the electronics that we use every day! We discovered that inside our electronics are PCBs which are used to build robust and efficient circuits. Datasheets also made an appearance, and we covered some tips on what information to look for and how to find them within the vast repository of the World Wide Web.

We learned more about the parts and pieces inside our electronics, including what tools to use to access them, what to look for and harvest, and how to use our observations to better understand circuits and electronic components.

Finally, we used our knowledge to explore the insides of electronics! I hope this chapter revealed all sorts of delightful information, including how much you already know about the parts and pieces inside our everyday electronics.

Index

F

Faraday's Law, 98

Far-right breadboard, 339, 376

FET N-Channel pinout
diagram, 251

Field-effect transistor (FET), 250, 261, 328

Flex sensor, 229

Force-sensing resistor (FSR), 246, 250

    converting, 229

    materials, 225

    schematic symbol, 231

    touch-sensitive light, 226

    written instructions, 226, 227

Free electrons, 32

Frequency, 70, 100

Full driver kit, 439

G

Gate pin, 251–254, 257–258, 260, 269, 274, 275, 287–289, 298, 302, 313, 329, 341, 345, 378

Goodwill or Salvation Army, 450

H

Hard disk drive (HDD), 357

Harvestable parts, 452, 453

Harvested motors, 477

Harvested parts, 478

Harvesting gears, 476

Harvesting parts, 461

electronic component, 464

electronic speaker, 462, 463

holders, 466

motors, 473–477

needle-nose pliers, 462

PCBs, 469–473

plastic bit, 465

wire connectors, 467, 468

Heat gun, 440

I

iFixit, 440

if-then statements, 198

Infrared (IR)

    break-beam schematic symbol, 242, 243

    receiver, 240

    sensors, 216, 236, 241

    transmitter, 237, 238

Integrated circuits (ICs), 218, 219, 380–384, 470

J

Jimmy, 440

Jumper wires, 136, 156, 327

Junction FETs (JFETs), 262

K

Kirchhoff's Current Law (KCL), 423, 425, 427

Kirchhoff's Voltage Law (KVL), 414, 417, 418, 425, 427

R

Printed in the United States
by Baker & Taylor Publisher Services